DESIGNING & MAKING

WOODEN TOYS

DESIGNING & MAKING
WOODEN TOYS

TERRY KELLY

GUILD OF MASTER CRAFTSMAN PUBLICATIONS

First published 1994 by
Guild of Master Craftsman Publications Ltd
116 High Street, Lewes
East Sussex BN7 1XU

© Terry Kelly 1994

ISBN 0 946819 43 2

Cover photograph, colour photographs and
black-and-white photographs of the painted projects
by A. I. Webster, Photech (Northern) Ltd.
All other black-and-white photographs by Terry Kelly.
Line illustrations by Tim Benké,
Top Draw (Tableaux).

Designed by Ian Hunt Design

Printed and bound in Great Britain by
Ebenezer Baylis & Son Ltd.

To John

ACKNOWLEDGEMENTS

I would like to give my appreciation to editor
Liz Inman and desk editor Joe Sheehan for their
help, guidance and patience, and to Ken Widdall and
Colin Wilson for their efforts. Finally, I would like
to thank my wife, Anne, who didn't help
(but who was extremely patient).

CONTENTS

MEASUREMENTS: CAUTIONARY NOTE

Although care has been taken to ensure that the imperial measurements are true and accurate, the plans for the projects were originally in metric, so the imperial measurements are conversions. Throughout the book instances will be found where a metric measurement has fractionally varying imperial equivalents (or vice versa), usually within $\frac{1}{16}$in either way. This is because in each particular case the closest imperial equivalent has been given, so that a measurement fractionally smaller will be rounded down to the nearest $\frac{1}{16}$in, and fractionally greater will be rounded up. If you are using imperial measurements, it is recommended, particularly on the smaller projects, that you draw a plan of the work using imperial measurements to ensure that nothing has been lost in the translation. (*See also* the Metric Conversion Table, page 182.)

INTRODUCTION

Being one of six children (the other five being girls), toys were something of a luxury. But what I and my sisters lacked in luxuries was more than made up for by an abundance of imagination. With imagination we created the most marvellous toys. A cardboard box became a dolls' house, a boat or a zoo. An old pram bogie did yeoman's service as a racing car. And the back of an armchair – with the aid of a blanket for a saddle and a piece of rope for a rein – was miraculously transformed into a high-spirited Arabian stallion. The same spirit of play, of imagination, that is required for playing with toys, is the essential ingredient in making toys as well.

Although woodworkers of all levels of expertise can enjoy this book, I have carefully designed it to ensure that beginners find all the information they need. Special introductory sections will acquaint you with the tools, materials and methods used throughout the book. If you are an expert, you may skip these sections and go directly to the projects. However, if you need a more detailed explanation of a method or tool, the information will be there for you to refer to.

Simple tools such as a fret saw, hammer, drill and screwdriver are all you need to make this wide range of wooden toys. If you own or have access to a band saw, router and pillar drill, then the job becomes easier and quicker. But these tools are by no means essential.

I have found few pleasures greater than that of seeing the joy on a child's face as he or she goes on the grand adventure of the imagination sparked by playing with a toy I have made. I hope that making these wooden toys kindles that spark of playful imagination in you, and that you go on to design and make your own creations.

MATERIALS

This chapter covers the materials used in making the toys. The timber-based materials required to make the toys in this book are readily available from your local DIY store or timber merchant.

Some of these items may not be easily obtained locally. You can still purchase these hard-to-find items through mail order companies. I have listed mail order suppliers at the end of the book (*see* Suppliers, page 181). Many suppliers will send you a catalogue, but please remember to enclose a stamped, addressed envelope.

SPECIALITY ITEMS

▪ Wooden balls
▪ Bronze bearings
▪ Piano hinge
▪ Plastic eyes
▪ Brass hinges
▪ Washers: steel and fibre
▪ Wheels: wood or plastic
▪ Wing nuts and bolts

KITS

Classic Wooden Toys (*see* Suppliers, page 181) will supply kits of wood for all the toys illustrated in this book. All kits include the wood and the necessary fittings, such as axle rods, bearings, etc., but do not include glue and paint.

If you can't find these items at your local DIY supplier, try mail order. Wheels (left), and, from top to bottom: steel axle rod, washers, lengths of steel rod (some with starlock washers and caps fitted), starlock washers and caps, screw cups and screws.

PLYWOOD

There are a number of different types of plywood. The best material for the toy maker is birch ply. It is easy to work and, having a fine grain, takes a good finish. Ply will be required in several thicknesses: ½in (12mm), ⅜in (9mm), ¼in (6mm), ⅛in (3mm) and ¹⁄₁₆in (1.5mm).

SOFTWOOD (PINE)

For some of the larger toys, softwood battens are used to support and strengthen the structure. The only size batten that will be required is the one commonly termed 'two-by-one' (PAR). Two-by-one means two inches by one inch nominal, and PAR means that the wood is planed on all faces. The finished size is normally 1¾in (44mm) by ¾in (18mm), but the finished size is not critical.

WOOD DOWEL (HARDWOOD)

Hardwood dowels are required for some of the toys. The diameters are: ¼in (6mm), 1in (24mm) and 1⅜in (30mm).

GLUE

There are so many brands of glue that it would be difficult to name them all here. The toys in this book call for two types of glue.

WOOD GLUE

Ask advice from your stockist and purchase a good quality, quick drying PVA (polyvinyl acetate) type for gluing wood. I can recommend Evo-Stick, Bostik and Humbrol, but you will eventually find a brand that suits your purposes best.

EPOXY RESIN GLUE

This type of glue is called for when materials of different types are to be bonded together. Epoxy resin, in an uncured state, consists of a resin and a hardener. The two must be mixed together for the curing process to begin. Epoxy resins are useful for bonding wood, glass, plastic, metal and other materials together. The brand I use is Araldite Rapid.

PANEL PINS

A selection of different sized pins will be needed. The following sizes will cover all your needs: 1in (25mm),

¾in (18mm), ½in (12mm) and ⅜in (9mm). These are available at your local DIY.

BRASS OR STEEL ROD

Metal rod (dowel) is used for axles, shafts and attaching moving or pivoting parts. Brass is preferable because it will not rust. The size called for is ¼in (6mm).

STARLOCK WASHERS AND CAPS

These fasteners fit on the ends of metal rods or axles. They consist of a self-locking washer and a chrome cap (the washer is integral with the cap). The size called for is ¼in (6mm). Once fitted, starlock washers and caps are almost impossible to remove without force, so don't secure them until the toy is completely finished, painted and ready for final assembly.

SCREWS

Brass screws are preferred (to prevent rusting) but steel screws are cheaper. Sizes and types (such as round-head or countersunk) are shown on the plans. Screws are best purchased as required from your local DIY stockist.

SCREW CUPS

Screw cups are recessed to take the head of a countersunk screw and will protect little fingers from the sharp edges of screw heads. They are available in brass or chrome finish. Purchase screw cups as required.

A two-part epoxy resin will securely attach plastic eyes to wood. Used in many of the toy animal projects.

Round-bladed Surform (top), filler (left), abrasive paper (middle) and a round file.

ABRASIVES (SANDPAPER)

Abrasives, usually called sandpaper or glasspaper, are available in many forms and grades. The choice can be confusing. It will help to understand that most abrasive papers (although fabric, too, is used as a backing material) are coated with one of three materials: garnet, aluminium oxide or silicon carbide. Silicon carbide is used in the wet-and-dry types of sandpaper. Aluminium oxide papers are good with high-speed machines. Garnet papers are not suitable for high-speed machines, but are good for hand or slower machine methods. Garnet papers rapidly remove wood down to

a fine finish. Your local supplier will be pleased to advise you on selection if you tell him or her your requirements.

Fabric-backed abrasives are useful. They can be torn into narrow strips, held between the finger and thumb of each hand and worked to and fro in order to round an edge over quickly.

PAINT

Any paint used for children's toys must be clearly labelled as non-toxic and conform to the British Standards. The best paints, in my experience, are Humbrol enamels. These paints are non-toxic and give a beautiful finish in gloss or matt finish. They are widely available from DIY and model shops. Acrylic paints are also of good quality and are obtainable from suppliers of artists' materials. Should you wish the grain of the wood to show through, non-toxic wood stains in a range of colours are also available.

BRUSHES

A cheap paintbrush can spoil all the hard work you have done in preparation. I have found that Daler and Windsor and Newton brushes, available from your local artists' supplies shop, are ideal for painting toys. Useful sizes are 1in (25mm), ½in (12mm) and one with a fine tip for detail work such as painting the eyes of a toy animal.

Enamel and acrylic paints with a useful selection of brushes.

TOOLS

All the toys illustrated in the book can be made using just a few hand tools, but if you possess some power tools the work is that much easier and quicker. Most tool manufacturers offer tools in a range of price and quality. Choose the best that you can afford.

Some good quality second-hand tools can be found advertised in the monthly woodworking magazines. Car boot sales are another potential source for second-hand tools.

TENON SAW

A tenon saw has a brass or metal reinforcement along the back of the saw blade. This stiffens the blade allowing a straighter, more accurate cut to be made. Unfortunately, the strip of reinforcement along the back of the blade limits the width of board that can be cut.

HANDSAW

Any cross-cut or panel saw will do for rough cutting.

FRET SAW

These saws have a frame that holds a thin blade under tension, which enables the user to cut shapes in wood. A variety of sizes of frames are available. The deeper frames allow the user to reach farther from the edge of the wood with the blade.

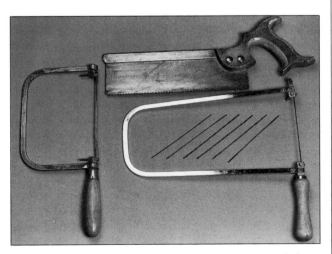

A selection of saws: tenon saw (top), coping saw (left) and fret saw (right).

COPING SAW

A type of fret saw that has a simple feature that allows the blade to be rotated at different angles within the frame. This allows the user to make cuts parallel to the edge of the wood.

HACKSAW

Used for cutting metal axle rod. For safety's sake, the metal rod should be gripped firmly in a vice before cutting with the hacksaw.

POWER FRET SAW

Performs the same job as a hand fret saw, but more quickly and with far less effort. An electric motor operates the saw blade, leaving both hands free to move the wood being cut.

BAND SAW

The band saw is another timesaver for sawing both straight and curved cuts.

BELT SANDER

The belt sander takes down wood rapidly and can be used across the grain or with the grain. Care needs to be taken, however, as mistakes can quickly ruin the work being sanded.

DISC SANDER

Disc sanders are useful for squaring off the ends of dowels and other pieces of wood. Many tool manufacturers offer an accessory that enables you to use an electric drill as a table-top disc sander.

RASP, FILE AND SURFORM

The rasp is used for the rougher shaping and rounding of the ply edges. This is followed by the file, which removes the rasp marks and leaves a surface fine enough for sanding. A half-round cabinet file will be found the most useful for these and other woodworking projects. The Surform is another tool, like the rasp, that can be used for the initial shaping and rounding steps. Surform tools are available in both planer (flat) and round shapes. The blades are replaceable.

The requisites for securing plywood: a good wood glue, panel pins, a punch, pliers and a light hammer.

SCREWDRIVERS

If you need to buy a screwdriver, bring along some of the screws you will be using in these projects and find a screwdriver to match.

HAMMER

Any light hammer will do for driving panel pins into the ply.

DRILL

You will be drilling holes ranging from $\frac{1}{8}$in (3mm) to $1\frac{3}{16}$in (30mm) in diameter. An electric drill or a pillar drill would fit the bill perfectly. A hand drill would be fine for drilling small holes but would be unable to drill the larger ones. A brace would easily bore the larger holes. A variety of drill bits that match your drill will be needed for the projects.

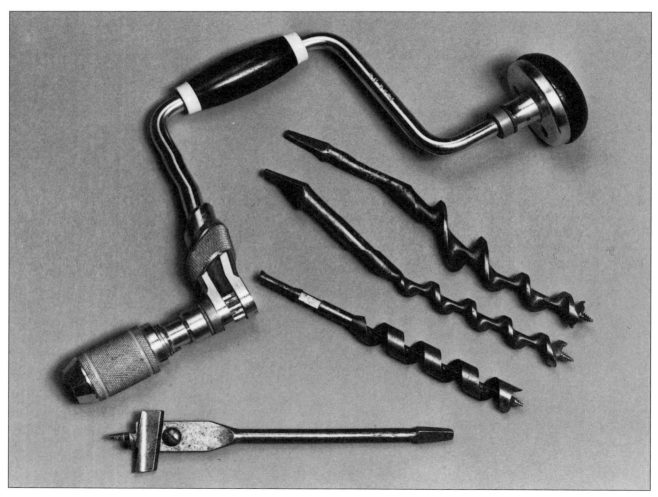

A brace with a selection of augers.

HOLE SAW

This could actually be considered a drill bit of sorts. It is a cylinder that attaches to a power drill chuck. The business end of the cylinder is toothed, like a saw, and cuts round holes. The hole saw attachment would be useful for cutting some of the larger holes, for instance, 1³⁄₁₆in (30mm), for some of the projects.

PINCERS OR PLIERS

Either one of these tools will be needed for removing protruding panel pins after temporarily pinning parts together for sawing or drilling.

SQUARE

This tool is used for marking wood and for testing that square edges are indeed square.

CRAMPS

A variety of sizes of G-cramps will useful for holding together parts while gluing, drilling sawing.

SLIDING BEVEL

This will be useful for projects (such as the Boot House, *see* page 85) where odd angles, that is, angles other than 90°, are needed for the edges of ply parts.

PUNCH

A punch will be needed for punching panel pins below the surface of the wood.

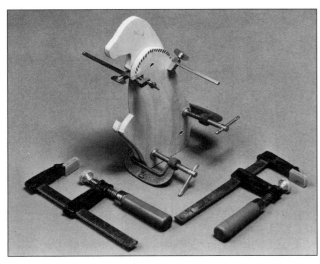

A variety of cramps will be useful for gluing, sawing and drilling.

TIPS FOR TOOLS

▎Keep tools sharp.
▎Renew fret saw blades as soon as they become dulled.
▎Use the correct tool for the job in hand.
▎If you do not have a fitted workshop or bench with drawers, make simple plywood boxes in which to keep your tools.

SAFETY

Safety in the workshop is the foremost priority. Injuries cause not only inconvenience and loss of time but sometimes severe disablement. Even the most experienced operators have lapses of concentration or allow the working area to become littered. This is when accidents happen.

By instituting these few simple rules you will keep your working environment safe. Toy making should be a pleasant and safe occupation.

▎Keep the workshop or working area tidy.
▎Wear protective goggles or visor when sharpening tools on powered grindstones.
▎Fingers should be kept clear of saw blades and drill bits.
▎Use a mask to cover the mouth and nose when sanding, even the dust from hand sanding can cause distress with some kinds of wood.
▎Do not wear loose clothing that may become entangled in power tools.
▎Keep long hair tied back.
▎Route power cables well clear of the working area, preferably fixed to walls in trunking.
▎Make sure small components are securely cramped to a table or workbench when drilling.
▎Do NOT hold workpieces or metal rod in the hand to drill or to cut. Place the part securely in a vice or cramped to a workbench. Place a piece of scrap wood beneath the part to protect the surface of the workbench from the drill bit.

These rules may seem a little tedious, but if practised regularly they will become second nature. They are even more important in the small workshop, where space is restricted.

Remember the old adage: A place for everything, and everything in its place.

TOY MAKING METHODS

ENLARGING PLANS

Many of the plans in this book use a grid. Each grid states the size square the grid is based on. To enlarge the shapes from the grid, make your own grid with a pencil and straight edge on some lightweight drawing paper. Base your grid on the size squares stated in the plan. Copy the shapes onto your grid. When you have refined your drawings, place a piece of carbon paper on the ply, put the drawing on top of the carbon paper, and trace the parts onto the ply.

A much quicker method of enlarging shapes is to use a photocopier with an enlarging feature. Simply work out how much the grid would have to be enlarged to match the dimensions of the squares the grid is based on. For example, the grid may say 'Based on 2in (50mm) squares', but actually measure out at 1in (25mm). The plan will have been reduced by 50% to fit into the format of the book. It needs to be doubled in order to get it back to its proper size. Set the photocopier at 150% and copy the plan. Take the enlarged copy and copy it again, again at 150%. This final copy will be enlarged a total of 200% (or twice as much). You can then trace the enlarged shapes onto the ply.

STACK SAWING AND DRILLING

Many of the projects require identical parts (usually two parts). If you have access to a power fret saw, you can cut out both parts in one operation. It is easier and more accurate to do so. Place the two pieces of roughly cut ply together by hammering two or three panel pins into them (leave the pin heads proud to aid easy removal). The pins will prevent the parts moving while cutting. Then cut with the fret saw as usual. After cutting, remove the pins with a pair of pliers and fill the holes with wood filler and sand flush.

You can drill holes in duplicate following the same steps.

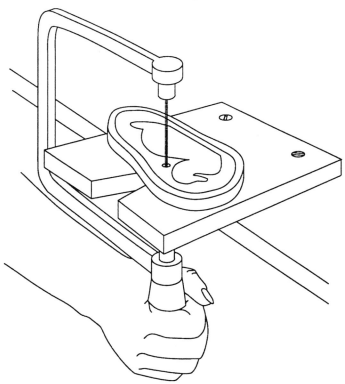

To saw interior shapes, drill a hole in the waste wood, loosen the blade from the top part of the saw frame, pass the blade through hole and secure it back on to the frame.

SAWING INTERIOR SHAPES

Some parts in these toys will require sawing in the interior. This is very easy to do. Simply drill a hole in the waste wood of the interior of the shape. Loosen the saw blade from the frame of your fret or coping saw (from the top of the frame). Pass the saw blade through the drilled hole and re-attach the blade to the saw frame. Then proceed to cut out the interior shape. If there is no waste wood involved, drill the passage hole on the border of the interior and exterior shape.

ASSEMBLY

Some of the projects involve animals whose shapes are formed by laminating two or more layers of shaped ply together. Certain parts would be difficult to shape once they are pinned and glued to the other shapes. Examples are the shoulders, cheeks areas around the eyes on the penguin (*see* page 27) and the kangaroo (*see* page 35). The areas to be shaped are indicated in the plans by diagonal shading. Make sure you shape and sand these parts before pinning and gluing. When gluing, wipe away any excess glue around the joint with a damp cloth as it would be difficult to remove at the finishing stage.

FINISHING

One of the most important aspects of toy making is the finishing. Finishing means the preparation of the surfaces to be painted, varnished, etc.

Any panel pins in the wood must be punched below the surface. The remaining hole, and any other blemishes, holes and countersunk screw holes, should be filled with wood filler and sanded flush with the surface.

PRIMING AND PAINTING

The first step to priming is to make sure the wood is clean and free from dust. Remove all traces of dust by going over the wood with a rag dampened with white spirit (turpentine substitute). Prime with a good-quality, non-toxic primer. Two coats of primer will provide a good base for painting. Sand lightly between each coat of primer.

The choice of finish is yours, but remember that children seem to like bright, bold colours.

SAFETY NOTES

▌All toys must be of sturdy construction – children are experts at demolition!

▌Round over all sharp edges.

▌Avoid pointed shapes in your designs.

▌Punch all panel pins below the surface and fill with wood filler.

▌Countersink screws or use screw caps. Fill countersunk screw holes with wood filler and sand flush with the surface.

▌Make sure all screws are really tight to prevent children from withdrawing them.

▌Use non-toxic primer and paints.

TOY DESIGN

All toys begin with an idea, a spark of imagination or inspiration that then must be translated into somewhat intractable materials – wood, metal, a bit of paint – to make the finished toy. Although I have given you plans for the twenty-four toys in this book, I hope you use them merely as a starting point to developing your own ideas. To that end I want to share some of the process I go through in making a toy, and hope that you may profit from the example.

THE DESIGN PROCESS

Having been lucky enough to spend a few months sailing in the Mediterranean one year, I was awed by the many schools of dolphins I saw there. The sheer beauty of these creatures as they leapt in perfect harmony in groups of two or three was a sight never to be forgotten.

Months later, back in my workshop, I tried to recapture these memories in the form of a toy. I scribbled some drawings of dolphins as I remembered them. These drawings were quite accurate, I thought, in terms of capturing the form of a dolphin. But I found I wasn't satisfied. I wanted something more. The something more that I wanted resolved itself into the form of a question, a puzzle: how could a toy express the leaping motion of a dolphin as it launches itself out of the water?

This is just the sort of problem I know from experience that my mind enjoys wrestling with. I made more drawings. Cams, wheels, axles floated through my

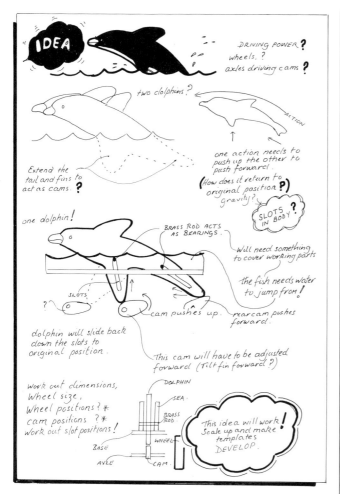

A page from my design notebook showing the development of an idea.

After I was finished with the rocking horse I settled down to work on the dolphin idea. I made a whole new series of drawings, but by this time I knew what I wanted: a dolphin pull-along toy. After I had worked out the mechanics of the movement using a few pieces of wood and some bearings and axles I had on hand, I drew up some plans based on my earlier sketches and began making the toy.

THE DESIGN NOTEBOOK

I hope you have noticed my most important design tool: drawing. If you are serious about designing toys, you'll need to keep a notebook with all your sketches and drawing of toy ideas. Don't limit your notebook to drawings, however. Magazine cuttings showing photos, photocopies of material from library books, everything that relates to toy ideas can go in the notebook or in folders. I find myself continually adding to and referring to my design notebooks. For example, two of the toys in this book are based on those early drawings of dolphins I made.

DESIGN REVIEW

After you have finished making a toy, either one of your own design or one of mine, go over the design once more. Is there anything you would change to make it work better, to make it more interesting or more attractive? Make notes of improvements you would like to incorporate the next time you make the toy. And make notes and drawings of any new versions of toys that may spring to mind as well.

Getting back to the pull-along dolphin, although nothing could do justice to the grace of the dolphins that occasionally accompanied the boat I was sailing on in the Mediterranean, I was delighted when the toy was accepted by a child who treasures it.

head and I scribbled them down on the paper, too. I still hadn't anything concrete when I went in for tea that evening, but I felt I was getting somewhere.

The thinking or designing process doesn't stop when I leave the workshop. That evening, and over the next few days as I was finishing up a commission – restoring a Victorian rocking horse, as it happened, I found myself visualizing the drawings I had done. Memories of the leaping dolphins superimposed themselves on the drawings of cams and wheels.

Animals With Young

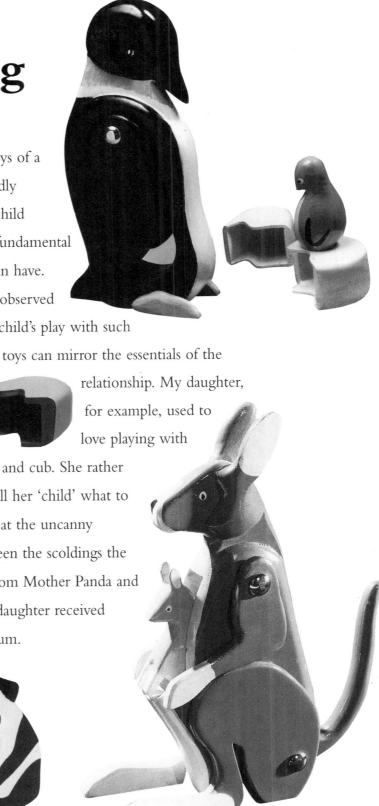

Children are often attracted to toys of a mother and a child. This is hardly surprising, I suppose, as the mother/child relationship must surely be the most fundamental a human being, or an animal, can have.

I have often observed how a child's play with such toys can mirror the essentials of the relationship. My daughter, for example, used to love playing with the panda and cub. She rather enjoyed having the 'mother' panda tell her 'child' what to do. I was always amused at the uncanny similarity between the scoldings the cub received from Mother Panda and the ones my daughter received from her mum.

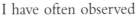

Panda and Cub

It would be hard to find a more endearing animal than a panda. If you haven't had a chance to see pandas at a zoo or in a nature film, you might want to go to the library and find some illustrated books on pandas. It never hurts to arm yourself with plenty of visual references when designing a toy. Colour photos are especially useful for deciding how to paint the finished toy.

MATERIALS

- birch ply 20 x 14 x ³⁄₈in (500 x 350 x 9mm)
- (2) steel or brass rod; length: 2¹¹⁄₁₆in (68mm); diameter ¼in (6mm)
- (4) ¼in (6mm) starlock washers and chrome caps
- (4) ¼in (6mm) steel or brass washers
- panel pins
- paints
- glue
- sandpaper (coarse, medium and fine) wood filler

TOOLS

- tracing paper
- carbon paper
- pencil
- saw (either hand or power fret saw)
- G-cramps
- hammer
- rasp
- pliers
- drill
- ¼in (6mm) drill bit
- punch
- brushes

Familiarize yourself with plans and photographs. You will be cutting out of ply two each of parts A, B, C, D and E.

TRACING THE DESIGN

Trace two of each part (labelled A, B, C, D and E) onto the plywood. (*See* page 8 for the methods used for enlarging plans and transferring patterns to the plywood.) Careful arrangement should allow all ten pieces to be cut from one piece of plywood, 20 x 17 x ³⁄₈in (51 x 43 x 9mm) with room to spare. Remember to leave ample room between each shape to allow for the saw blade. Label the parts with a pencil.

CUTTING THE SHAPES

Using either a hand fret saw or a power fret saw, cut out all of the shapes from the sheet of plywood (*see* Figs 1.2 and 1.3). Cut just outside the pencil line.

CUTTING IDENTICAL PARTS

If you have access to a power fret saw, you can cut out the identical parts at the same time. It is easier and more accurate to do so. Place the two pieces of roughly cut ply together and hammer two or three panel pins into them (leave the pin heads proud to aid easy removal). The pins will prevent the parts moving while cutting. Make sure the pins are placed so they are not near the path of the saw blade. Then cut with the fret saw as usual. After cutting, remove the pins with a pair of pliers and fill the holes with wood filler and sand flush with the surface of the wood.

GLUING

Take up the two A parts. Apply a thin layer of glue to one side of each part. Place them together, making sure the edges of both pieces are matched and flush. Either pin the two parts together or use two cramps to hold them together while the glue dries. Set aside until dry. Follow the glue manufacturer's suggestions for drying times.

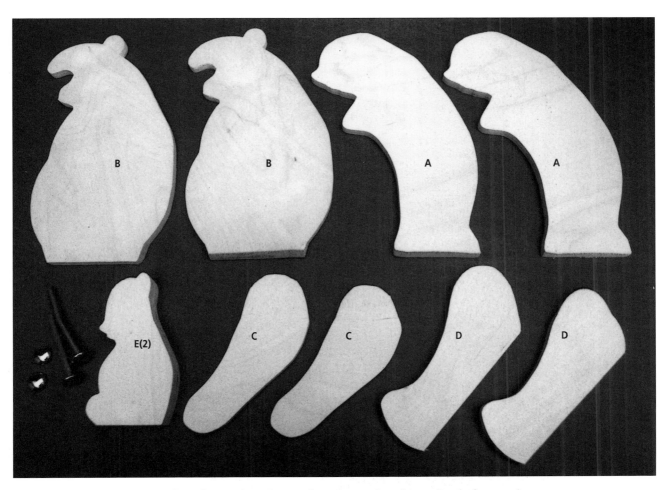

Fig 1.1 Parts A, B, C, D and E after sawing. Parts E have been pinned together before sawing.

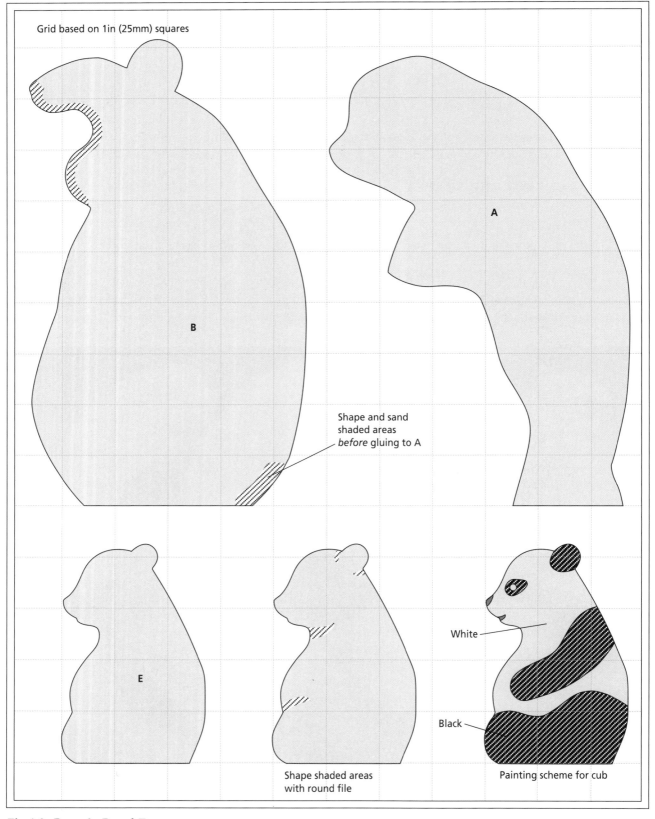

Grid based on 1in (25mm) squares

A

B

Shape and sand
shaded areas
before gluing to A

E

Shape shaded areas
with round file

White

Black

Painting scheme for cub

Fig 1.2 Parts A, B and E.

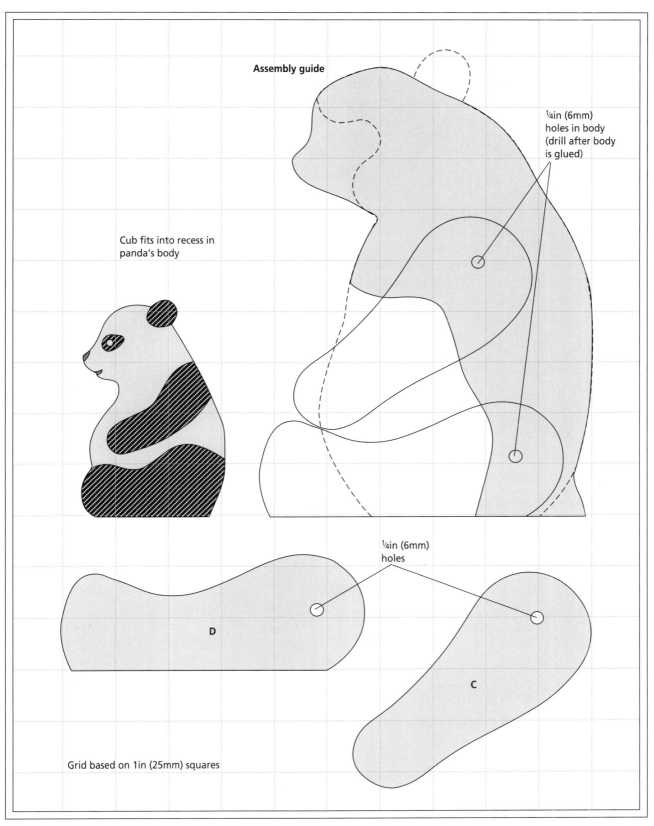

Assembly guide

¼in (6mm) holes in body (drill after body is glued)

Cub fits into recess in panda's body

¼in (6mm) holes

D

C

Grid based on 1in (25mm) squares

Fig 1.3 Parts C and D. An assembly guide is also shown.

THE LEGS

Drill the ¼in (6mm) holes in the fore (C) and hind (D) legs in the positions shown in Fig 1.3.

With the rasp, shape all four legs so that the edges are rounded over smoothly. Remove the rasp marks with sandpaper.

When the panda's body, consisting of parts A and B glued together, has completely dried, mark the positions for the two ¼in (6mm) holes with a pencil. Then drill the holes. The location of the holes is shown in Fig 1.3. These holes will receive the metal dowels on which the legs will fit. Fig 1.9 shows the drilled holes.

Shape the body with a rasp and the ¼in round file. Your aim in shaping should be to visually join the glued pieces as though they were one solid piece. All edges should have a smooth, well-rounded appearance. Fill any pin holes and blemishes with wood filler and sand level. A close-up of the head is shown in Fig 1.6 and the shaped body in Fig 1.9.

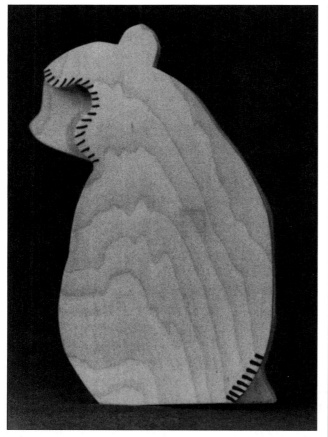

Fig 1.4 Shape the areas with heavy diagonal lines with the rasp.

Take up the two parts B. These two parts will form the outermost body of the mother panda. Notice in Fig 1.4 the heavy diagonal lines. These lines indicate areas that must be shaped. With a rasp, shape these areas around the eyes, cheeks and lower body around the tail on the outer body sections.

Smooth the marks left by the rasp with sandpaper: first coarse, then medium grade, then fine. Parts B are shaped at this stage as it would be difficult to shape them properly when fixed to the combined parts A. Fig 1.5 shows the finished shaping round the eye and cheek on one part B.

When the glued parts are dry, glue one B to each side of the A assembly, making sure the bases of all pieces are level. Align the outlines as best you can, but don't worry if they don't match up perfectly. You will remove any small irregularities on the outline of the body at a later stage after the glue has dried. Set aside until the glue has dried completely.

Fig 1.5 The head area of part B after shaping with a rasp, then sanding.

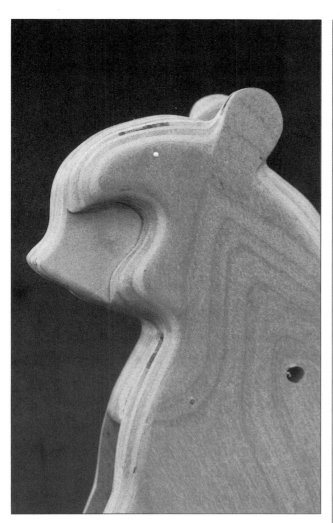

Notice in Fig 1.2 the heavy diagonal lines. These lines indicate areas where heavy shaping is needed with the rasp.

After shaping, go over the edges with sandpaper. First use coarse to remove the marks of the rasp, then medium, then finish up with fine. Fig 1.7 shows the cub with the edges nicely rounded by the rasp and smoothed with sandpaper. The cub is now ready for painting and can be set aside for the moment.

PREPARATION FOR PAINTING

Punch all panel pins below the surface of the wood. Fill the holes left by the panel pins and all other blemishes with wood filler. Allow the wood filler to thoroughly dry, then sand until the filler is flush with the surface of the ply.

Sand all parts using a progression of coarse, medium and fine paper until they are perfectly smooth.

Fig 1.6 Notice how the contours of A and B merge into one curved shape.

THE CUB

Glue the two sections of the cub (E) together. Use either pins or cramps to hold the two pieces together while the glue has a chance to dry. Set aside until the glue has dried.

Sand both sides of the cub until it slides easily into the aperture in the panda's body (the aperture is clearly seen at Fig 1.8). Use coarse sandpaper and sand quite heavily. Your aim here is to take down the thickness of the cub to such a degree that when it is painted it will still slide into the aperture in the panda without rubbing or sticking. When you have removed enough wood (so that the cub slides into the aperture quite loosely), you may begin shaping the contours of the cub. Rasp the edges until rounded.

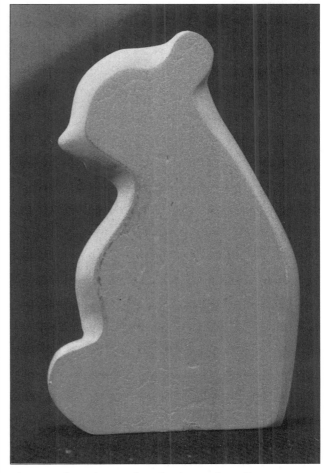

Fig 1.7 The cub (E) after shaping and sanding.

PAINTING

Fit the legs temporarily in position on the metal dowels to check for correct fitting and free movement (*see* Fig 1.9). If any parts are tight, disassemble the part and enlarge the holes with a small round file. Only a few light strokes with the file will be required. When you are satisfied with the movement of the legs, disassemble them and prime all parts. Prime twice, sanding lightly between coats. Then, when the primer has dried, paint all the parts using your own colour scheme or the colours shown in the picture of the finished toy (*see* the colour section). I added a little red to the black to make a warmer colour. For the white parts of the panda and her cub I used an off white to prevent harshness.

FINAL ASSEMBLY

When all the parts are completely dry, insert the two metal dowels through the holes in the panda's body, place a brass washer on each end of the dowels and fit the fore and hind legs in position. Check the legs for free movement. If the limbs are a little tight, clean out the holes in the limbs with a small round file. When you are satisfied with the movement of the legs, and the washers are in position between the body and the legs, fit the starlock washers and caps by pushing them firmly onto the ends of the dowels until they are fully engaged.

NOTE: Once fitted, these caps are almost impossible to remove without destroying them.

Fig 1.8 Parts A and B after gluing, shaping and drilling. The cub fits into the aperture in the panda's body.

Fig 1.9 Assemble the parts before priming to check for fit.

Duck and Duckling

The mother duck lifts her wing to reveal an egg. When the egg is removed from the duck and opened, her little chick emerges. After play, the chick can be stored inside the egg, and the egg inside the duck.

MATERIALS

- birch ply 20 x 7 x $^3/_8$in (508 x 178 x 9mm)
- birch ply 6 x 3 x $^1/_4$in (153 x 76 x 6mm)
- birch ply 6 x 4 x $^1/_8$in (153 x 102 x 3mm)
- steel or brass rod; length: $2^{11}/_{16}$in (68mm); diameter: $^1/_4$in (6mm)
- (2) $^1/_4$in (6mm) starlock washers and chrome caps
- panel pins
- primer
- paints
- brushes
- wood glue
- sandpaper (coarse, medium and fine)
- wood filler

TOOLS

- tracing paper
- carbon paper
- pencil
- straight edge
- coping saw or fret saw (or power fret saw if available)
- drill
- drill bit (small, just larger than the saw blade you plan to use)
- drill bit $^1/_4$in (6mm)
- G-cramps (various sizes)
- rasp
- file
- small round file
- light hammer
- pliers
- punch

TRACING THE DESIGN

If you will be using a power fret saw, you will need to trace each shape onto the plywood only once, for you can save time by cutting duplicate shapes. If you are using hand tools, trace two of each part onto the correct thickness of plywood. All the parts except parts D and F are to be traced onto ⅜in (9mm) ply.

Part D should be traced onto ¼in (6mm) ply, and F should be traced onto ⅛in (3mm) ply. All the parts except D are shown in Fig 2.1. Part D may be seen in Fig 2.5.

CUTTING OUT THE SHAPES

With either a coping saw or a fret saw, cut out all the shapes from the ply except for parts C. To cut out parts C from parts A and B you must first drill a small hole just on the line describing part C. Use a drill bit that is barely larger than the diameter of the saw blade you will be using. Pass the saw blade through the hole and re-attach the blade to the saw frame (*see* pages 8 and 9 in the Toy Making Methods). Fig 2.2 shows where to drill the saw hole. Then proceed to cut out parts C.

If you have a powered fret saw, stack the ply with panel pins and cut out the shapes in duplicate. You'll save a lot of time because you will only have to draw and cut out each shape once. Moreover, the parts will be identical from the start. If sawing by hand, cut each piece as accurately as possible to avoid a lot of work truing edges at a later stage. Label all the parts lightly with a pencil.

GLUING

Glue and pin together the two inner body parts (A). Make sure the bases are level and the outlines line up as evenly as possible. Keep the pins clear of the area where the hole will be drilled. See Fig 2.2 for the hole position. Set aside the parts A assembly until the glue has dried.

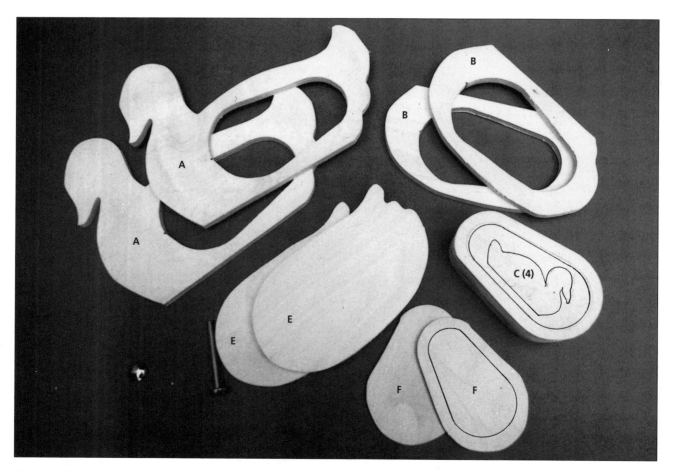

Fig 2.1 All the parts (except D, which is shown in Fig 2.4) after cutting from the plywood.

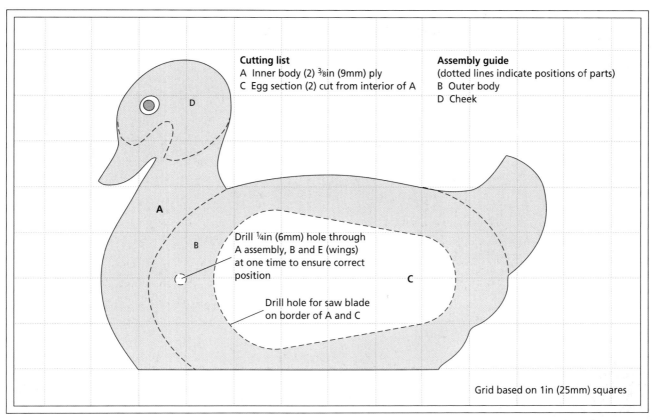

Fig 2.2 Cutting list for parts A and C. Assembly guide.

[Text within figure:]

Cutting list
A Inner body (2) ³⁄₈in (9mm) ply
C Egg section (2) cut from interior of A

Assembly guide
(dotted lines indicate positions of parts)
B Outer body
D Cheek

Drill ¼in (6mm) hole through A assembly, B and E (wings) at one time to ensure correct position

Drill hole for saw blade on border of A and C

Grid based on 1in (25mm) squares

SHAPING

Note in Fig 2.3 the diagonal lines drawn on the edges of parts B and D. These lines indicate areas that need to be shaped before B and D can be glued to the A assembly. With a rasp, shape the two B and two D parts in the areas indicated by shading. Figs 2.4 and 2.5 show the parts fully shaped. After rasping, sand the areas you have shaped with sandpaper, using first coarse, then medium, then fine sandpaper.

GLUING

Glue and pin one part B and one cheek piece (D) to each side of part A in the positions shown in Fig 2.2. Again, refer to Figs 2.4 and 2.5 for examples of the correct placement of parts before gluing. Make sure that the egg-shaped cut-outs on parts A and B are lined up and that their bases are level.

After the glue has dried, take the duck's body, which now consists of parts A, B and D glued together. With the rasp, shape and blend the contour of part A to the parts you have glued onto it (B and D). Figs 2.4 and 2.5

should again prove useful examples of how the contours of one shape can be made to blend into the contours of another shape. Note especially the shaping around the bill and head in Fig 2.5.

Don't forget the interior egg shape. Use the rasp to smooth any edges that may be uneven. With rasp in hand, it is a good time to take up parts E, the wings. Round and smooth the contours of the wings. Fig 2.6 shows a shaped wing. After rasping, remove all rasp marks by sanding, first with coarse sandpaper, then with medium, and then fine sandpaper.

DRILLING AND FITTING

Drill the ¼in (6mm) holes in the body and wings in the positions shown in Figs 2.2 and 2.6. Insert a metal dowel through the hole in the body and place a wing on each end of the dowel as shown in Fig 2.6. Check that the wings raise clear of the hole into which the egg fits. Remove the wings from the metal dowel and then the dowel from the hole. Set the dowel aside for the time being.

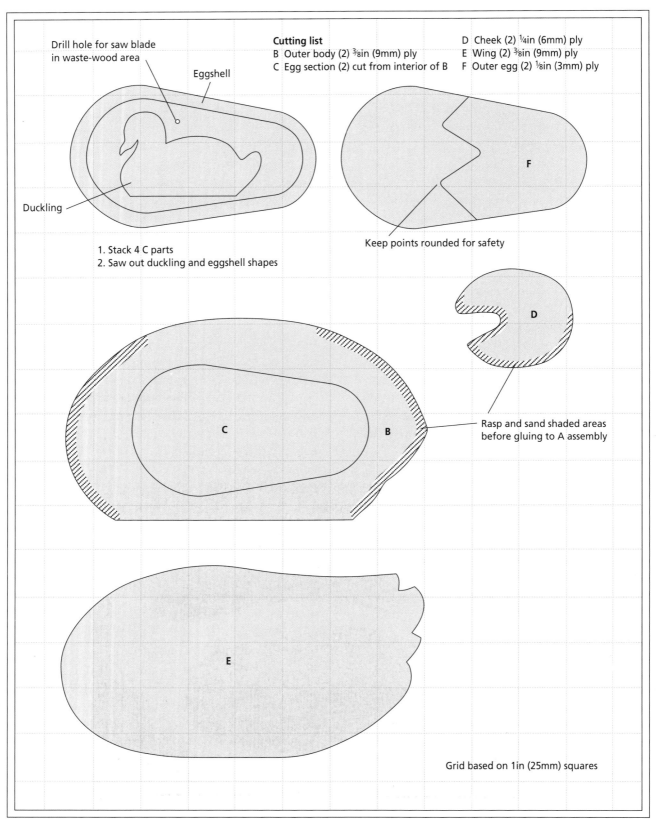

Drill hole for saw blade
in waste-wood area

Eggshell

Duckling

Cutting list
B Outer body (2) ⅜in (9mm) ply
C Egg section (2) cut from interior of B

D Cheek (2) ¼in (6mm) ply
E Wing (2) ⅜in (9mm) ply
F Outer egg (2) ⅛in (3mm) ply

Keep points rounded for safety

F

1. Stack 4 C parts
2. Saw out duckling and eggshell shapes

D

Rasp and sand shaded areas
before gluing to A assembly

C

B

E

Grid based on 1in (25mm) squares

Fig 2.3 Cutting list for the remainder of the parts.

FINISHING THE MOTHER DUCK

Fill all pin holes and blemishes in both of the wings and the duck's body with wood filler. When the wood filler has dried, sand the filler flush with the wood. Then sand the wings and the duck's body with medium, then fine sandpaper to achieve a smooth, flawless finish. Pay particular attention to the cutout into which the egg fits.

THE EGG AND THE DUCKLING

At last we'll get a chance to put those four duplicate shapes labelled C to work. As they have come from inside the duck's body, I suppose it is fitting that they will be used to make an egg and a duckling. Parts C are shown in Fig 2.7 resting on top of the two parts F.

If you will be cutting the shapes with hand tools, you will need to trace the shapes of the inner egg section and the chick from the plan (*see* Fig 2.3) onto the four parts C. Using a drill bit only slightly larger in diameter than the diameter of the saw blade you intend to use, drill a hole in the waste area of each part C. Pass the saw blade through the hole and re-attach the blade to the saw frame. With the saw, cut out the inner egg shape first. Then saw out the duckling from the waste wood.

SAWING WITH A POWERED FRET SAW

If you possess a powered fret saw, you can cut the inner egg shape and the duckling by 'stack sawing'. Glue all the parts C together and cramp until the glue is dry. Make sure the edges of all parts are absolutely flush. You will need to trace the shapes for the inner egg and duckling only once, on the top of the stack.

Fig 2.8 shows the glued stack with the outline of the inner egg, the duckling and the hole for the saw blade. Drill a small hole in the waste part of the egg. Release one end of the blade from the fret saw and pass the blade through the hole. Then reconnect the blade and cut out the smaller egg-shaped section from the centre of the egg. Then cut the duckling from the waste wood. Fig 2.9 shows the inner egg and duckling shapes cut out of the parts C with a powered fret saw.

GLUING

If the sawing has been done by hand, carefully glue and cramp together the four outer egg sections, taking care to keep the edges even and the bottoms level. Glue and cramp the four pieces of the duckling as well and leave both assemblies to dry. When dry, glue and cramp parts F (the two outer egg sections), one to each side of the egg. Set aside the egg until the glue has dried.

Fig 2.4 Parts B and D have been fully shaped with the rasp and sandpaper, then glued and pinned to the A assembly.

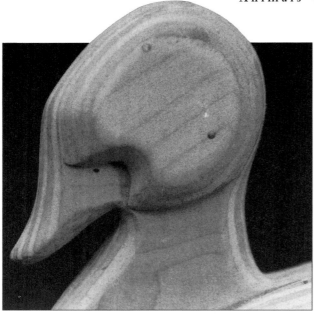

Fig 2.5 The contours of parts D and A have been blended nicely using the rasp and sandpaper.

SHAPING AND FINISHING THE EGG

When the glue has dried completely, take up a rasp and round off the corners and edges of the egg. Remove the marks made by the rasp with coarse sandpaper. Continue sanding with medium sandpaper.

If there are any nicks or blemishes, fill them with wood filler. When the wood filler has dried, sand it flush with the surface of the wood. Then finish off the sanding with fine sandpaper until the egg is perfectly smooth.

'CRACKING OPEN THE EGG'

Draw a zigzagging line on the surface of the egg (*see* Fig 2.3). Avoid making a line with sharp points. With a fret saw, saw the egg into two parts along the line (*see* Fig 2.10). Sand the inside of the egg and the sawn edges of the line so that there are no sharp corners.

Fig 2.6 The contours of the wing (E) and the duck's body are rounded and smoothed with a rasp and sandpaper.

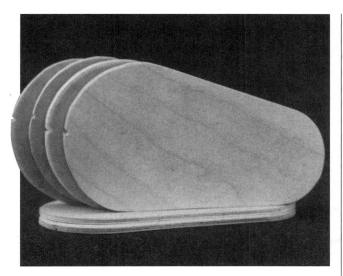

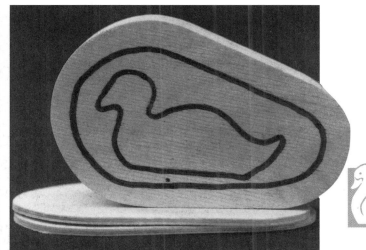

Fig 2.7 Parts C and F. The semicircular notches are from the hole drilled to pass the saw blade through.

Fig 2.8 Four parts C have been stacked in order to cut them together with a power fret saw. Note the hole drilled to allow passage of the saw blade.

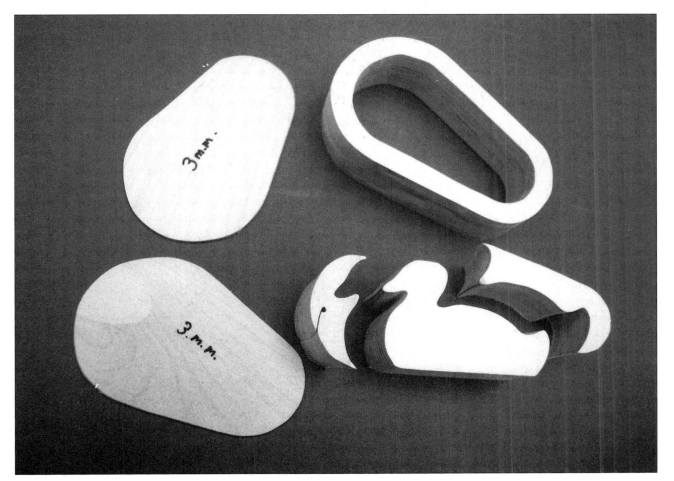

Fig 2.9 The eggshell and duckling cut with a power fret saw. Parts F (marked '3mm') are ready to glue onto the stacked eggshell parts.

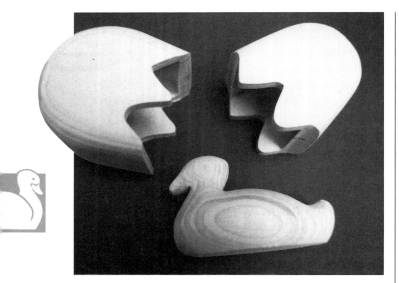

Fig 2.10 The egg assembly after sawing. The duckling
has been shaped with a rasp and sandpaper.

SHAPING THE DUCKLING

Fig 2.11 shows the parts of the duckling that need to be
removed in order to give the duckling its shape. Facing
the front of the chick, draw the outline of the duckling.
Then cut away the waste areas with a coping saw.
Looking down on the duckling from above, plan the
path of your saw, then make your cuts. With the rasp,
round and shape all corners and angles until they blend
into a nicely rounded duckling like that shown in

Fig 2.10. Follow the rasping with sanding, first with
coarse, then with medium and lastly with fine
sandpaper. If there are any holes or blemishes in the
duckling, fill them with wood filler and, when the filler
has dried, sand the filler smooth.

PAINTING AND ASSEMBLY

You should now have a duck, an egg and a duckling all
ready for painting and assembly. Use the same colours I
used (*see* the finished toy in the colour section) if you
wish, or make up a colour scheme of your own.
Remember to prime twice, sanding lightly between
coats. Then paint.

When the paint has thoroughly dried, fit the wings
by inserting the $2^{11}/_{16}$in (68mm) metal dowel through
the hole in the body. Should any paint be clogging the
hole, clean it out with a small round file. Fit the wings
into position. Place a washer onto each end of the
dowel. Place the wings so they are holding the egg in
position. Then push the caps firmly onto the ends of
the dowel.

NOTE: You will have noticed that the egg is $^1/_4$in
(6mm) wider than the body. An allowance has been
made for a little play in the wings to compensate for
the extra thickness of the egg. The wings hold the egg
firmly in position.

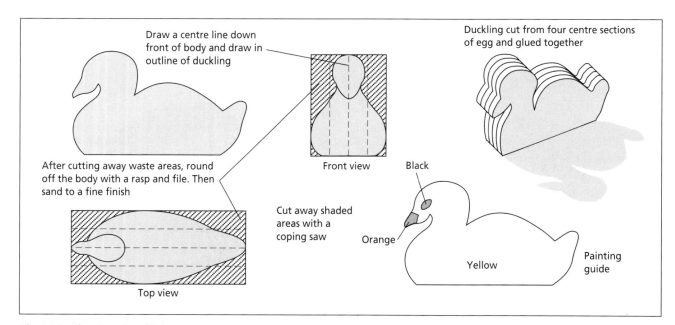

Fig 2.11 Shaping the chick.

Penguin and Chick

The penguin's flippers lift up to reveal an egg. Inside the egg is a tiny penguin chick. I'm not sure what noises a baby penguin makes after it hatches, but I'm sure a child will have no trouble improvising!

MATERIALS

▌ birch ply 16 x 16 x ³⁄₈in (420 x 420 x 9mm)
▌ birch ply 5 x 6 x ¹⁄₈in (130 x 150 x 3mm)
▌ steel or brass rod; length: 2¹¹⁄₁₆in (68mm); diameter: ¼in (6mm)
▌ (2) ¼in (6mm) starlock washers and chrome caps
▌ panel pins
▌ primer
▌ paints
▌ brushes
▌ wood glue
▌ sandpaper (coarse, medium and fine)
▌ wood filler

TOOLS

▌ tracing paper
▌ carbon paper
▌ pencil
▌ straight edge
▌ coping saw or fret saw (or power fret saw if available)
▌ drill
▌ drill bit (small, just larger than the saw blade you plan to use)
▌ drill bit ¼in (6mm)
▌ G-cramps (various sizes)
▌ rasp
▌ light hammer
▌ pliers
▌ punch

Familiarize yourself with the plans and photographs. You will be cutting two each of parts A, C, D, E and F from the ³⁄₈in (9mm) ply. Parts B will be cut from the inside of parts A and C, so you will end up with four parts B. Part G is cut from the ¹⁄₈in (3mm) ply. You will be cutting two parts G. The chick will be cut from the interior of the four parts B. Parts B will also provide, along with G, the parts that will make up the egg.

TRACING THE DESIGN

Trace parts A, B, C, D, E and F from Fig 3.2 and transfer the shapes onto the ⅜in (9mm) ply. Trace part G on the ⅛in (3mm) ply. You will be needing two of each of these parts, so be sure to trace each shape onto the ply twice. Note that, as part B comes from the interior of A and C, you will have four parts labelled B. If you wish, you may label each part with the appropriate letter.

SAWING OUT THE SHAPES

With either a coping saw or a fret saw, cut out all the shapes except for parts B from the plywood. To cut out parts B from parts A and C you must first drill a small hole just on the line describing part B (*see* Fig 3.2 for saw hole locations). After drilling, pass the saw blade through the hole and re-attach the blade to the saw frame. Then cut out the inner shape B. Set aside the four B parts for later. You will be using them to construct the egg and the chick.

If you have a powered fret saw, stack the shapes with pins and cut them out in duplicate. If sawing by hand, cut each piece as accurately as possible to avoid a lot of work truing up edges at a later stage. Fig 3.1 shows all the parts after they have been cut out of the ply.

GLUING AND PINNING

Glue and pin the two parts A, taking care to align their outlines as closely as possible. Make sure that the bases of both parts are flush. Allow the A assembly to dry.

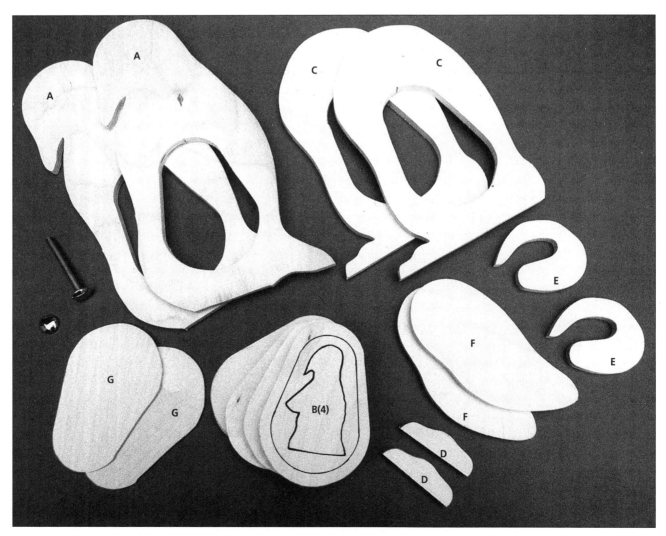

Fig 3.1 All the parts after sawing from the plywood, ready for gluing, pinning and shaping.

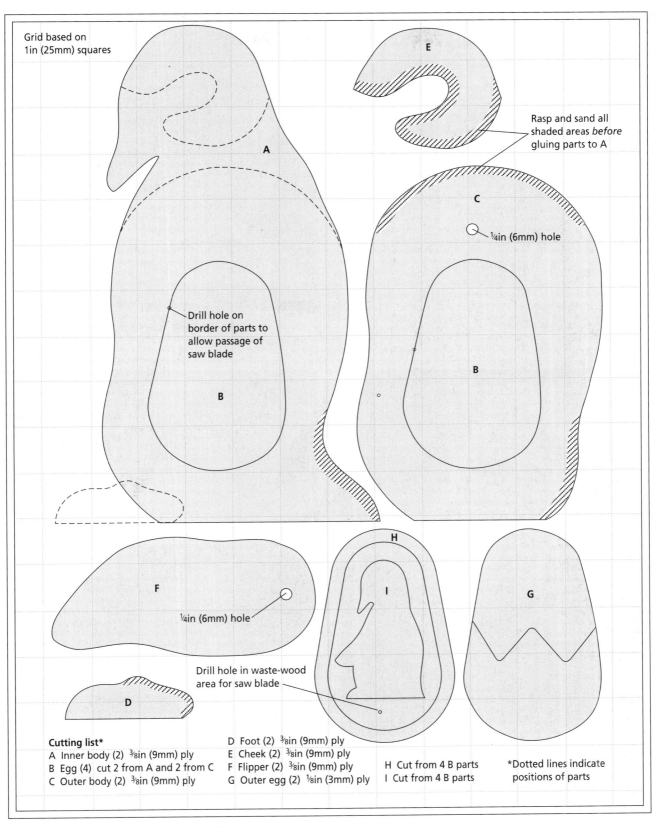

Grid based on 1in (25mm) squares

Rasp and sand all shaded areas *before* gluing parts to A

¼in (6mm) hole

Drill hole on border of parts to allow passage of saw blade

A

E

C

B

B

F

¼in (6mm) hole

Drill hole in waste-wood area for saw blade

D

H

I

G

Cutting list*
A Inner body (2) ⅜in (9mm) ply
B Egg (4) cut 2 from A and 2 from C
C Outer body (2) ⅜in (9mm) ply

D Foot (2) ⅜in (9mm) ply
E Cheek (2) ⅜in (9mm) ply
F Flipper (2) ⅜in (9mm) ply
G Outer egg (2) ⅛in (3mm) ply

H Cut from 4 B parts
I Cut from 4 B parts

*Dotted lines indicate positions of parts

Fig 3.2 Cutting list and assembly guide.

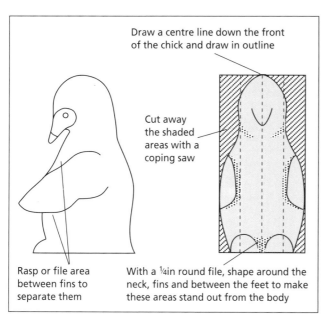

Draw a centre line down the front of the chick and draw in outline

Cut away the shaded areas with a coping saw

Rasp or file area between fins to separate them

With a ¼in round file, shape around the neck, fins and between the feet to make these areas stand out from the body

Fig 3.3   Shaping the chick.

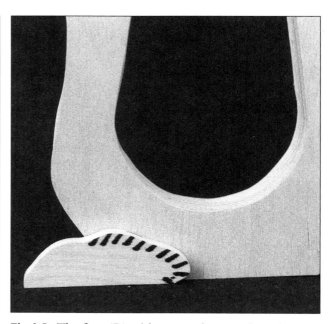

Fig 3.5   The foot (D) with area to be rasped marked with diagonal lines.

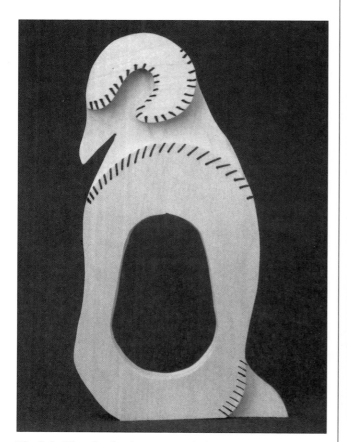

Fig 3.4   The cheek piece (E) and the outer body (C) must be shaped (as indicated by diagonal shading lines) before attaching to the inner body (A).

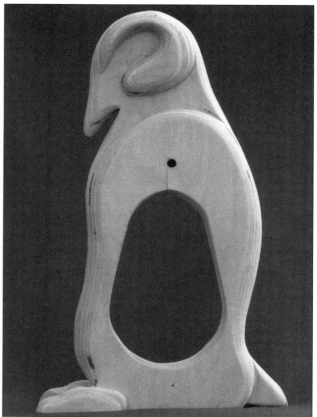

Fig 3.6   The penguin's body after all the shaping has been completed.

SHAPING

Take parts C, D and E. All of these parts will be affixed to the A assembly and will form the outermost body of the penguin. Notice in Figs 3.2, 3.4 and 3.5 the diagonal lines. These lines indicate areas that must be shaped before assembly. With a rasp, shape these areas. Use Fig 3.6 as a guide to how the finished shapes should look. Smooth the marks left by the rasp with sandpaper. First use coarse, then medium grade, then fine. These parts are shaped at this stage as it would be difficult to reach them with a rasp once they were fixed to the A assembly.

Notice in Fig 3.2 the diagonal shading on the tail area of shape A. Shape this area with a rasp and sandpaper just as you did with the other parts. It should be somewhat rounded, as in Fig 3.6.

When you have finished sanding the tail area, glue and pin one C, D and E part to each side of the A assembly. Fig 3.2 shows the location of the parts on the A assembly. Make sure the bases of C and D are level with the base of the A assembly. Align the edges of the shapes as best you can, but don't worry if they don't match up perfectly. You will remove any small irregularities on the outline of the body at a later stage after the glue has dried. Set aside until the glue has dried completely.

When the penguin's body (consisting of the glued and pinned parts A, C, D and E) has dried, mark from Fig 3.2 the position for the ¼in (6mm) hole. Drill the hole.

Now you may finish shaping the body with a rasp. You will be working on rounding the edges of the A parts and, where they meet with parts C, D and E, blending the layers of ply into one rounded shape. Fig 3.7 shows how the rasp has been used to blend the cheek piece (E) into the head of the A assembly. All edges should have a smooth, well-rounded appearance. Do not neglect the interior egg shape, which should also be gone over with the rasp to smooth out any irregularities in outline.

After shaping with the rasp, go over the same areas with sandpaper to remove the marks of the rasp. Then sand the whole of the penguin's body to a smooth finish. Use coarse sandpaper first, followed by medium, then fine. Fill any pin holes and blemishes with wood filler and sand level. Fig 3.6 shows the penguin's body after shaping and sanding.

THE CHICK AND THE EGG

Gather together the four B parts and the two G parts. Note from Fig 3.2 that you will need to drill a hole in the waste area of each part B to allow for the passage of a saw blade into the interior of the shape. You will then be cutting out two parts from each B part: the eggshell (H) and the chick (I). You will then have four H parts and four I parts.

TRACING THE SHAPES, THEN SAWING

If you will be cutting the shapes with hand tools, you will need to trace the shapes of the eggshell (H) and the chick (I) (*see* Fig 3.2) onto each of the four B parts. After tracing the shapes, drill a hole in the waste area of each part C. Pass the saw blade through the hole and re-attach the blade to the saw frame. Saw out the eggshell shape (H) first. Then saw out the chick (I) from the waste wood.

SAWING WITH A POWERED FRET SAW

If you possess a powered fret saw you can cut the inner eggshell shape and the chick by 'stack sawing.'

Glue all four B parts together and cramp until the glue is dry. Make sure the edges of all parts are absolutely flush.

You will need to trace the shapes for the inner eggshell and the chick only once, on the top of the stack. Drill a small hole in the waste part of the egg. Release one end of the blade from the fret saw and pass the blade through the previously drilled hole. Then reconnect the blade and saw out the smaller egg-shaped section from the centre of the egg. Cut the chick from the waste wood. Fig 2.9 from the Duck and Duckling project shows similar egg and chick shapes cut out with a powered fret saw.

GLUING

If the sawing has been done by hand, carefully glue and cramp together the four eggshell sections (H), taking care to keep the edges even and the bottoms level. Glue and cramp the four pieces of the chick (I) as well and leave both assemblies to dry. When dry, glue and cramp parts G, one to each side of the egg. Make sure the edges of G are flush with the egg assembly. Set aside the combined G and H assembly until the glue has dried.

Fig 3.7 **Use the rasp to blend contours from one part to another.**

SHAPING AND FINISHING THE EGG

When the glue has dried completely, take a rasp and round off the corners and edges of the egg (the G and H assembly). Remove the marks made by the rasp with coarse sandpaper. Continue sanding with medium sandpaper. If there are any nicks or blemishes, fill them with wood filler. When the wood filler has dried, sand it flush with the surface of the wood. Then finish off the sanding with fine sandpaper until the egg is perfectly smooth.

'CRACKING OPEN' THE EGG

Draw a zigzagging line on the surface of the egg (*see* Fig 3.2). Avoid making a line with sharp points. With a fret saw, saw the egg into two parts along the line (*see* Fig 3.8). Sand the inside of the egg and the sawn edges of the line so that there are no sharp corners.

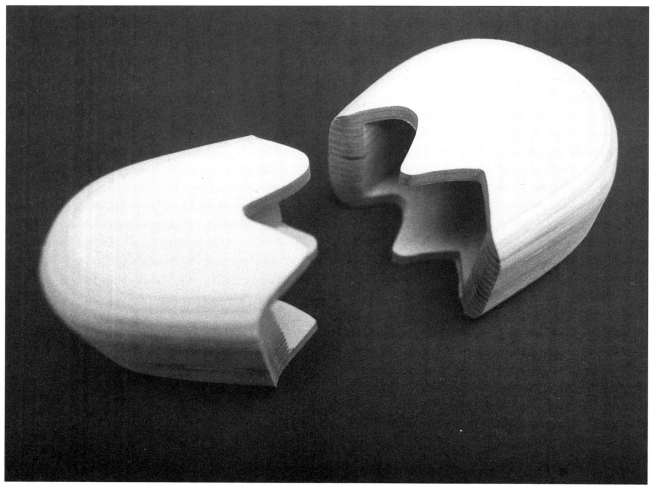

Fig 3.8 **Use a softened zigzagging line for the crack line.**

SHAPING THE CHICK

Fig 3.3 shows the parts of the chick that need to be removed in order to give the chick its shape. Facing the front of the chick, draw its outline. Then cut away the waste areas with a coping saw. Referring still to Fig 3.3, shape the chick with a rasp to give it a sense of fullness and roundness. Use the rasp also to open up areas between the flipper and feet along the belly. Follow the rasping with sanding, first with coarse, then with medium and lastly with fine sandpaper. Fill any holes or blemishes in the chick with wood filler. When the filler has dried, sand the surface smooth.

THE FLIPPERS

The egg is approximately ¼in (6mm) wider than the body of the penguin, but an allowance has been made on the metal dowel for the flippers to have a little movement to compensate for this. Fig 3.9 shows the position of the egg (before shaping) in the penguin's body.

Drill a ¼in (6mm) hole in each of the two flippers (F) at the position marked in Fig 3.2. Round off the edges of the flippers (F) with the rasp so that there are no sharp edges or corners. Remove the rasp marks by sanding with coarse sandpaper. Then sand the whole of the flippers with medium paper. If there are any holes

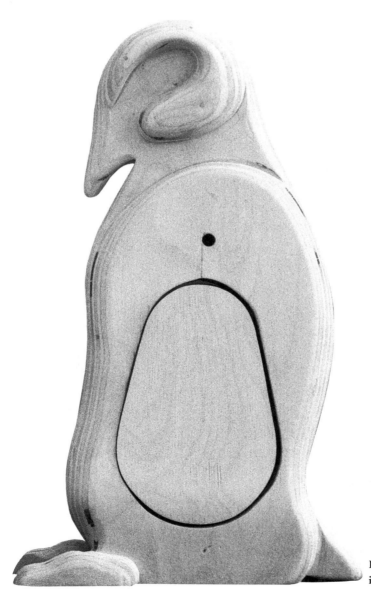

Fig 3.9 The egg will fit inside the penguin's body.

or blemishes in the flippers, fill them with wood filler. When the wood filler has dried, sand it level with the wood. Then go over the flippers with fine sandpaper until perfectly smooth.

`Insert the metal dowel through the ¼in (6mm) hole in the penguin's body and place a flipper over each end to test that the flippers clear the hole into which the egg fits (*see* Fig 3.10). Remove the flippers and the metal dowel in preparation for painting.

PRIMING AND PAINTING

Gather together all of the parts for painting. You should have the penguin, the flippers, the egg and the chick. All parts have already been filled and sanded to a perfectly smooth finish. Prime each part twice, sanding lightly between each coat, then paint to your choice of colour scheme.

You may want to paint the chick a light grey. While the paint is still wet, brush a little black around the eye area. This will create an area that appears to recede,

forming an eye socket. When dry, paint the eye and beak black.

FINAL ASSEMBLY

When the paint is completely dry, insert the steel dowel through the body. Fit the flippers onto the metal dowel. Place a ¼in (6mm) starlock washer over each end of the dowel. Lift one of the flippers out of the way and place the egg in the penguin's body. Lower the flipper over the egg. With the flippers holding the egg firmly in position, place the caps onto the ends of the metal dowel and apply firm pressure to lock them onto the dowel.

The flippers do not swing loosely when the egg is placed inside the penguin's body. They hold the egg firmly in position.

NOTE: When cutting out these parts, use the finest fret saw blade you have available. A coarse blade will give a wider cut and may leave some parts loose.

Fig 3.10 Check the fit of the flippers (F) on the metal dowel before painting.

Kangaroo and 'Joey'

There's something about kangaroos that children are intrigued by. Perhaps
it's just the idea of having someone do all the work while you just go along for the ride.
(I know my children used to love riding on my shoulders.)
Children are sure to have the joey insist on being carted about, safe and sound, in its
mother's pouch. And when the joey is feeling adventurous, it can hop out and play on its own.

MATERIALS

▌ birch ply 24 x 12 x ³⁄₈in (600 x 300 x 9mm)

▌ steel or brass rod; length: 2¹¹⁄₁₆in (68mm); diameter: ¼in (6mm)

▌ (4) ¼in (6mm) starlock washers and chrome caps

▌ panel pins

▌ primer

▌ paints

▌ brushes

▌ wood glue

▌ sandpaper (coarse, medium and fine)

▌ wood filler

TOOLS

▌ tracing paper

▌ carbon paper

▌ pencil

▌ straight edge

▌ coping saw or fret saw (or power fret saw if available)

▌ drill

▌ drill bit (small, just larger than the saw blade you plan to use

▌ drill bit ¼in (6mm)

▌ G-cramps (various sizes)

▌ rasp

▌ light hammer

▌ pliers

▌ punch

Familiarize yourself with Figs 4.1–4.3. Notice the eight shapes labelled A–H. You will be cutting out two of each shape using ³⁄₈in (9mm) birch ply.

TRACING THE SHAPES

Trace two of each part onto the ³⁄₈in (9mm) ply. Remember to leave ample room for the saw blade between each shape.

CUTTING OUT THE SHAPES

With either a coping saw or a fret saw, cut out two of each shape from the ply. If you have a powered fret saw, stack the shapes with pins and cut them out in duplicate. If sawing by hand, cut each piece as accurately as possible to avoid a lot of work truing up edges at a later stage. Label each part lightly with a pencil.

GLUING

Glue and pin together the two A parts keeping the edges flush and the bottom edges level. Keep the pins clear of the areas where the holes will be drilled later. Set aside the A assembly until the glue has dried.

Glue and pin the two G parts together, carefully matching the edges before pinning. Set aside until the glue has dried.

SHAPING WITH THE RASP

Notice in Figs 4.2 and 4.3 the diagonal lines on parts B, C and F. These lines indicate areas that need to be shaped before the parts can be glued to other parts. (After shaping, B and C will be glued to the A assembly. F will be glued to E.)

With a rasp, shape B, C and F (there are two of each part, so shape both!) in the areas indicated by the diagonal lines. Fig 4.4 shows B before and after shaping. Figs 4.5 and 4.6 show parts C and F before and after shaping.

After rasping, sand the areas you have shaped. Use coarse sandpaper in order to remove the rasp marks. Follow the coarse sandpaper with medium, then fine.

GLUING

Glue and pin one B and one C to each side of the A assembly. Refer to Fig 4.2 for locations. Make sure the edges of the A assembly and the B parts are flush and that their bases are level before pinning.

Fig 4.1 All parts except for H, which may be seen at Fig 4.10, after cutting from the plywood.

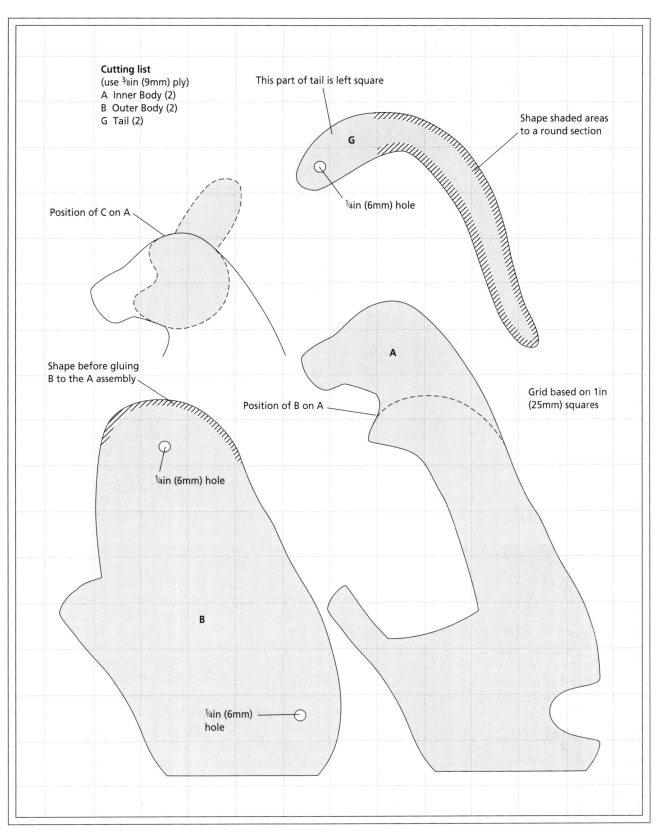

Cutting list
(use ³⁄₈in (9mm) ply)
A Inner Body (2)
B Outer Body (2)
G Tail (2)

This part of tail is left square

Shape shaded areas
to a round section

G

¼in (6mm) hole

Position of C on A

Shape before gluing
B to the A assembly

A

Position of B on A

Grid based on 1in
(25mm) squares

¼in (6mm) hole

B

¼in (6mm)
hole

Fig 4.2 Cutting list for A, B and G.

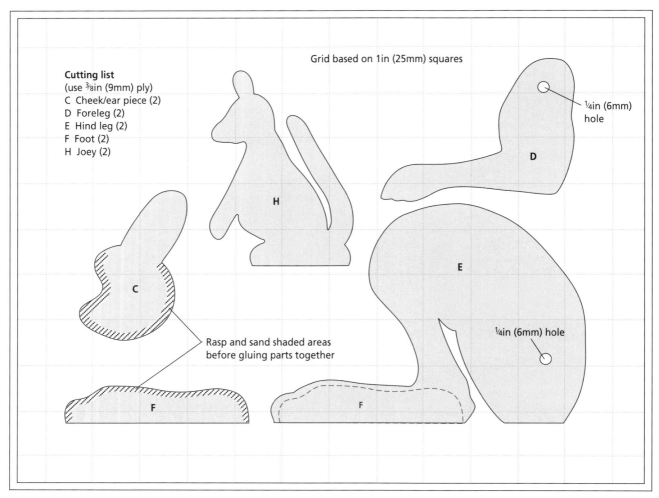

Cutting list
(use ³⁄₈in (9mm) ply)
C   Cheek/ear piece (2)
D   Foreleg (2)
E   Hind leg (2)
F   Foot (2)
H   Joey (2)

Grid based on 1in (25mm) squares

¹⁄₄in (6mm) hole

D

H

C

E

¹⁄₄in (6mm) hole

Rasp and sand shaded areas
before gluing parts together

F

F

Fig 4.3 Cutting list for the remaining parts.

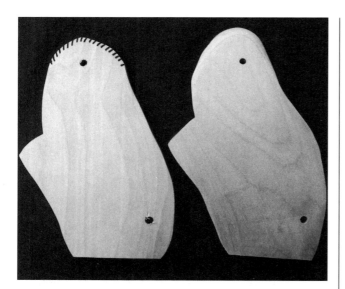

Fig 4.4 Part B, before and after shaping the shoulder area with the rasp.

Glue and pin one F to each of the two E parts. Figs 4.3 and 4.8 show where F is to be glued onto part E. Set aside the body assembly and the two hind leg assemblies until the glue has dried.

DRILLING

Several of the parts and assemblies will need to have holes drilled in them. Referring to Fig 4.2, find the locations of the two drill holes shown on part B and mark the locations with a pencil on the body.

Still referring to Fig 4.2, mark the position of the drill hole on the tail.

Refer to Fig 4.3 to find the locations of the drill holes in the forelegs (D) and the hind legs (E). Mark the locations of the holes on the parts with a pencil. Fit your drill with a ¹⁄₄in (6mm) drill bit and drill the holes.

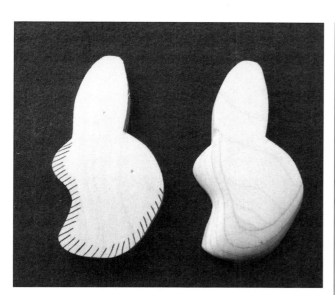

Fig 4.5 Part C, before and after rasping and sanding.

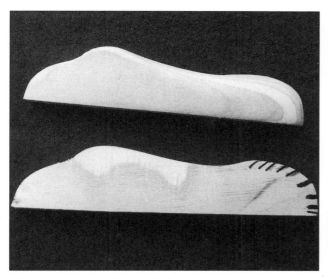

Fig 4.6 Part F, before and after rasping and sanding.

FITTING THE PARTS

Insert one of the two 2¹¹⁄₁₆in x ¼in (68 x 6mm) metal dowels into each of the two holes in the body. Before inserting dowel into the lower hole, fit the tail (G) into place in the recess in the body as shown in Fig 4.9. Then place the fore and hind legs temporarily in position on the ends of the dowels to check for free movement (*see* Fig 4.7). If the movement of any of the parts is stiff, remove the part and open up the hole slightly with a small round file. When you are satisfied with the movement of all parts, disassemble the parts and remove the metal dowels.

MORE SHAPING

Now you may finish the shaping of the disassembled parts and prepare their surfaces for painting. Take up the body first. With the rasp, round the edges of the A parts and, where they meet with parts B and C, smooth out any irregularities in the outlines and merge the edges to a single rounded contour. Shape the hind legs (E) and the forelegs (D) in the same way. All edges should have a smooth, well-rounded appearance. Refer to the finished toy in the colour section for an idea of how the shapes should appear.

Refer to Fig 4.2. Notice the dotted line near the base of the tail (G). This line indicates the boundary where shaping should end. Take up the rasp and round off all edges of the tail. Give the tail a round cross-section. Do not rasp on the base side of the dotted line.

Fig 4.7 Assembling the parts to check the fit.

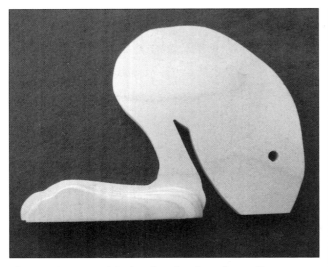

Fig 4.8 Part E, with the already shaped part F attached.

PREPARING THE WOOD FOR PAINTING

After you have finished shaping all parts with the rasp, remove the rasp marks by sanding with coarse sandpaper. Punch all panel pins below the surface of the wood. Fill all pin holes and blemishes with wood filler. When the filler has dried, sand it level. Then sand the entire surface of all parts to a smooth finish using medium, then fine paper. The parts are now ready for painting and may be set aside for the time being.

THE 'JOEY'

At last it's time to make the baby kangaroo. Glue and pin the two H parts together as shown in Fig 4.10. Make sure the bases and edges are flush before pinning. Set aside the joey until the glue has dried.

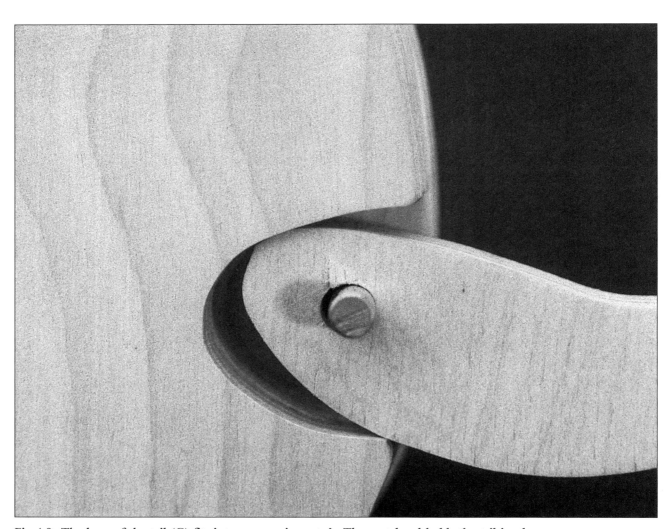

Fig 4.9 The base of the tail (G) fits into a recess in part A. The metal rod holds the tail in place.

When the glue is dry, refer to Fig 4.11 and plan where you will be shaping with the rasp. The diagonal lines indicate where wood needs to be removed with the rasp. Shape the joey with the rasp, rounding all edges. When you have finished shaping, go over all the areas of wood you have shaped with coarse sandpaper to remove the rasp marks (*see* Fig 4.12). Punch all panel pins below the surface of the wood. Fill all pin holes and other blemishes with wood filler. When the filler has dried, sand it flush to the surface of the wood. Then go over the whole of the joey with medium, then fine, sandpaper until the surfaces are perfectly smooth. The joey is now ready for priming and painting.

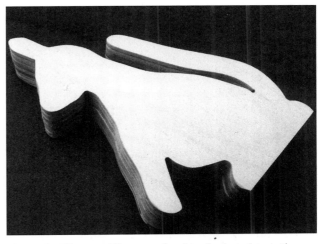

Fig 4.10 The two H parts, glued and pinned together.

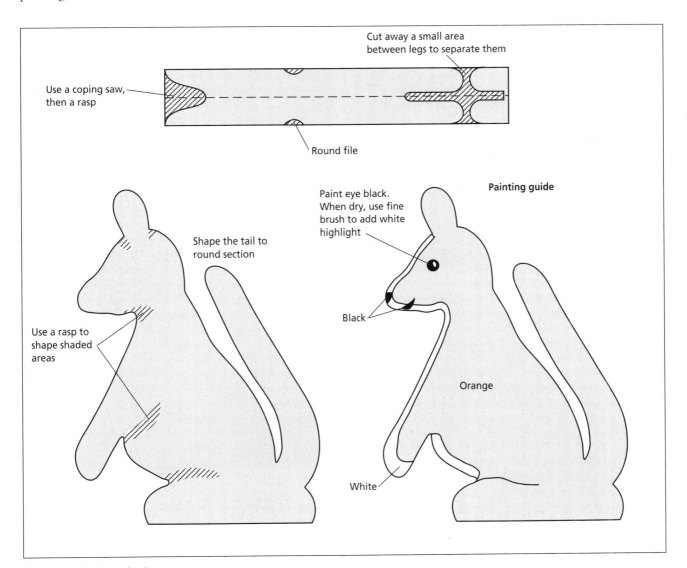

Fig 4.11 Shaping the joey.

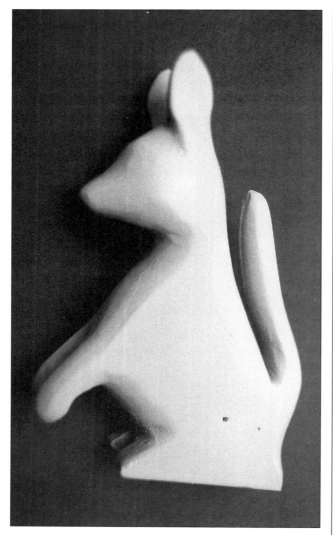

Fig 4.12 The rasp has been used to undercut areas around the neck and ears, which helps define these features and give the figure a sense of roundness.

PRIMING AND PAINTING

You may wish to come up with your own colour scheme. Or you can refer to the finished toy in the colour section and copy my colour scheme. Fig 4.11 contains a few notes on how I painted the joey. Whatever colour scheme you decide to follow, prime all parts twice, sanding lightly between coats. This will provide a perfect base upon which to paint your colours.

FINAL ASSEMBLY

When the paint has thoroughly dried, place the base end of the tail into the recess of the kangaroo's body and insert a steel dowel through hole in the body and tail (*see* Fig 4.9). Insert the other metal dowel through the hole in the shoulder area of the kangaroo. Should paint be clogging any of the holes, clean them out with a small round file.

Fit the forelegs onto the upper metal dowel and the hind legs onto the lower metal dowel. Place the starlock washers and caps onto the ends of the dowels and press them firmly into place. Fig 4.13 shows how the joey fits inside the kangaroo's pouch.

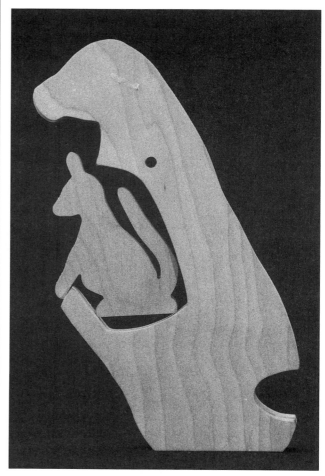

Fig 4.13 Parts A and H demonstrate how the joey will fit into the kangaroo's pouch.

Toys Based on Geometric Shapes

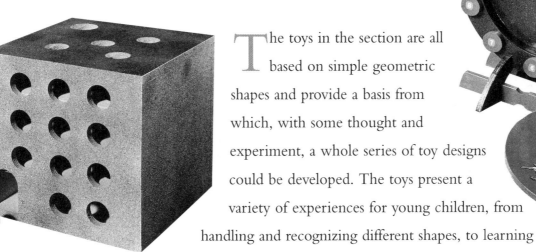

The toys in the section are all based on simple geometric shapes and provide a basis from which, with some thought and experiment, a whole series of toy designs could be developed. The toys present a variety of experiences for young children, from handling and recognizing different shapes, to learning how to tell time. And, if you use bright, bold colours, children will enjoy the toys even more.

As you work on these designs consider how each design could be changed or adapted to form a different toy from the same basic shape. Get into the habit of making notes and sketches of your ideas.

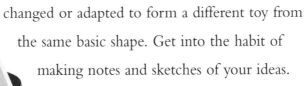

Clock (circle)

The first toy in this section is a clock that incorporates a stand into which the clock fits.
The stand itself, which fits like a jigsaw into the body of the clock and must be slotted together
to make the stand, will help a child develop manipulative skills and provide tactile experiences.
The clock can be used to teach a child to tell the time.

MATERIALS

- (3) birch ply $12^3/_{16}$ x $12^3/_{16}$ x $^3/_8$in (310 x 310 x 9mm)
- paint
- primer
- wood filler
- sandpaper
- wood glue
- pins
- epoxy resin
- (2) thin fibre washers with $^1/_4$in (6mm) diameter holes
- $^1/_4$in (6mm) starlock washer and cap
- $^1/_4$in (6mm) steel spring washer
- $^1/_4$in (6mm) brass or steel dowel, $1^1/_4$in (33mm) in length
- (2) 1in (25mm) brass round-head screws
- (2) spring washers with $^5/_{32}$in (4mm) holes

TOOLS

- light hammer
- hack saw
- handsaw
- fret saw with very fine saw blade (size 0/3)
- pencil
- compass
- straight edge
- router (optional)
- $^1/_4$in (6mm) round file
- protractor
- brushes
- drill
- $^5/_{32}$in (4mm) drill bit
- $^1/_4$in (6mm) drill bit
- file (for metal)
- cramps
- punch
- file (for wood)

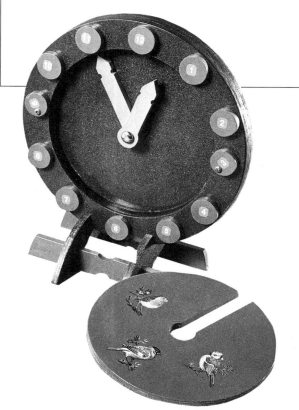

With a handsaw, cut three squares of $^3/_8$in (9mm) birch ply $12^3/_{16}$in x $12^3/_{16}$in (310mm x 310mm). The parts required are circular, but it will be easier to mark out the designs from the straight edges of the squares.

BASE

On one of these squares draw diagonal lines from corner to corner to form a cross (*see* Fig 5.1). The centre of the cross marks the centre of the square. Place the point of a compass on the centre mark and draw a circle $11^{13}/_{16}$in (300mm) in diameter. Now mark out the four small $1^3/_8$in (35mm) discs in the outer waste section.

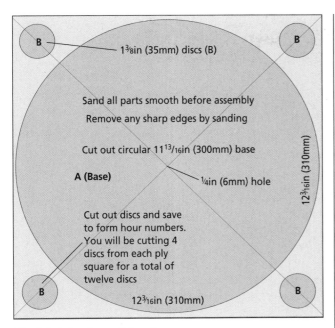

Fig 5.1 The first of the ply squares.

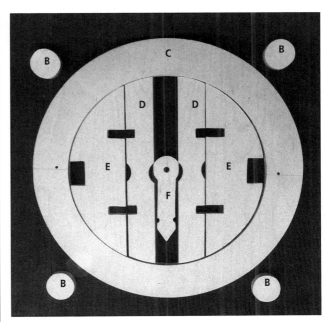

Fig 5.3 Parts B, C, D, E, and F sawn from the second ply square.

Cut out the 11¹³⁄₁₆in (300mm) circle (A) carefully and then cut out the 1³⁄₈in (35mm) discs (B) from the waste outer part. Drill a hole with a ¼in (6mm) bit in the centre of part A. Use the mark where you placed the point of the compass as a drilling mark. If you own a router, the large disc can be cut out perfectly using a circle cutting guide attached to the base of the router.

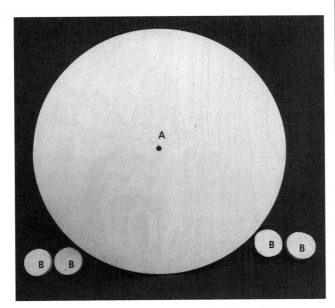

Fig 5.2 Parts A and B sawn from the first of the ply squares.

Fig 5.2 shows the parts: A (the base) and B (the four 1³⁄₈in (35mm) discs) sawn from the first of the plywood squares.

CENTRE SECTION

Fig 5.3 shows all the parts you will be cutting from the second of the three squares of plywood: the outer ring (C), the parts for the stand (two parts each labelled D and E), the four 1³⁄₈in (35mm) discs (B, again) and part F.

Mark out the second square piece of ply as shown in Fig 5.4. After you have completed the design, cut out the 11¹³⁄₁₆in (300mm) diameter disc with a fret saw. Then cut out the 8¹¹⁄₁₆in (220mm) diameter centre disc. This will give you the outer ring (C) and a centre disc. From the centre disc cut out parts D, E and F. (The areas in Fig 5.4 with diagonal shading are waste wood.) Parts D and E will form the stand on which the body of the clock will rest when assembled for play, and part F will form the hour hand.

Drill a ¼in (6mm) hole in the hour hand (F) as shown in Fig 5.4. The decorative semicircular notches can be shaped with a ¼in (6mm) round file.

Next, carefully cut out with the fret saw the four 1 ³⁄₈in (35mm) discs (B) from the outer waste area. You should now have eight parts B for your collection.

TOP SECTION

Take up the remaining ply square and, referring to Fig 5.5, again find the centre of the square by drawing diagonal lines from corner to corner. With a compass, draw the outer 11¹³⁄₁₆in (300mm) circle (C) and the inner 8¹¹⁄₁₆in) (220mm) circle (G). Draw the four 1³⁄₈in (35mm) discs (B) in the outer waste section.

Before you begin to saw the parts out of the square you must draw some more lines in order to locate the positions of the twelve clock numbers. Draw a horizontal line across the centre of the board and a vertical line to cross the horizontal line at the centre. These lines will mark the positions for the hour number discs (B) at 12, 3, 6, and 9 o'clock on the outer

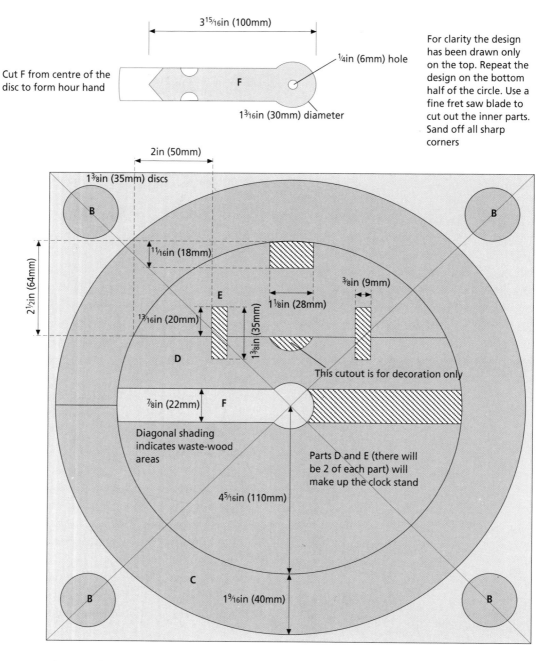

Fig 5.4 Plan for laying out the parts to be cut from the second ply square.

ring (the part C cut from this ply square). From the horizontal line mark off the remaining positions (1, 2, 4, 5, 7, 8, 10 and 11 o'clock) at 30° divisions (*see* Fig 5.5)

With a fret saw, cut the outer 11¹³⁄₁₆in (300mm) disc (C), the retaining disc (G) and the four 1³⁄₈in (35mm) hour number discs (B). You now have twelve discs (B),

one for each hour of the clock. From part G cut out the minute hand (H). The decorative semicircular notches can be shaped using a ¼in (6mm) round file.

Drill ¼in (6mm) hole in the base of the minute hand. Drill a ⁵⁄₃₂in (4mm) hole in two of the hour discs (B) as shown on Fig 5.5.

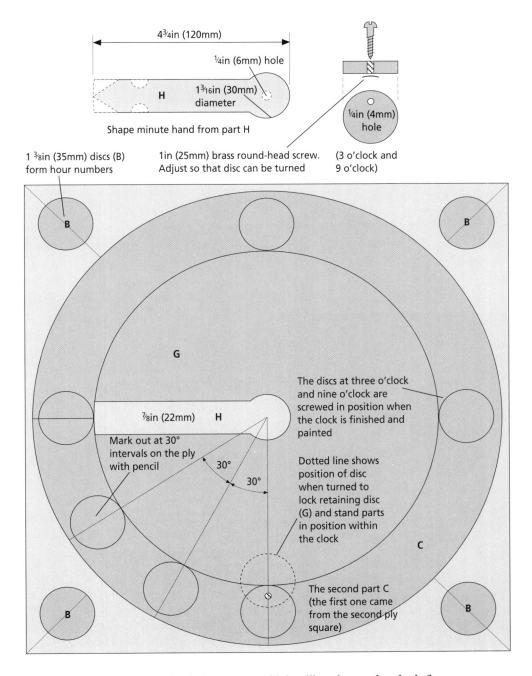

4¾in (120mm)

¼in (6mm) hole

H   1³⁄₁₆in (30mm) diameter

Shape minute hand from part H

¼in (4mm) hole

1³⁄₈in (35mm) discs (B) form hour numbers

1in (25mm) brass round-head screw. Adjust so that disc can be turned

(3 o'clock and 9 o'clock)

B

B

G

⁷⁄₈in (22mm)   H

Mark out at 30° intervals on the ply with pencil

30°

30°

The discs at three o'clock and nine o'clock are screwed in position when the clock is finished and painted

Dotted line shows position of disc when turned to lock retaining disc (G) and stand parts in position within the clock

C

The second part C (the first one came from the second ply square)

B

B

Fig 5.5 The plan for the third ply square, which will make up the clock face.

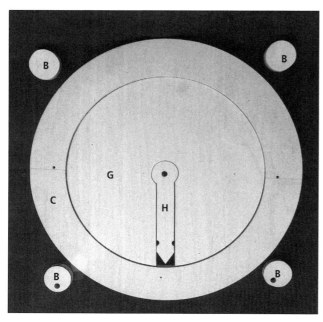

Fig 5.6 Parts B, C, G and H sawn from the third ply square.

Fig 5.6 shows the parts: outer ring (C), retaining disc (G), hour number discs (B) and the minute hand (H) that have all been sawn from the third plywood square.

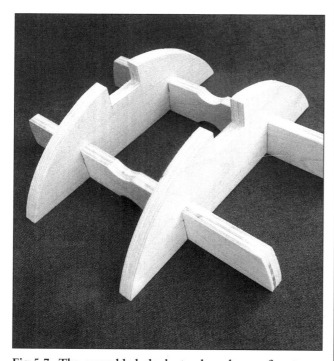

Fig 5.7 The assembled clock stand made up of parts D and E.

ASSEMBLING THE STAND

Take parts D and E. You should have two of each. Fill any small defects with wood filler. When the filler has dried, sand D and E to a smooth finish. Sand all edges to round them off slightly. Make sure no sharp corners remain.

Assemble the stand as shown in Fig 5.8. Check for a good fit. If the parts are tight, file or sand the notches so that they are easy for a child to assemble. Take down extra wood while sanding to allow for the thickness of the paint when finished. Fig 5.7 shows the assembled stand.

ASSEMBLING THE CLOCK BODY

Glue and pin the two rings (C) together. Make sure you face the side of the second part C (on which you have marked the positions of the hours) outwards (*see* Fig 5.8). When this assembly is dry, countersink the pin heads, fill any small defects with wood filler and sand smooth. Round the inner edge of the top ring with sandpaper just enough to remove the sharp edge. Don't bother sanding the outer edge of the assembly as this will be done at the next stage.

Glue and pin the base (A) to the bottom of the C assembly (*see* Fig 5.8). Again, keep the side with hour locations facing outwards. Countersink and fill the pin holes and any defects with wood filler. When the filler is dry, sand to a good finish. Now sand the outer rim of the completed assembly until smooth. Round the outer edges to remove the sharp corners.

FIXING THE HANDS TO THE CLOCK

For assembling the hands to the clock body you will require the following: two thin fibre washers, a $\frac{1}{4}$in (6mm) starlock washer and cap, a $\frac{1}{4}$in (6mm) steel spring washer and a $\frac{1}{4}$in x $1\frac{5}{16}$in (6mm x 33mm) brass or steel dowel. Cut a $1\frac{5}{16}$in (33mm) length of $\frac{1}{4}$in (6mm) metal dowel with a hacksaw. This is slightly longer than required for reasons that will be explained shortly.

Press the starlock washer and cap firmly onto one end of the metal dowel, then place the steel spring washer over the dowel and against the starlock washer. Slide the hour hand (F) onto the dowel, followed by a fibre washer. Now place the minute hand (H) and the remaining fibre washer in position (*see* Fig 5.8).

Insert the end of the metal dowel into the ¼in (6mm) hole in the centre of the base. (Make sure that none of the parts fall off the dowel during assembly!) The dowel will be a tight fit in the hole and it will be necessary to tap it through with a light hammer. This helps to compress the steel spring washer and hold the clock hands firmly in place so that they can be turned but still maintain their position. You will now find that the metal dowel protrudes through the back of the base slightly; this is because it is difficult to estimate the exact length of the dowel due to the compression of the spring washer. It is now a simple matter to carefully

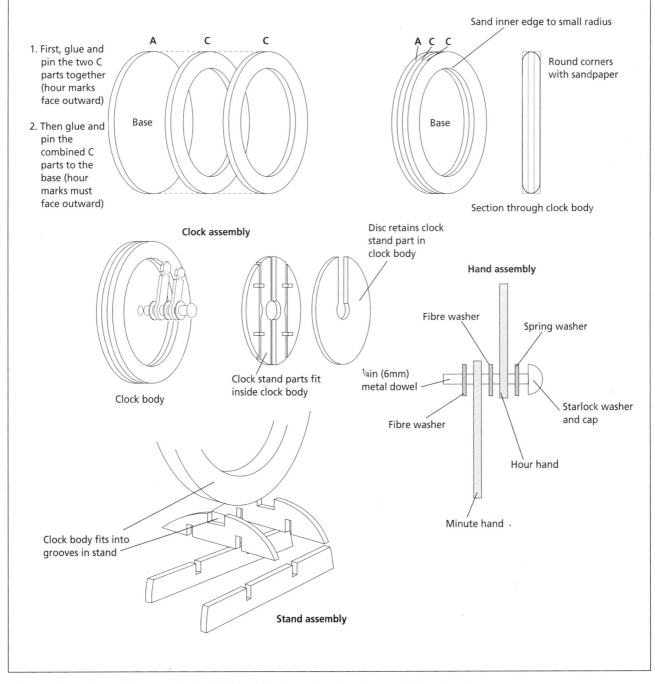

Fig 5.8 Assembly guides for the clock body, clock stand and minute and hour hands.

Fig 5.9 The assembled clock (the hour discs are not yet attached).

file the dowel flush with the base to obtain a perfect fit. Dismantle the assembly by tapping out the steel dowel with a punch and a light hammer.

THE HOUR NUMBERS

The twelve small 1⅜in (35mm) discs (B) are used to indicate the hours 1 to 12 on the clock face. Two of these discs (at 3 o'clock and 9 o'clock) will be used to secure the retaining disc (G) in position so that it will keep the stand parts within the clock body when the toy is not in use (*see* Fig 5.10).

Sand all twelve discs (B) and remove any sharp edges. Glue ten of the discs (excluding the discs with holes drilled in them, which will be used at 3 o'clock and 9 o'clock) in the positions you previously marked on part C (*see* Fig 5.5). Fig 5.9 shows the clock assembled but for the hour discs (B). Fig 5.10 shows the stand parts packed away beneath part G. Part G is locked in position by the two hour discs at 3 and 9 o'clock. The remaining hour discs have yet to be glued into position. (*See* Fig 5.8 for details of the order of packing.)

PAINTING AND ASSEMBLY

Make sure blemishes and small holes on all parts have been filled with wood filler and sanded smooth. Prime and paint to your selected colour scheme.

When all the painted parts are completely, dry fix the hand assembly to the clock body by smearing a little epoxy resin (Araldite Rapid is ideal) into the ¼in (6mm) hole in the base. A toothpick is useful for applying small amounts of resin. Then tap in the metal dowel containing the hand assembly (be careful not to get any resin on the inner face of the clock). Clean away any excess adhesive from the back of the base and retouch with paint if necessary.

Paint the hour numbers 1–12 on the small discs (B). You may wish to use the self-adhesive numbers available from stationer's and art shops. They are neat and easy to apply.

Using brass round-head screws and a spring washer beneath the disc (*see* Fig 5.5), fix the two discs at 3 o'clock and 9 o'clock as shown in Figs 5.5 and 5.10, then adjust the screws so that a child can turn the discs without too much effort (but don't make them too loose).

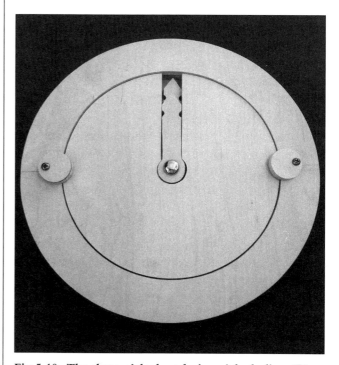

Fig 5.10 The three o'clock and nine o'clock discs (B) rotate to hold the clock stand beneath the retaining disc for storage.

Jigsaw Puzzle (octagon)

The design for this toy is based on an octagon and is a good exercise in straight line, internal and angled cutting. The shapes contained within the toy can be used to make a variety of constructions. They are arranged to form a layered jigsaw when the toy is packed. The brightly coloured pieces and the shape-building element will stimulate a child's imagination.

MATERIALS

- (4) birch ply 10 x 10 x ³⁄₈in (255 x 255 x 9mm)
- (4) wood dowel; length: 1⁵⁄₈in (42mm); diameter: ⁹⁄₁₆in (14mm)
- paint
- primer
- wood filler
- sandpaper (coarse, medium and fine)
- wood glue
- panel pins

TOOLS

- light hammer
- handsaw
- fret saw or coping saw
- pencil
- compass
- straight edge
- protractor
- brushes
- drill
- small drill bit (slightly larger than fret saw blade)
- ⁹⁄₁₆in (16mm) drill bit
- file
- punch

METHOD OF CONSTRUCTION

No grid is necessary for enlarging the parts for this toy. You will be marking out the design for the octagon and the internal parts from squares of ply. Cut four 10 x 10in (255 x 255mm) squares from ³⁄₈in (9mm) birch ply. These will form the base, two centre sections and the top.

BASE

On one of the squares, mark the centre by drawing diagonal lines from corner to corner to form a cross. Place the point of a compass on the centre and draw a circle of 7¹⁄₈in (180mm) diameter (*see* Fig 6.1). Cut the circle out at an angle of approximately 15°. This will prevent the piece from falling out when the toy is packed. If the fret sawing is done by hand, try to keep the blade at a constant angle. The angle is easily cut on a motorized fret saw by tilting the table 15°. The detail

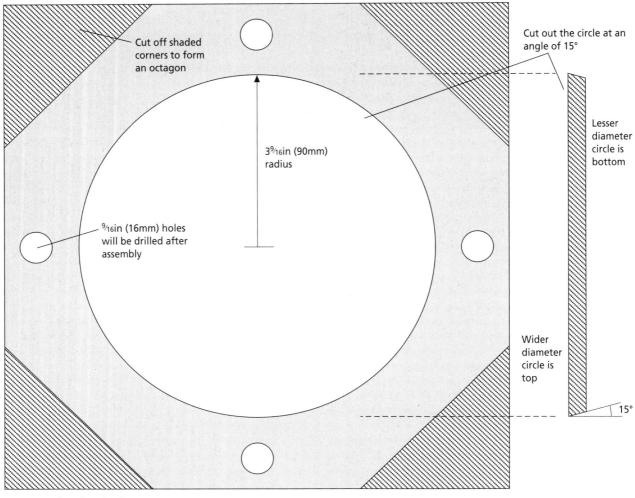

Cut off shaded corners to form an octagon

Cut out the circle at an angle of 15°

Lesser diameter circle is bottom

$3\frac{9}{16}$in (90mm) radius

$\frac{9}{16}$in (16mm) holes will be drilled after assembly

Wider diameter circle is top

15°

Fig 6.1 Plan for the base.

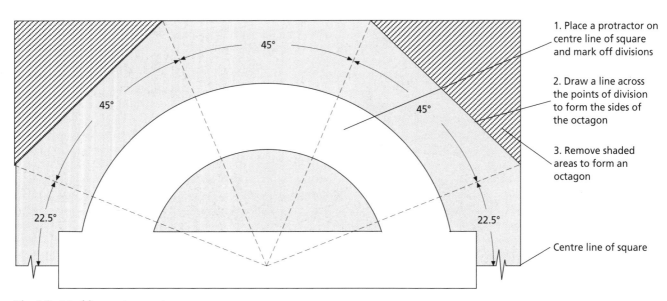

45°

45°

45°

22.5°

22.5°

1. Place a protractor on centre line of square and mark off divisions

2. Draw a line across the points of division to form the sides of the octagon

3. Remove shaded areas to form an octagon

Centre line of square

Fig 6.2 Marking out an octagon.

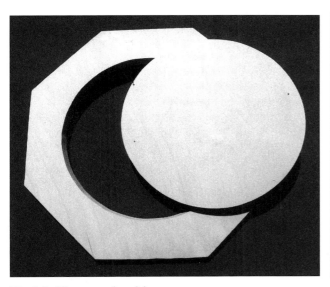

Fig 6.3 The completed base.

of the angle is shown in Fig 6.1, and the reason for it will become clear as you progress.

Mark out the octagon as shown in Fig 6.2, then cut off the corners shaded in the diagram to form the octagon. The ⁹⁄₁₆in (14mm) diameter holes shown on the plan (*see* Fig 6.1) need not be drilled at this stage as it is easier and more accurate to drill the four holes through the completed assembly, which will be explained later. The completed base is shown in Fig 6.3. The wider diameter of the circle is to be kept uppermost when finally assembling the toy.

THE TWO CENTRE SECTIONS

On two of the three remaining squares of ply, mark out the octagon on each piece as shown in Figs 6.4 and 6.5.

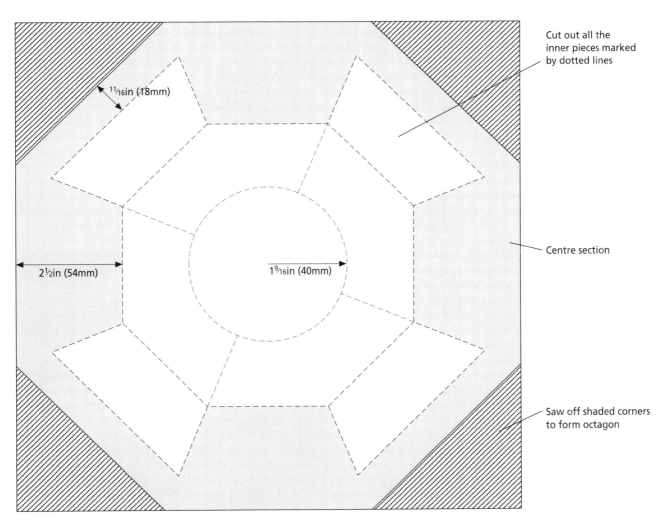

Cut out all the inner pieces marked by dotted lines

Centre section

Saw off shaded corners to form octagon

¹¹⁄₁₆in (18mm)

2½in (54mm)

1⁹⁄₁₆in (40mm)

Fig 6.4 Plan for one of the centre squares.

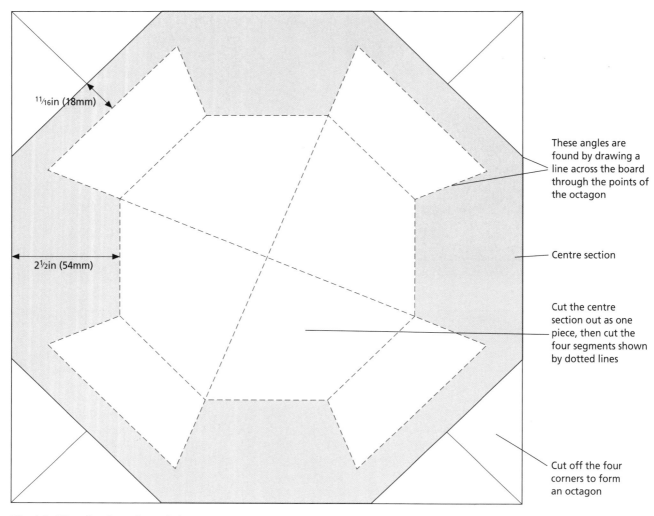

11/16in (18mm)

2 1/2 in (54mm)

These angles are found by drawing a line across the board through the points of the octagon

Centre section

Cut the centre section out as one piece, then cut the four segments shown by dotted lines

Cut off the four corners to form an octagon

Fig 6.5 Plan for the other of the centre squares.

Refer to Fig 6.2 for directions on how to mark out an octagon. Trace each of the designs shown on the plan by dotted lines onto the two centre sections. Now carefully fret saw all the parts shown by a dotted line and then cut off the shaded corner areas to form the octagon.

The parts cut from the two centre sections are shown in Figs 6.6 and 6.7.

TOP

On the remaining square of ply, mark out the 4 1/8 x 4 1/8in (105 x 105mm) square and the corners of the octagon as shown in Fig 6.8. The square is cut from the centre of the octagon at an angle of 15° (to retain the piece when the toy is packed after play). Cut off the shaded corners to form the octagon.

Fig 6.6 Parts cut from a centre square.

Fig 6.7 Parts cut from the other centre square.

| 2¹⁵⁄₁₆in (75mm) | 4⅛in (105mm) | 2¹⁵⁄₁₆in (75mm) |

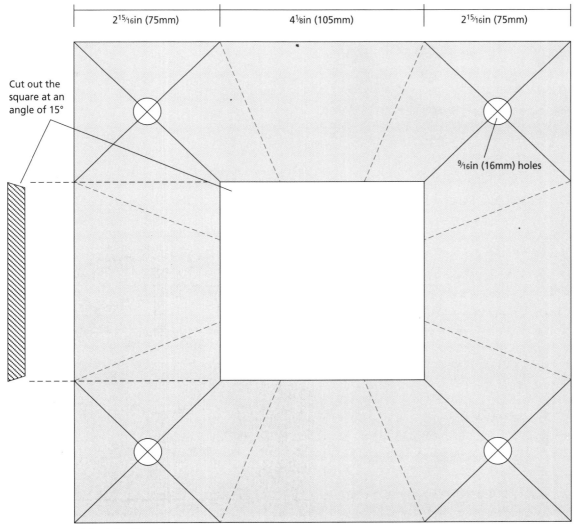

Cut out the
square at an
angle of 15°

⁹⁄₁₆in (16mm) holes

Fig 6.8 Plan for the top.

METHOD OF ASSEMBLY

Set aside all the pieces sawn from the inner parts of the two centre sections, then glue and pin together the two octagonal parts remaining from the two centre sections as shown in Fig 6.9. Wipe away any excess glue with a damp cloth.

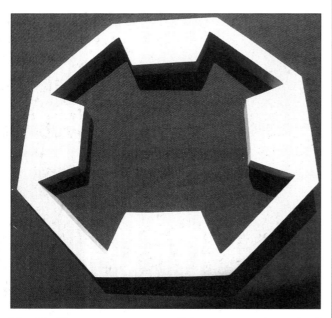

Fig 6.9 The two outer parts of the centre sections glued and pinned together.

When the glue is dry, sand all sawn inner edges to a smooth finish. (The outer edges will be sanded smooth when the parts are assembled.)

When the glued octagonal parts are dry, place in position on top of the base and then place the top onto this assembly (make sure the face with the larger square is uppermost). Keep all sides of the assembled octagon level. Fig 6.10 shows the order and placement of the parts for drilling and assembling.

DRILLING

Tape (masking tape is ideal) or pin the parts together temporarily and drill the four $^9/_{16}$in (14mm) holes in the positions marked from the plan (*see* Fig 6.8) through the complete assembly. Place a piece of scrap ply beneath the work to prevent splintering when the drill bit breaks through.

GLUING THE DOWELS

Cut the four wooden dowels to length and bevel the top of each with sandpaper to remove the sharp edges. Remove the tape or pins. Glue the four wooden dowels, with the bevelled edge of the dowels uppermost, into the holes in the base (*see* Fig 6.11). Make sure that the base is the correct way up (*see* Fig 6.10) and the bottom of the dowels are level and flush

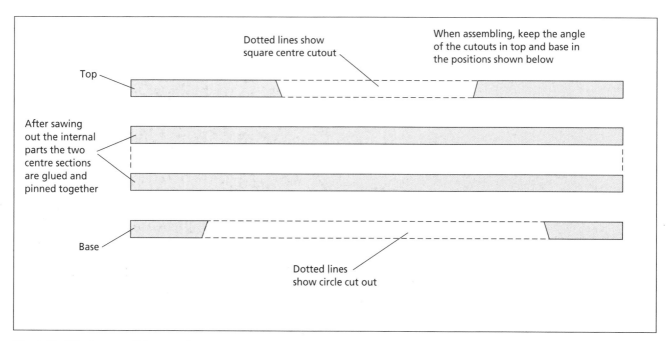

Fig 6.10 The layers of the puzzle.

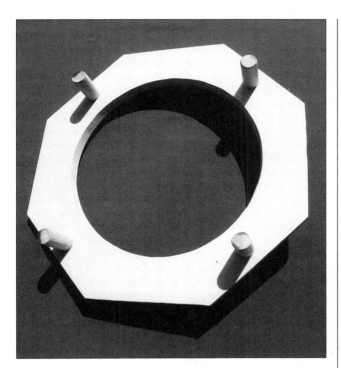

Fig 6.11 Glue the four dowels into the holes in the base.

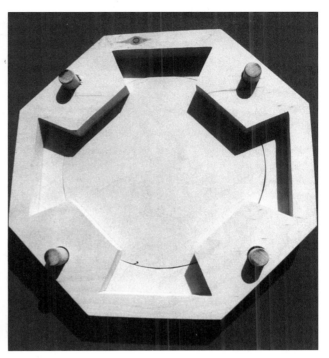

Fig 6.12 The laminated centre sections placed over the dowels in the base.

with the underside of the base. Fill any defects with wood filler and sand smooth.

FINISHING

The ^{9}/₁₆in (14mm) holes in the laminated centre sections should fit snugly over the protruding dowels in the base (see Fig 6.12). The top fits in position by simply placing it over the dowels. With these parts assembled, sand all the outer edges of the octagon smooth and level.

Fig 6.13 shows all the inner parts sawn from the centre sections fitted into position. The bottom layer is not visible but the two layers are interchangeable as complete units and the order of fitting is unimportant.

Countersink and fill any pin heads and defects with wood filler and sand all parts to a fine finish. Sand and remove any sharp edges of all the loose pieces that fit into the main structure like a jigsaw.

PAINTING

Give all parts two coats of primer, sanding smooth between coats. Then paint to your choice of colour scheme. Bright, contrasting colours are a good choice. They make shapes more attractive to a child.

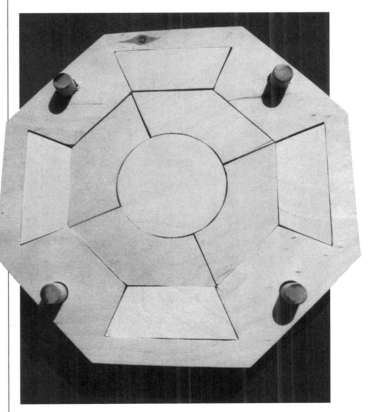

Fig 6.13 The inner parts, which were sawn from the centre sections, placed back into position.

Skittles (rectangle)

A rectangle is the basis of this toy, which is designed from the old game of table skittles.
Skittles was once popular amongst young and old alike and was often found in public houses,
where it was used for gambling purposes.
The game can be played by two children, who can take turns aiming the ball at the soldiers
(skittles). The player with the most points (soldiers knocked down) after a pre-arranged number of
'tries' wins. When opened, the lid of the box acts as a scoreboard.

MATERIALS

- birch ply 44 x 16 x ³⁄₈in (1000 x 400 x 9mm)
- wooden ball 1⁷⁄₁₆in (37mm) diameter
- metal rod 1¹³⁄₁₆ x ¼in (46 x 6mm)
- (2) metal rods 8⁷⁄₁₆ x ¼in (214 x 6mm)
- (6) ¼in (6mm) starlock washers and caps
- (4) brass hinges 1 x ½in (25 x 12mm)
- bolt and wing nut; 2¼ x ¼in (57 x 6mm)
- bolt and wing nut; ³⁄₈ x ¼in (35 x 6mm)
- paint
- primer
- wood filler
- sandpaper (coarse, medium and fine)
- wood glue
- panel pins

TOOLS

- lightweight drawing paper such as newsprint
- carbon paper
- light hammer
- handsaw
- fret saw or coping saw
- pencil
- straight edge
- brushes
- drill
- ¹⁄₁₆in (1.5mm) drill bit
- ¼ (6mm) drill bit
- 1in (25mm) drill bit
- file
- punch

THE BOX

Transfer the dimensions of the ends, base, top and sides (*see* Fig 7.1) to ³⁄₈in (9mm) ply. These parts form the rectangular box that contains the game. Mark the positions of the two ¼in (6mm) holes in the sides.

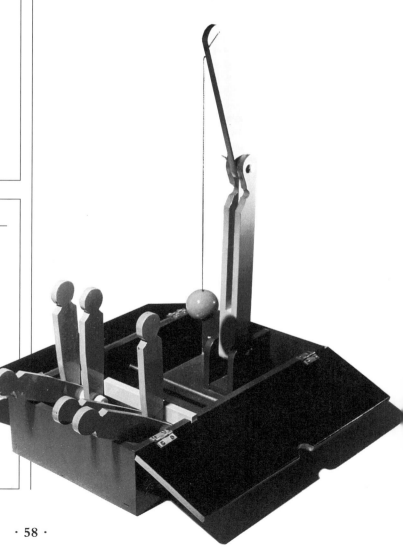

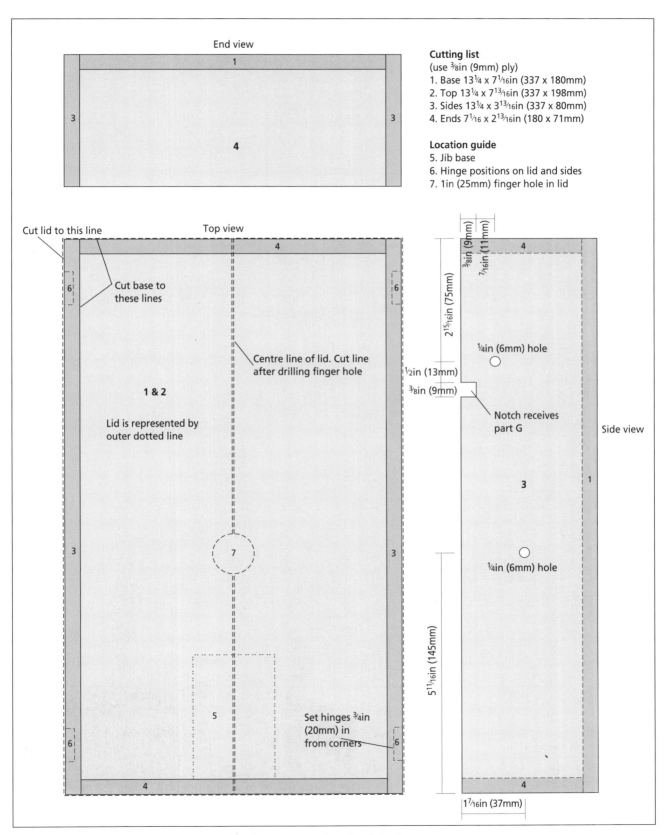

End view

Cutting list
(use ³⁄₈in (9mm) ply)
1. Base 13¼ x 7¹⁄₁₆in (337 x 180mm)
2. Top 13¼ x 7¹³⁄₁₆in (337 x 198mm)
3. Sides 13¼ x 3¹³⁄₁₆in (337 x 80mm)
4. Ends 7¹⁄₁₆ x 2¹³⁄₁₆in (180 x 71mm)

Location guide
5. Jib base
6. Hinge positions on lid and sides
7. 1in (25mm) finger hole in lid

Cut lid to this line

Top view

Cut base to these lines

Centre line of lid. Cut line after drilling finger hole

1 & 2

Lid is represented by outer dotted line

³⁄₈in (9mm)
⁷⁄₁₆in (11mm)

2¹⁵⁄₁₆in (75mm)

¼in (6mm) hole

½in (13mm)
³⁄₈in (9mm)

Notch receives part G

Side view

¼in (6mm) hole

Set hinges ¾in (20mm) in from corners

5

5¹¹⁄₁₆in (145mm)

1⁷⁄₁₆in (37mm)

Fig 7.1 Plans and cutting list for the sides, base, top, and ends of the box.

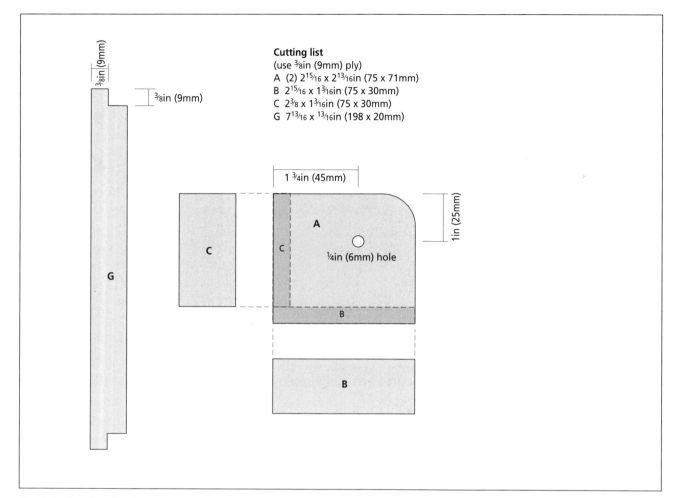

Cutting list
(use ³⁄₈in (9mm) ply)
A (2) 2¹⁵⁄₁₆ x 2¹³⁄₁₆in (75 x 71mm)
B 2¹⁵⁄₁₆ x 1³⁄₁₆in (75 x 30mm)
C 2³⁄₈ x 1³⁄₁₆in (75 x 30mm)
G 7¹³⁄₁₆ x 1³⁄₁₆in (198 x 20mm)

³⁄₈in (9mm)

³⁄₈in (9mm)

1 ³⁄₄in (45mm)

1in (25mm)

A

C

¼in (6mm) hole

B

G

C

B

Fig 7.2 Cutting list for A, B, C and G.

TOP

The top is cut lengthwise into two pieces (at a later stage) to form a hinged lid that, when open, is used as a scoreboard. This piece can be set aside until a later stage.

SIDES

Pin the two sides together temporarily and drill the ¼in (6mm) holes. Cut out the notch on the top edge of the sides as seen in Fig 7.1. The notch will take part G, which will be explained at a later stage in construction.

Separate the sides by removing the pins. Glue and pin the sides to the base, making sure the drilled holes and the notches are opposite each other. The positions of the sides on the base are indicated in Fig 7.1 by dotted lines.

ENDS

Glue and pin the two ends to the sides and the base to form a box. Wipe away any excess glue with a damp cloth and leave assembly to dry.

THE JIB ASSEMBLY

Transfer the dimensions of parts A, B and C from Fig 7.2 to ply. Then enlarge (with the grid) and trace parts D, E and F from Fig 7.3 and transfer these to the ply.

Drill the ¼in (6mm) holes in A. These holes take the 2¼ x ¼in (57 x 6mm) bolts on which the jib is assembled. Sand smooth all parts. Glue and pin parts B and C between the A parts in the positions shown in Fig 7.2. Allow the glue to dry. When the glue has dried, glue and screw the jib base to the box in the position shown in Fig 7.1. Fig 7.4 shows the box with the jib base in place.

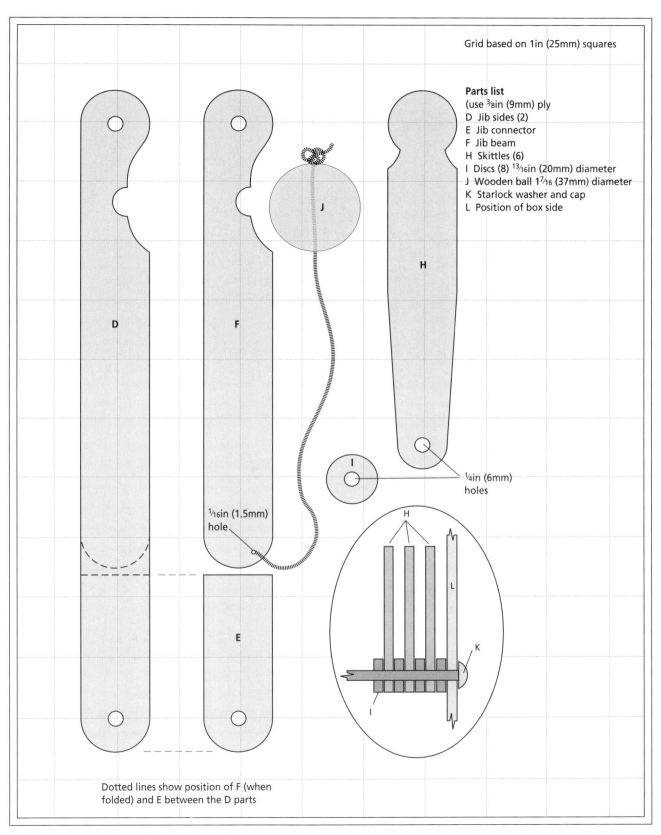

Grid based on 1in (25mm) squares

Parts list
(use ³⁄₈in (9mm) ply
D Jib sides (2)
E Jib connector
F Jib beam
H Skittles (6)
I Discs (8) ¹³⁄₁₆in (20mm) diameter
J Wooden ball 1⁷⁄₁₆ (37mm) diameter
K Starlock washer and cap
L Position of box side

¹⁄₄in (6mm) holes

¹⁄₁₆in (1.5mm) hole

Dotted lines show position of F (when folded) and E between the D parts

Fig 7.3 Cutting list for D, E, F, H and I.

Fig 7.4 The box with the base for the jib assembly in place. Note the position of the holes for the two metal rods and the notches cut out to accept part G.

Drill a ¹⁄₁₆in (1.5mm) hole in F as shown in Fig 7.3. This hole accepts a length of string to which a wooden ball is attached. Drill a ¼in (6mm) hole in the base of F to take a 1³⁄₈ x ¼in (35 x 6mm) bolt and wing nut, which allows F to fold between the jib sides (D) when the toy is packed after play. Part F is fitted (after painting) between the jib sides (*see* Fig 7.5).

The lower part (D) is fixed in position (after painting) between the sides of the jib base (A) with a ¼in (6mm) bolt and wing nut. The completed jib assembly may be seen in Fig 7.7.

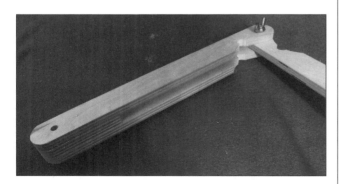

Fig 7.5 Part F fits between the two D parts.

THE SKITTLES

Transfer the design for the six soldiers (skittles) to the ply and saw to shape. Then drill the ¼in (6mm) hole in the base of each one.

The eight spacer discs (I) are best drawn on one strip of ³⁄₈in (9mm) ply and the ¼in (6mm) holes drilled before sawing to shape as the small discs would be difficult (and dangerous!) to hold.

Fig 7.6 shows the sawn and drilled skittles (H) and spacer discs (I).

FINAL CUTTING AND DRILLING

Cut G to the dimensions shown in Fig 7.2. This piece slots into the notches that were cut from the sides of the box and prevents the skittles falling forward during play.

Drill a ¹⁄₁₆in (1.5mm) hole through the centre of the wooden ball to accept a length of string for attaching to F.

TRIAL ASSEMBLY

To check that all parts move freely, temporarily assemble (do not fit starlock washers and caps at this stage) the skittles and spacer discs onto the metal rod

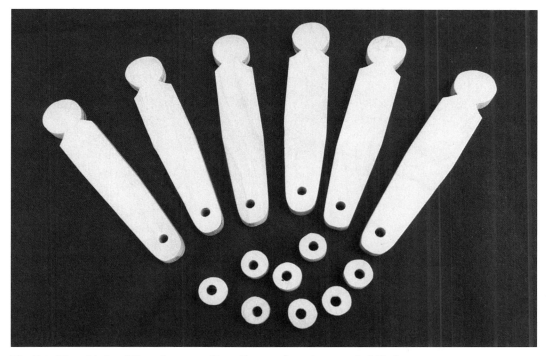

Fig 7.6 The skittles (H) and spacer discs (I) sawed to shape and drilled.

in the order shown in Fig 7.3. Fit part G into the notches in the box sides. Lean all the skittles forward onto G and then temporarily attach the wooden ball to F with a length of string.

Adjust the string and jib until the ball strikes the skittles at head height. Then test that the skittles fall backward easily onto the edge of the box when struck (*see* Fig 7.7).

FINISHING

Disassemble the parts and countersink all panel pins. Fill all holes left by panel pins and any defects with wood filler. Sand all parts smooth, then prime.

THE LID

Mark out the centre of the top (lid) by drawing lines diagonally from corner to corner. Drill a 1in (25mm) hole at this point. This is a finger hole to open the top. Cut the top in half along its length to form two lids. These will be hinged (after painting) to the box so that the cover may close (*see* Fig 7.8).

PAINTING AND ASSEMBLING

Paint the underside of the two parts of the lid (the scoreboards) with blackboard paint. You will probably

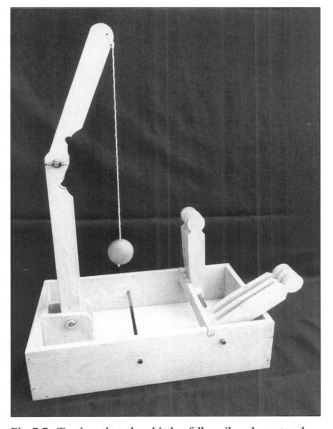

Fig 7.7 Testing that the skittles fall easily when struck by the wooden ball.

Fig 7.8 The box closes up neatly with all the parts inside.

need two coats. Paint all other parts to your own colour scheme.

When all painted parts are completely dry, assemble the toy as previously described. Fit the starlock washers and caps to both the ends of the metal rod that holds the skittles and the metal support rod on which the skittles rest. Fit the lid with the four hinges. Hinge positions are shown in Fig 7.1.

To pack the toy after play, remove G from the notches in the box sides and place it in the box. Lean the skittles forward so that they rest horizontally on the metal support rod. Loosen the two wing nuts on the jib assembly and fold F between the D parts and rest it on the metal rod on which the skittles are mounted (*see* Fig 7.9). Add a piece of chalk for scoring and close the lid to complete.

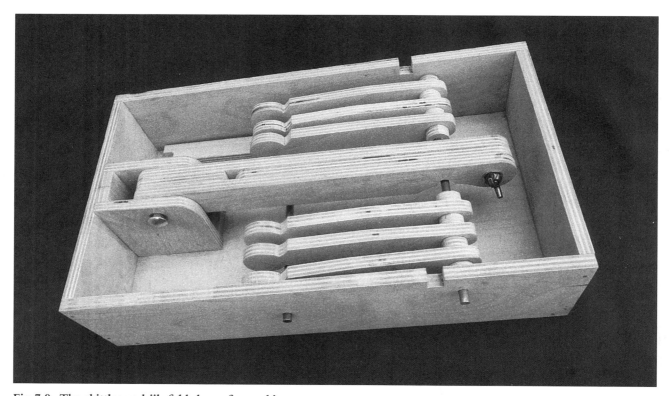

Fig 7.9 The skittles and jib fold down for packing.

Ball-in-a-Cube Game (square)

*The ball-in-a-cube game is easy to make and leaves the maker plenty
of scope to alter the design to make it more difficult to play. I have included guidance
(should you need it) at the end of the instructions on how this can be achieved. But if you have
your own ideas to make the game more devious and difficult, go right ahead!
The game consists of a simple enclosed box with floors. A wooden ball is dropped through a hole in
the top of the box and is guided by the player through holes in each floor until it is finally retrieved
through a door-shaped hole in the front of the box on the ground floor.*

MATERIALS

▮ birch ply 21 x 21 x $^3/_8$in (530 x 530 x 9mm)
▮ 1in (25mm) diameter wooden ball
▮ paint
▮ primer
▮ wood filler
▮ sandpaper (coarse, medium and fine)
▮ wood glue
▮ panel pins

TOOLS

▮ light hammer
▮ handsaw
▮ fret saw or coping saw
▮ pencil
▮ compass
▮ straight edge
▮ brushes
▮ drill
▮ small drill bit (slightly larger than fret saw blade)
▮ $^7/_8$in (22mm) drill bit
▮ 1$^3/_{16}$in (30mm) drill bit
▮ file
▮ punch

SAWING AND DRILLING THE PARTS

Cut out all the parts shown in the plans from $^3/_8$in (9mm) birch ply. Label each part lightly with a pencil as you go.

TOP

Draw diagonal lines from corner to corner of the square to find the centre as shown in Fig 8.1. Then mark out the positions for the three $^7/_8$in (22mm) diameter holes and the 1$^3/_{16}$in (30mm) diameter hole. Drill the holes. The wooden ball is passed through the 1$^3/_{16}$in (30mm) hole in play; the smaller $^7/_8$in (22mm) holes allow light into the interior of the box.

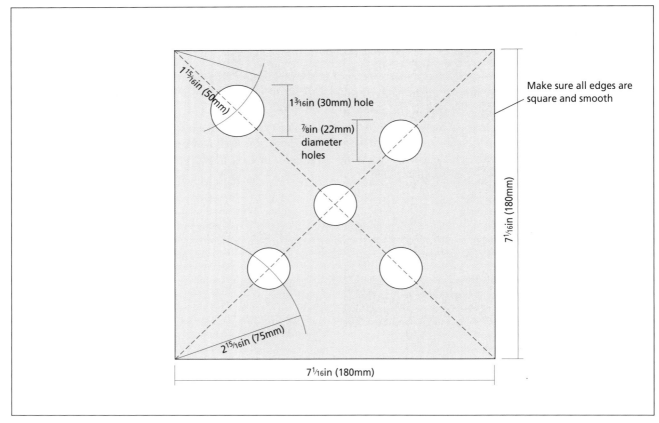

Fig 8.1 The top.

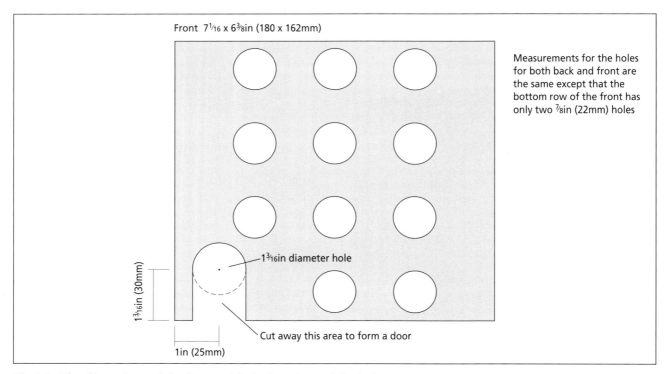

Fig 8.2 The dimensions of the front, with the locations of the holes.

Fig 8.3 The front completed.

FRONT

From Fig 8.2 mark out the positions for the eleven ⅞in (22mm) holes and the 1³⁄₁₆in (30mm) hole that forms the door.

Cut out the doorway shape as shown on the plan. Drill all the holes. The front is shown in Fig 8.3.

BACK

From Fig 8.4 mark out the positions for the twelve ⅞in (22mm) holes and then drill them carefully.

FLOORS

Mark the position from Fig 8.5 for the 1³⁄₁₆in (30mm) hole on each of the three floors and then drill.

SIDE AND BASE

The two sides and the base are left plain (*see* Fig 8.6), but you might wish to incorporate an idea of your own into these pieces.

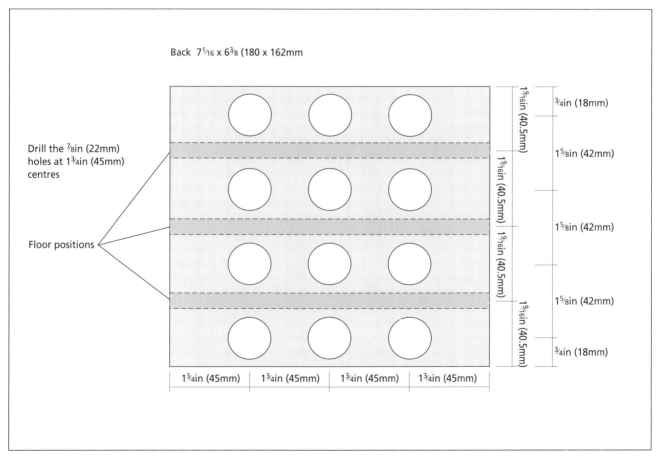

Back 7¹⁄₁₆ x 6³⁄₈ (180 x 162mm)

Drill the ⅞in (22mm) holes at 1¾in (45mm) centres

Floor positions

1⁹⁄₁₆in (40.5mm)   ¾in (18mm)

1⁹⁄₁₆in (40.5mm)   1⁵⁄₈in (42mm)

1⁹⁄₁₆in (40.5mm)   1⁵⁄₈in (42mm)

1⁹⁄₁₆in (40.5mm)   1⁵⁄₈in (42mm)

¾in (18mm)

1¾in (45mm)   1¾in (45mm)   1¾in (45mm)   1¾in (45mm)

Fig 8.4 The back.

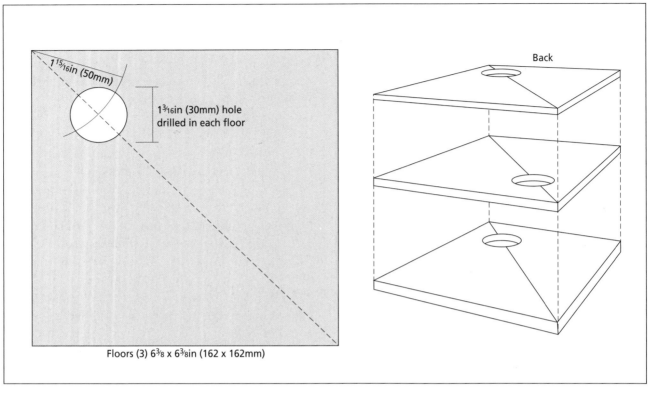

Fig 8.5 The dimensions for the floors, and the arrangement of the floors within the box.

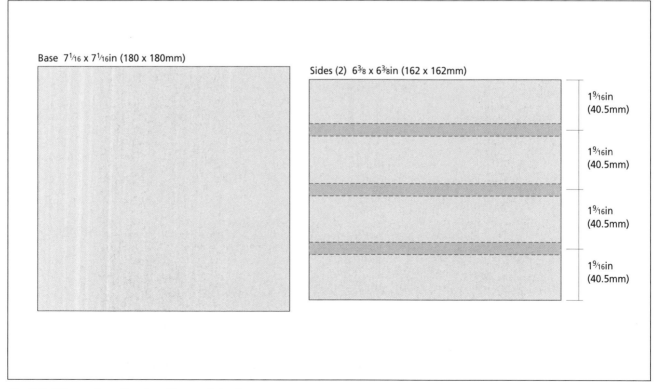

Fig 8.6 Dimensions for the sides and the base.

Fig 8.7 **The back and the two sides are pinned to the base.**

PAINTING THE INTERIOR

With a pencil, mark out the positions of the floors on the back (*see* Fig 8.4) and the two sides (*see* Fig 8.6). The lines should show on the inside of the box during construction and are a guide to fitting the floors in position.

The interior of the box would be very difficult to paint when assembled so it is advisable to paint or varnish these parts before assembly. Establish the parts to be painted and mask off the areas where the floors will be fixed (the glue will not adhere to painted or varnished areas). Also, leave the edges of the floors unpainted. Use a clear varnish or white paint so that the interior of the box is light.

ASSEMBLY

Glue and pin the back to the base. The back fits on top of and flush with the back edge of the base. Make sure the four rows of holes run horizontally (*see* Fig 8.7).

Glue and pin a side to the base and the back in the position shown in Fig 8.7. Then fix the opposite side in the same manner. Note in Fig 8.7 the pencil lines indicating the position of the floors.

Glue and pin the top to the two sides and the back. The large hole should be at the front right.

Fix the top shelf in position (using the previously drawn pencil lines as a guide) by gluing and pinning to the sides and back. The large hole is positioned to the back and right of the box. The middle shelf is fitted with the large hole to the front right and the lower shelf with the large hole to the back right using the

Fig 8.8 **The three floors pinned and glued into position on the sides and back.**

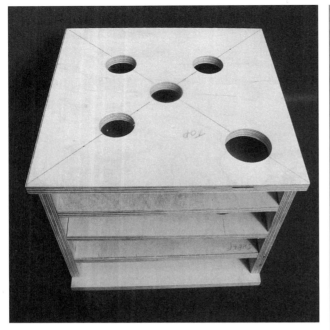

Fig 8.9 The base and top are pinned and glued into position.

pencil lines as a guide for their positions. Fig 8.8 shows the floors glued and pinned in position to the sides and back. Fig 8.5 also shows the arrangement of the floors.

You will note in Fig 8.9 that the base and the top protrude forward from the sides. Slot the front into position between the protruding top and base, and glue and pin it into place with the door to the bottom left of the box (*see* Fig 8.10).

FINISHING

Countersink the panel pins and fill the holes and any blemishes with wood filler. Sand smooth all the box surfaces, paying particular attention to the edges of drilled holes. Sand a small radius on all the box edges, then prime and paint to your colour scheme. Paint the wooden ball to contrast with the colour of the box.

Here are a few ideas to make the game more difficult to play for older children (or adults).

• Each floor could have a series of small holes drilled in them, leaving an erratic pathway.
• Small walls could be constructed in the manner of a maze (including dead ends), through which the ball is guided.
• The two outer blank walls could have the odd $1\frac{3}{16}$in (30mm) hole drilled in them at floor level so that the ball could fall out before reaching its destination.

I'll refrain from making any more suggestions as I'm sure at this stage you will have developed some ingenious ideas of your own.

Fig 8.10 The front fits between the protruding ends of the base and the top.

Toys Based on Everyday Articles

In this section I hope to stimulate your imagination into developing toy ideas from objects found around the house. My daughter selected the items for the toys in this section (in around three seconds!), challenging me to create toys from the following objects: a pop-up toaster, a ladies' long leather boot, a teapot and a carpet sweeper.

It is an act of pure invention to conjure up ideas from seemingly mundane items like a toaster or a carpet sweeper, but creative exercises such as these can result in unexpected and fascinating toys. You will come up against stumbling blocks – I did – but these will be overcome. I prefer to work on two or three designs at the same time. When ideas stop flowing on one theme I continue with another. This method usually clears the block and leaves the mind open to new ideas and possibilities.

When designing your own toys you will find that some good ideas will have to be omitted for the sake of safety or some other factor. Don't discard the idea! It might be useful for a time when you might be designing toys for adults. There are many adult collectors of wooden toys, especially of automatons (mechanical toys).

Pop-up Toaster

I think a child will appreciate the humour of a mouse sharing his or her breakfast, and, like all pets, this mouse wants serving first.

MATERIALS

- birch ply 32 x 16 x $^3/_8$in (800 x 400 x 9mm)
- (3) brass or steel dowels; length: $3^7/_8$in (98mm); diameter: $^1/_4$in (6mm)
- (6) starlock washers and caps
- (4) $^3/_4$in (18mm) eyescrews
- (2) springs (The springs will have to be selected by trial and error and can be purchased in assorted packs from a supplier at the back of the book.)
- (4) $^3/_4$in (18mm) No 6 brass round-head screws
- masking tape
- panel pins
- primer
- paints
- brushes
- wood glue
- sandpaper (coarse, medium and fine)
- wood filler

TOOLS

- tracing paper
- carbon paper
- pencil
- straight edge
- coping saw or fret saw (or power fret saw if available)
- (2) saw blades: one fine for turning sharp corners and one a bit wider to ease the cutting of straight lines
- drill
- (3) drill bits: $^1/_{16}$in (1.5mm), $^1/_8$in (3mm) and $^1/_4$in (6mm)
- rasp
- file
- light hammer
- pliers

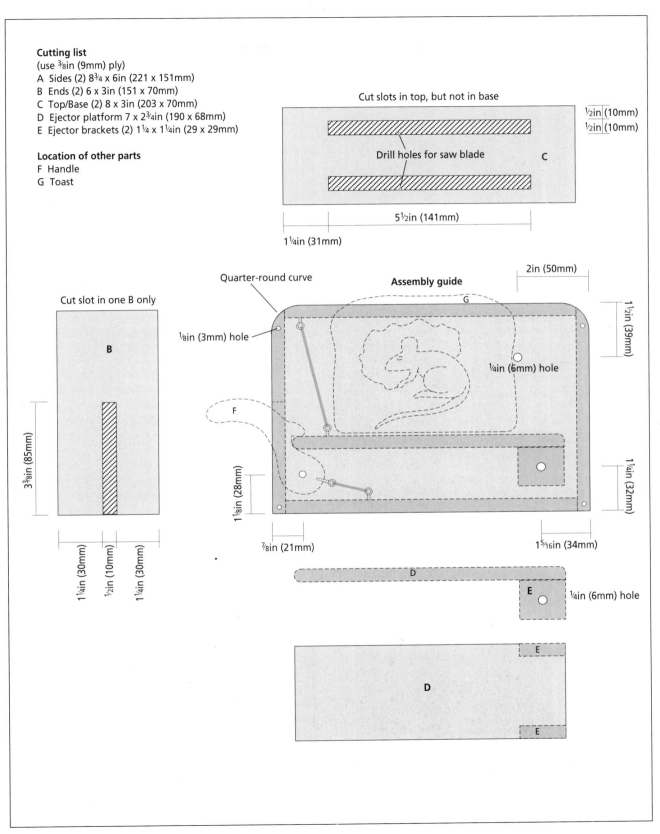

Cutting list
(use ⅜in (9mm) ply)
A Sides (2) 8¾ x 6in (221 x 151mm)
B Ends (2) 6 x 3in (151 x 70mm)
C Top/Base (2) 8 x 3in (203 x 70mm)
D Ejector platform 7 x 2¾in (190 x 68mm)
E Ejector brackets (2) 1¼ x 1¼in (29 x 29mm)

Location of other parts
F Handle
G Toast

Cut slots in top, but not in base

Drill holes for saw blade

C

½in (10mm)
½in (10mm)

5½in (141mm)

1¼in (31mm)

Cut slot in one B only

B

3⅜in (85mm)

1¼in (30mm)   ½in (10mm)   1¼in (30mm)

Quarter-round curve

Assembly guide

G

2in (50mm)

1½in (39mm)

⅛in (3mm) hole

¼in (6mm) hole

F

1⅛in (28mm)

⅞in (21mm)

1¼in (32mm)

1⁵⁄₁₆in (34mm)

D

E

¼in (6mm) hole

E

D

E

Fig 9.1 Cutting list and assembly guide.

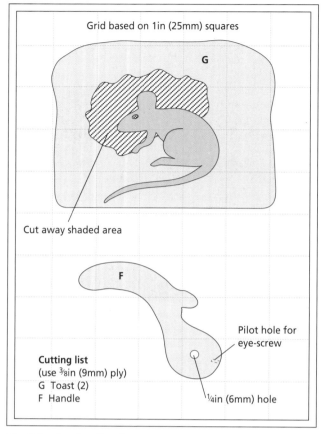

Grid based on 1in (25mm) squares

G

Cut away shaded area

F

Pilot hole for
eye-screw

Cutting list
(use ³⁄₈in (9mm) ply)
G Toast (2)
F Handle

¹⁄₄in (6mm) hole

Fig 9.2 Cutting list for parts F and G.

Familiarize yourself with Figs 9.1 and 9.2. Notice the seven shapes labelled A–G. You will be cutting two each of A, B, C, E and G and one each of D and F. All parts will be cut from ³⁄₈in (9mm) plywood.

LAYING OUT THE DIMENSIONS

You will need to transfer only two shapes, F and G, from a grid onto plywood. The remaining parts can easily be laid out on the plywood using a straight edge to measure the dimensions and a square to keep the right angles true. Choose one of the two C parts for the top of the toaster. Measure and mark on this piece of wood the two slots for the toast as shown in Fig 9.1. Choose one of the two B parts to be the end of the toaster that will have a slot for the handle (*see* Fig 9.1). Mark on the wood the location of the slot.

Refer to Fig 9.1. Mark with a pencil the locations of the ¹⁄₄in (6mm) drill holes on parts A, E and F. Choose one of the parts A and mark the four ¹⁄₈in (3mm) drill holes in that part.

Note in Fig 9.1 the locations of the ¹⁄₁₆in (1.5mm) pilot holes to be drilled in C, D and F. These locations are not engraved in stone; much will depend on the strength of the springs used. Experiment with the springs to find the best locations for the pilot holes.

CUTTING OUT THE SHAPES

Use either a coping saw or a fret saw with a fine blade to cut out the two G parts and the one F part from the ply. Notice in Fig 9.2 the areas of diagonal shading in the interior of the toast shape. This area indicates waste wood that needs to be sawn out of the toast. Drill a small hole anywhere in the waste-wood area. After drilling, pass the saw blade through the hole and re-attach the blade to the saw frame. Then proceed to saw out the inner shape from each of the G parts.

The fine saw blade in the coping or fret saw will also be needed to make the interior cuts in one of the B parts and one of the C parts. Notice in Fig 9.1 that the two slots are located in the interior part C. You will need to drill a hole in the waste-wood areas of each slot to allow passage of the saw blade.

The rest of the parts can be cut using a heavier, wider saw blade, as this blade will keep more easily to a straight line than a fine blade.

The two A parts are best cut in duplicate. Temporarily pin together the two pieces of wood from which the parts will be cut. Then cut both A parts in one operation. Pay particular attention to the rounded corners to produce identical parts. Fig 9.3 shows part A cut to shape.

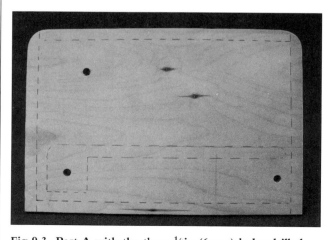

Fig 9.3 Part A with the three ¹⁄₄in (6mm) holes drilled. Dotted lines indicate the positions of the ends (B), the top and base (C) and the toast ejector assembly (D and E).

DRILLING

While the two A parts are still pinned together, fit your drill with a ¼in (6mm) bit and drill the three holes you have marked in A. Drilling in duplicate will ensure that the holes are in identical locations. Drill the ¼in (6mm) holes in parts E and F as well.

Remove the panel pins holding together the two A parts. Fit a ⅛in (3mm) bit to the drill. Drill four holes in one of the A parts, one hole in each corner as shown in Fig 9.1.

Fit a ¹⁄₁₆in (1.5mm) drill bit to your drill. Fig 9.1 shows the general locations of the ¹⁄₁₆in (1.5mm) pilot holes. These holes will accept the eyescrews to which the springs will be attached. Drill the holes. Don't go all the way through the wood! The holes are merely to guide the screws into the wood.

SHAPING AND SANDING

Parts G and part F will need light shaping with the rasp. The aim here is to remove any irregularities the saw blade has left behind. Don't neglect the interior shapes of the two G parts. The object there will be to make the shapes look like the mice have been eating away at the bread (*see* Fig 9.4).

A file may be used to smooth the interior of the slots in parts B and C.

Fig 9.5 The interior of the toaster.

Part D will need some attention with the rasp. Refer to Fig 9.1 to see how one end of D is fully rounded and the other end is half rounded. Sanding with coarse sandpaper should follow any shaping with the rasp in order to remove the rasp marks from the wood. Follow the coarse sandpaper with medium, then fine.

The faces and edges of all parts should now be sanded until smooth. All sharp edges should be sanded until slightly rounded. Fill all holes left by the panel pins and any blemishes with wood filler. When the filler has dried, sand it level. The object of this sanding step is twofold: to prepare the surfaces for painting and to true all edges so that they fit snugly when assembled.

THE TOASTER

The first step in assembling the toaster is simply making a box as shown in Fig 9.5. Glue and pin the two ends (B) to the base (the C part without slots) and the top (the C part with slots). Immediately before the glue has had a chance to dry, take the A part that does not have the four ⅛in (3mm) holes. Glue and pin this A part in place on the side of the box. Your box should now be a strong assembly with one side open as shown in Fig 9.5. The open side will allow you access to the interior of the toaster so that you can assemble its inner workings. Set aside the toaster assembly until the glue is dry.

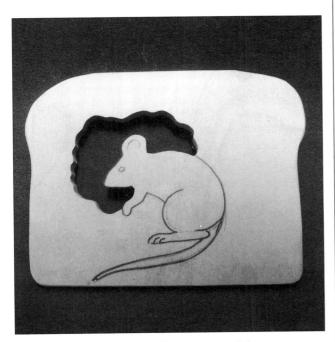

Fig 9.4 The mouse eating its way out of the toast.

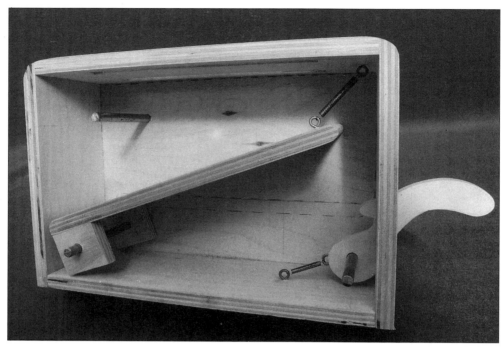

Fig 9.6 The inner workings of the toaster.

THE TOAST EJECTOR

Glue and pin the two E parts to part D. Study the toast ejector assembly in Fig 9.1 before gluing so you are sure of the correct position of the parts. After pinning, set aside until the glue is dry.

PAINTING THE INTERIOR SURFACES

You needn't bother with the outside of the toaster at this time, but the inside surfaces and anything that goes inside (that is, the toast ejector assembly and part F) must be painted before the toaster is permanently closed.

Mask off with masking tape the rim of the toaster assembly, that is, the faces that will abut part A when the toaster is completely assembled. Mask off the corresponding areas on part A, that is, the area along the edge of part A that will abut the edges of the toaster assembly. Prime the interior of the toaster, the handle and the inside of part A. Sand lightly when dry and apply another coat of primer. Sand lightly once more, then paint. You may, of course, use whatever colours you wish, but I like the effect a bright fire-engine red gives, with black for the handle and for the inside rim of the slots at the top of the toaster. The red makes the toaster

appear as if it were glowing from the inside. Set aside all painted parts until the paint has thoroughly dried.

ASSEMBLING THE INNER WORKINGS

Refer to Figs 9.1 and 9.6 to see how the eyescrews have been put in position. Screw into position all four eyescrews. If you have difficulty tightening the eyescrews with your fingers, insert the end of a nail into the eyehole to use as a lever.

Next, insert the three metal rods through the three holes in the toaster assembly. Put the handle (F) through the slot in the side and work the rod through the hole in the handle. Hook one end of a spring on the eyescrew in the handle, the other end of the spring on the eyescrew in the base.

Slide the toast ejector assembly into position on the rod at the base of the toaster opposite the handle. (The third rod, by the way, serves simply as a guide for the toast to glide out of the slots at the top of the toaster.) Fit one end of a spring through the eye of the screw fixed to the top of the toaster assembly and the other end of the spring to the eyescrew on part D. Although this sounds complicated, it is quite straightforward, and Fig 9.6 shows the setup clearly.

Now test the tension of the springs by working side A into place on the toaster assembly with the three metal dowels sticking through the holes in part A. Hold part A into position with hand pressure. Insert the two pieces of toast into the slots in the top and press down. As the toast is depressed, the notch in the handle should engage with the toast ejector (*see* Fig 9.1). After the handle has engaged, press it down. The toast should pop up from the slots as shown in Fig 9.7. If the toast is ejected too hard, or not hard enough, or if the sprung lever does not engage with the toast ejector, try springs of different lengths or strengths until the correct tension is obtained.

FINAL SHAPING, SANDING AND ASSEMBLY

When you are satisfied, affix the remaining side A to the toaster assembly with four brass round-head screws, one in each corner of A in the holes you have previously drilled.

Take the rasp again and go over the top edges where the curved sides of the toaster meet the ends and top. Blend the abutting edges smoothly into the curve of the toaster top. Remove the rasp marks with coarse sandpaper. Then sand the shaped areas with medium and then fine sandpaper to bring the whole to as perfect a finish as the rest of the toaster. You may have to backtrack a little and fill any blemishes in the newly rasped areas with filler and then, when the filler has dried, sand it flush with the surface.

When all surfaces are perfectly smooth, unscrew the four brass screws and once again remove part A from the toaster assembly for painting. Take the two slices of toast (G) for a moment. Go over the outlines of the mice with a ballpoint pen (*see* Fig 9.4). This will allow the outline of the mice to show through the primer. Prime the outside surfaces of part A, the toaster assembly and the two slices of toast twice, sanding between coats. Then paint the toaster and toast to your choice of colour scheme.

When the paint is completely dry, fix side A in position over the three metal dowels and secure with four brass round-head screws through the holes drilled previously at each corner. Fit the starlock washers and caps to the ends of the metal dowels and the toy is complete.

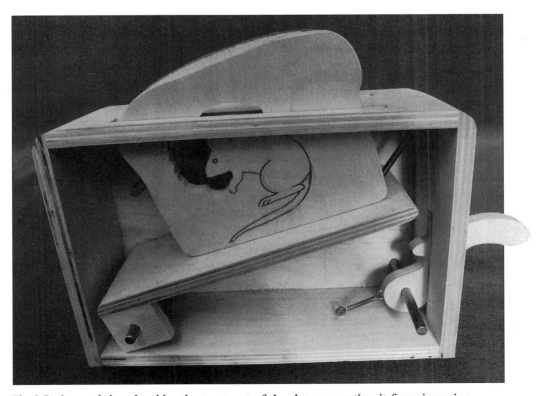

Fig 9.7 A metal dowel guides the toast out of the slot, preventing it from jamming.

Teapot House

The design for this toy is very simple and leaves the maker ample opportunity to include individual ideas for improvement.

MATERIALS

- birch ply 48 x 9 x ³⁄₈in (1175 x 255 x 9mm)
- wooden ball 1in (24mm) in diameter with ⁷⁄₁₆in (12mm) stem (stem can be made with a short length of ⁷⁄₁₆in (12mm) wooden dowel)
- lightweight drawing paper such as newsprint
- carbon paper
- pencil
- masking tape
- panel pins
- primer
- paints
- brushes
- wood glue
- sandpaper (coarse, medium and fine)
- wood filler

TOOLS

- drawing compass
- straight edge
- square
- coping saw or fret saw (or power fret saw if available)
- drill
- ⅛in (3mm) drill bit
- file
- rasp
- light hammer
- pliers
- punch

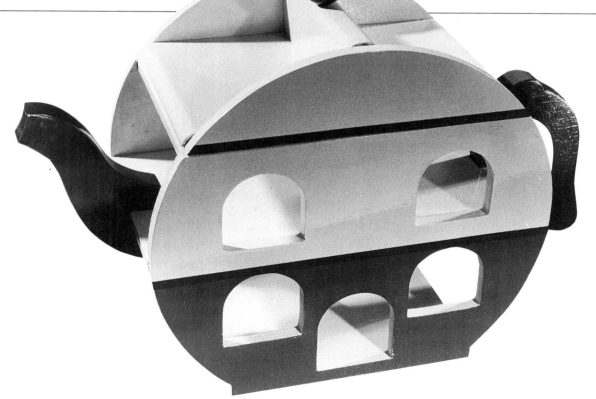

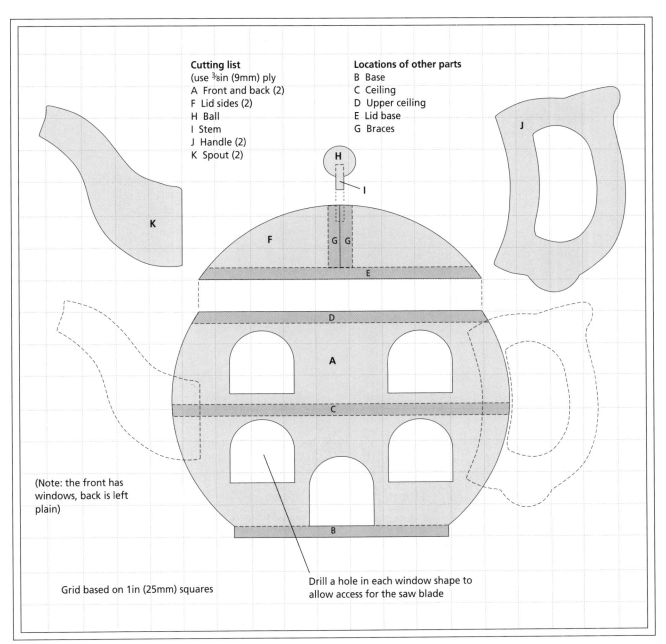

Within the figure:

Cutting list
(use ³⁄₈in (9mm) ply
A Front and back (2)
F Lid sides (2)
H Ball
I Stem
J Handle (2)
K Spout (2)

Locations of other parts
B Base
C Ceiling
D Upper ceiling
E Lid base
G Braces

(Note: the front has
windows, back is left
plain)

Grid based on 1in (25mm) squares

Drill a hole in each window shape to
allow access for the saw blade

Fig 10.1 Transfer the shapes of A, F, J and K to ply using the grid.

Familiarize yourself with Figs 10.1 and 10.2. The toy is made up of eleven shapes, labelled A–K. Shapes A, F, G, J and K will be duplicated for a total of sixteen parts. Note that one part A will have windows cut in it and the other part A will be left plain.

MARKING OUT THE DIMENSIONS

Make a grid with 1in (25mm) squares. Draw shapes A, F, J and K onto the grid following the plan at Fig 10.1.

Make sure you draw the window shapes in part A. Trace the shapes onto the plywood. You will be sawing out the shapes in duplicate, so you will only need to trace each shape once.

The dimensions of the remaining parts, except for the ball (H) and stem (I), can easily be marked out on the plywood using a straight edge and a square. The dimensions of B, C, D, E, and G are given in Fig 10.2. Label each part lightly with a pencil.

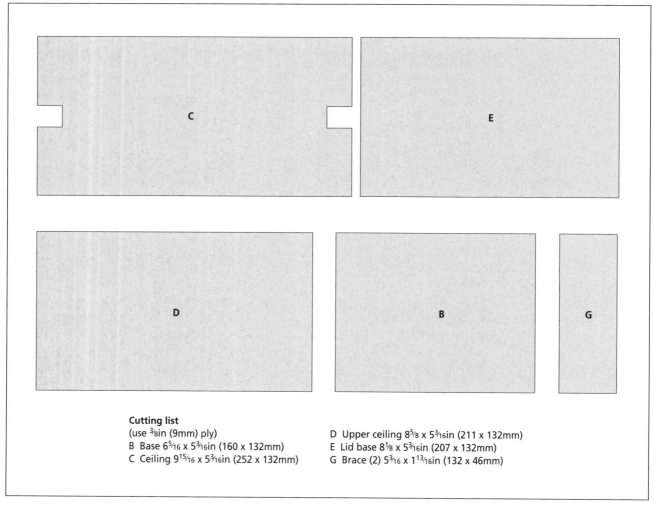

Cutting list
(use ⅜in (9mm) ply)
B Base 6⁵⁄₁₆ x 5³⁄₁₆in (160 x 132mm)
C Ceiling 9¹⁵⁄₁₆ x 5³⁄₁₆in (252 x 132mm)

D Upper ceiling 8⁵⁄₈ x 5³⁄₁₆in (211 x 132mm)
E Lid base 8⅛ x 5³⁄₁₆in (207 x 132mm)
G Brace (2) 5³⁄₁₆ x 1¹³⁄₁₆in (132 x 46mm)

Fig 10.2 Cutting list for B, C, D, E and G.

CUTTING OUT THE SHAPES

Temporarily pin the two pieces of ply that will form the front and back of the teapot (A) with panel pins. Do the same for the pieces of ply that will form parts F, J and K. Parts J and K should be glued (and the glue given a chance to dry) before pinning, as these parts will remain permanently together. Parts A and F will be separated after cutting, so the panel pins holding these parts together should be driven in only part way. They may then easily be removed with a pair of pliers after sawing. You should now have four separate stacks. With a coping or fret saw, saw out shapes A, F, J and K in duplicate. Do not saw out the window shapes from parts A at this time.

After sawing, remove the panel pins with a pair of pliers from the A and F stack and separate the parts.

Saw out B, C, D, E, and G from the ply.

Refer to Fig 10.1. Only the part A that is to form the front of the teapot will have windows cut from it. Take up the part A that already has the window shapes marked in it and drill a small hole in each window area. The diameter of the hole should be large enough to allow access for the saw blade. Remove the top end of the saw blade from the coping or fret saw frame. Pass the saw blade through the hole and re-attach the blade to the saw frame. Then proceed to cut the windows (*see* Fig 10.3).

Take up the J stack. Drill a hole to allow passage of the saw blade into the interior of the shape. Pass the top of the saw blade through the hole and re-attach it to the saw frame. Saw out the waste-wood area in the J stack. Fig 10.4 shows J after sawing.

Fig 10.3 One part A has windows cut in it.

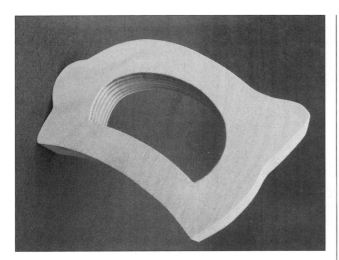

Fig 10.4 The handle (J) after cutting.

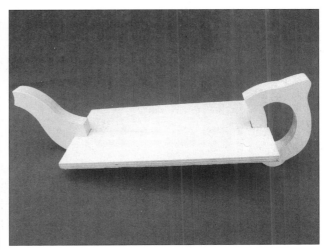

Fig 10.5 The handle (J) and spout (K) are glued into place in the slots cut in C.

FILLING, SANDING AND FILING

Fill the holes left from the panel pins in parts A and F with wood filler. Fill any blemishes or holes in any of the parts with wood filler. When the filler has dried, sand it flush with the surface of the wood.

With a file, smooth out any irregularities on the edges of the parts that the saw blade may have left. Also with the file, carefully trim the interior of the notches in part D. Do this a little at a time, fitting the spout (K) and the handle (J) into the notches temporarily and filing only enough to allow a snug fit for both of these parts. The file can be used to smooth out the bases of the windows in part A as well.

Sand all surfaces of all parts until perfectly smooth. Start with medium sandpaper and follow with fine sandpaper. Do not neglect to sand the interior shapes of A and J. With the sandpaper, round off all sharp corner and edges.

THE SPOUT AND HANDLE ASSEMBLY

Refer to Fig 10.5. Glue the handle (J) and the spout (K) into the slots in D. Set aside the assembly until the glue has dried.

PAINTING THE INTERIOR

The inner surfaces of the teapot must be painted before construction, otherwise it would be difficult to reach some of the areas with a paintbrush.

Mask off with masking tape the surfaces on both parts A that will abut the base (B) and the two ceilings (C and D). Fig 10.6 shows one part A with the masking tape applied. You needn't mask the edges on parts B, D and the handle/spout assembly (C, J and K) that will eventually form the glue joints with parts A. Just be careful, when painting, to keep those edges free of paint. Paint the inner surfaces of A, B, D and the handle/spout assembly. After painting, remove the masking tape and set aside the parts until dry.

NOTE: If using enamel paints, remove the masking tape while the paint is still wet or the paint may chip or flake at the edges.

CONSTRUCTING THE TEAPOT

Glue and pin B, D and the handle/spout assembly to the side A that has no windows (*see* Fig 10.7). Glue and pin the remaining side A as shown in Fig 10.8.

Fig 10.6 Masking tape prevents paint from covering surfaces that later become glue joints.

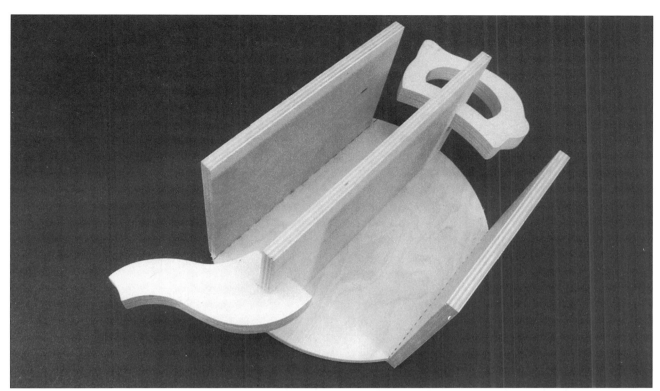

Fig 10.7   Parts B, D and the handle/spout assembly are glued and pinned into place on one part A.

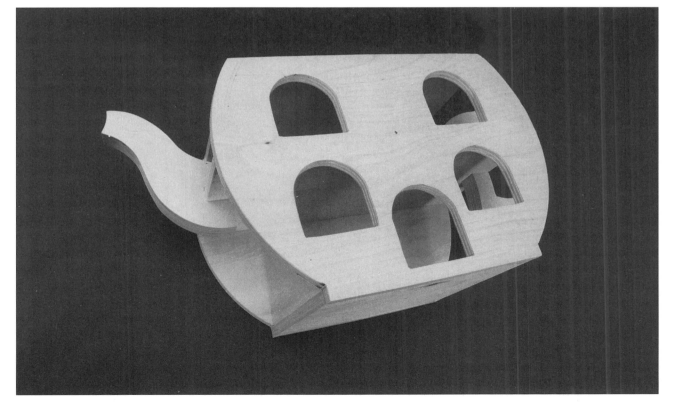

Fig 10.8   Part A (with windows) is glued and pinned into place.

CONSTRUCTING THE LID

Glue and pin the two G parts together. Refer to Fig 10.9 to see the glued together parts as they appear in the finished lid. Glue and pin the G assembly to the base (E) of the lid. Then glue and pin the two side of the lid (F) in place. Set aside the lid assembly to dry.

When the glue has dried, round over the top edges of the G parts as shown in Fig 10.9 with a rasp. Remove the rasp marks with coarse sandpaper. Follow by sanding with medium, then fine sandpaper.

Drill a $^7\!/_{16}$in (12mm) hole in the centre of the glued together braces (G) on the lid assembly. Drill the hole very slightly longer than the stem of the wooden ball. Apply glue to the stem and slide the stem into the hole in the lid. Set aside the completed lid assembly until dry.

If you have difficulty in obtaining a wooden ball with a stem, a stem can easily be added to a plain ball. Drill a $^7\!/_{16}$in (12mm) diameter hole to a depth of approximately $^1\!/_2$in (13mm) in a 1in (25mm) wooden ball. Hold the ball securely in a vice while drilling. Glue a 1in (24mm) length of $^7\!/_{16}$in (12mm) wood dowel into the hole. You now have a ball with a stem that may be attached to the lid assembly.

PREPARING SURFACES FOR PAINTING

Examine the constructed toy. Although you have already filled and sanded all the surfaces, subsequent operations will have marred some of those surfaces. Countersink all panel pins and fill all holes left by the panel pins with wood filler. Check over all the other parts and fill any blemishes with wood filler. When the filler has dried, sand it level with the surface of the wood.

FINAL PAINTING

Complete the teapot house by painting to your choice of colours.

Fig 10.9 The lid assembly.

Boot House

The dome of the boot house gives it a decidedly Turkish flavour.
A child could have hours of fun arranging furniture on the floors while his or her
pet mouse scrambled up the ladders formed by the wooden shoelaces.

MATERIALS

- birch ply 38 x 19 x $^3/_8$in (950 x 470 x 9mm)
- (11) wood dowel 5$^9/_{16}$ x $^1/_4$in (140 x 6mm) diameter
- lightweight drawing paper such as newsprint
- carbon paper
- pencil
- masking tape
- $^{11}/_{16}$in (18mm) panel pins
- primer
- paints
- brushes
- wood glue
- sandpaper (coarse, medium and fine)
- wood filler

TOOLS

- drawing compass
- straight edge
- square
- coping saw or fret saw (or power fret saw if available)
- (2) saw blades: one fine blade for turning sharp corners and one wider blade for cutting straight lines
- drill
- (3) drill bits: $^1/_4$in (6mm), $^{15}/_{16}$in (24mm) and 1$^3/_{16}$in (30mm)
- file
- light hammer
- pliers
- punch

Familiarize yourself with Figs 11.1–11.3. The toy is made up of eleven shapes, labelled A–K. Two of the shapes will be duplicated (A and K) to give a total of thirteen parts.

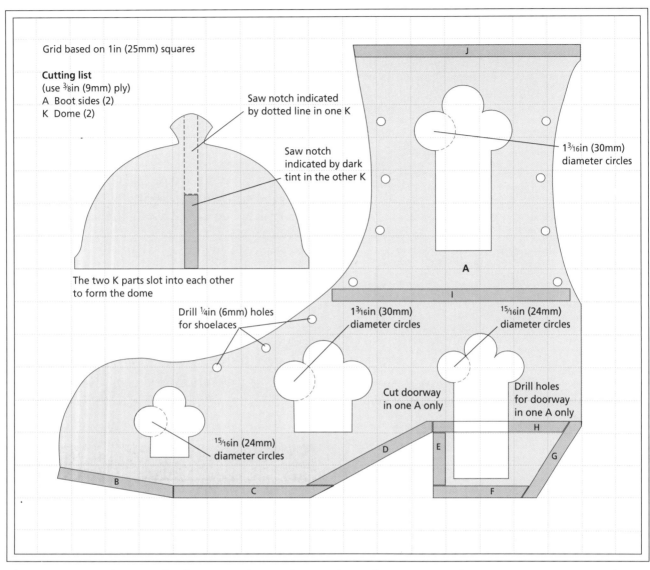

Grid based on 1in (25mm) squares

Cutting list
(use ³⁄₈in (9mm) ply)
A Boot sides (2)
K Dome (2)

Saw notch indicated by dotted line in one K

Saw notch indicated by dark tint in the other K

1³⁄₁₆in (30mm) diameter circles

The two K parts slot into each other to form the dome

Drill ¼in (6mm) holes for shoelaces

1³⁄₁₆in (30mm) diameter circles

1⁵⁄₁₆in (24mm) diameter circles

Cut doorway in one A only

Drill holes for doorway in one A only

1⁵⁄₁₆in (24mm) diameter circles

Fig 11.1 Use a grid to transfer shapes A and K to ply. Locations of parts B–I are shown.

LAYING OUT THE DIMENSIONS

Make a grid with 1in (25mm) squares. Draw shapes A and K on the grid following the plan at Fig 11.1. Trace the shapes onto the plywood. Try cutting out parts A and K in duplicate; there will be much drilling and sawing, especially in parts A, and cutting in duplicate will save a lot of time and will ensure accuracy. If you will be sawing out the shapes in duplicate you will only need to trace each shape once. If you are going to saw out each shape separately, trace two each of A and K onto the ply.

The remaining parts can easily be laid out on the plywood using a straight edge to measure the dimensions and a square to keep the right angles true. Label each part lightly with a pencil.

A note about parts K: Fig 11.1 shows slots to be cut in the two parts. Don't bother marking the positions of the slots for now. This will be taken up in a later step.

Mark on part I the position of the two holes to be drilled. Mark the position of the twelve holes to be drilled in parts A. If you are working with the A parts in duplicate, you will only need to mark these positions on one of the two pieces of ply for parts A. Mark the slot in part H and the interior shapes in A and I. Use a compass to draw the circular parts of these interior shapes.

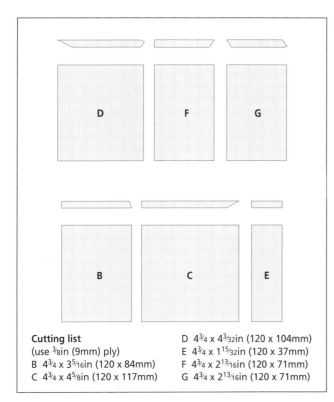

Fig 11.2 **Cutting list for B–G, which will form the sole and heel of the boot.**

Cutting list
(use ³⁄₈in (9mm) ply)
B 4³⁄₄ x 3⁵⁄₁₆in (120 x 84mm)
C 4³⁄₄ x 4⁵⁄₈in (120 x 117mm)
D 4³⁄₄ x 4³⁄₃₂in (120 x 104mm)
E 4³⁄₄ x 1¹⁵⁄₃₂in (120 x 37mm)
F 4³⁄₄ x 2¹³⁄₁₆in (120 x 71mm)
G 4³⁄₄ x 2¹³⁄₁₆in (120 x 71mm)

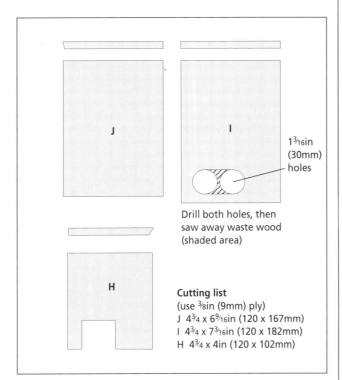

1³⁄₁₆in (30mm) holes

Drill both holes, then saw away waste wood (shaded area)

Cutting list
(use ³⁄₈in (9mm) ply)
J 4³⁄₄ x 6⁹⁄₁₆in (120 x 167mm)
I 4³⁄₄ x 7³⁄₁₆in (120 x 182mm)
H 4³⁄₄ x 4in (120 x 102mm)

Fig 11.3 **Cutting list and cross-sectional views for parts H, I and J. H will form part of the heel.**

CUTTING OUT THE SHAPES

If you will be sawing out the shapes in duplicate, temporarily pin the two pieces of ply that will form the boot sides (A) with panel pins. Pin the two pieces of ply that will form the dome (K) as well. Saw out the parts from each stack.

Carefully saw out the rest of the parts from the ply. Notice the sectional views of the parts in Figs 11.2 and 11.3. The sectional views show the edges of the parts at various angles. These angles will be shaped with a with a file at a later stage and may be ignored for now. Do not attempt to cut the wood at these angles; simply cut with the saw blade at the usual straight up-and-down angle.

Separate the two K parts and remove the panel pins with a pair of pliers (the pin holes will be filled later). Refer to Fig 11.1. Notice that the two parts will fit together in an interlocking arrangement (*see also* Fig 11.5). Mark the position of the lower slot on one part K and the position of the upper slot on the other part K. Then saw out these slots with a coping or fret saw. A fine blade will be useful for turning the sharp corners of the slots.

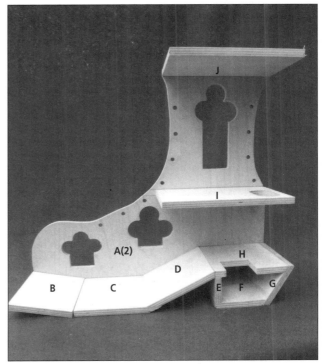

Fig 11.4 **The positions of the parts that make up the sole and heel, and parts I and J.**

DRILLING

Notice in Fig 11.1 the doorway in the boot near the heel in part A. This doorway is to be cut in one side of the boot (A) only. Do not drill the three holes for the doorway at this time. You should, however, drill the other nine $^{15}\!/_{16}$in (24mm) and $1^3\!/_{16}$in (30mm) holes as well as the eleven $^1\!/_4$in (6mm) holes in the stacked A parts.

While you have the drill fitted with the $1^3\!/_{16}$in (30mm) drill bit, drill the two holes in part I.

MORE STACK SAWING

With a coping or fret saw, cut out the areas of the three club shapes in the A stack that remain after drilling. The drill holes provide access for the saw blade to the interior of the club shapes.

Take up the stack with the I parts. Remove the waste areas from part I with the coping or fret saw. Again, the drilled holes will provide access for the saw blade.

FINAL DRILLING AND SAWING IN PART A

Separate the two A parts and remove the panel pins with a pair of pliers. Take up one part A and drill the three holes for the doorway (*see* Fig 11.1).

Take up the part A in which you have just sawn the three holes. With a coping or fret saw, and cut out the rest of the final club shape. You now have one part A with a doorway and one without. Fig 11.4 shows the A that has no doorway and Fig 11.7 shows the A with the doorway.

Referring to Fig 11.1, mark the position of part I on the inner face of the two parts A.

Fig 11.5 The two K parts slot together to form the dome.

FILING THE ANGLES

Parts B–H make up the sole and the heel of the boot (*see* Figs 11.1 and 11.4. The parts butt up against each other at angles. These angles are achieved by filing.

Begin by making the heel as a complete unit (*see* Fig 11.6). Bevel the edges of parts F, G and H with a file and sandpaper to the angles shown in the section view of each part (*see* Figs 11.2 and 11.3). Check the fit of the parts occasionally as you go along. When the edges of the parts fit together snugly, glue and pin F and H to E. When the assembly has dried, glue G to the edges of F and H (do not pin G as it will slide out of position due to the angles). The finished heel assembly is show at Fig 11.6.

While the heel assembly is drying, file and sand the edges of parts B, C and D to the angles shown in the section view of each part at Fig 11.2. These parts make up the sole of the boot.

Check the fit of the parts as you go along. When you are satisfied with the angles of the parts, it is time to backtrack a bit and make sure all parts are in good shape for painting and assembling.

SURFACE PREPARATION

Fill all holes left by the panel pins in parts A and K with wood filler. Check over all the other parts and fill any blemishes with wood filler. When the filler has dried, sand it level with the surface of the wood. Sand smooth all sawn and filed edges, paying particular attention to the door and window cutouts.

PAINTING THE INNER FACES OF THE HEEL

The inward-facing surfaces of parts E, F, G and H must be painted before beginning construction, or they would be hard to reach with a paintbrush afterwards. Consider the areas of each part that will eventually be covered with glue upon assembling the toy. These parts must be masked off with masking tape before painting, otherwise the glue joint would be weakened. Mask off those areas on A–I.

Prime the inner faces twice, sanding lightly between coats. Then paint to your choice of colour scheme. As the boot is going to be home to a child's favourite small toys, perhaps, you might find yourself considering what sort of decor these toys might prefer. The heel will, of

course, be the cellar of the boot house, so you may wish to paint accordingly.

When the paint is dry to the touch, strip off the masking tape and allow the paint to thoroughly dry.

CONSTRUCTING THE BOOT

Glue and pin the heel assembly to one of the A parts in the position shown in Fig 11.1. Then glue and pin parts B, C and D to the same side A as well. Again refer to Fig 11.1 for the positions of the parts and to Fig 11.4 for an example of the pinned and glued parts. Allow the assembly to dry. Then fill any slight gaps in the joints with wood filler. When the filler has dried, sand it level.

PAINTING THE INTERIOR OF THE BOOT

Mask off with masking tape the faces of parts I and J that will eventually be glued to the A parts. Mask off the corresponding areas on A that will form the glue joints with I and J.

Prime the interior surfaces of the boot, both sides of part I and the side of part J that will form the 'ceiling' of the uppermost floor in the boot house. Apply two coats of primer, sanding lightly between coats. Then sand lightly again and paint.

When the paint is dry to the touch, strip off the masking tape and allow the paint to thoroughly dry.

Fig 11.6 The heel assembly consists of E, F, G and H.

FINAL CONSTRUCTION

Glue and pin part I to the side of part A in the position you have marked from Fig 11.1. Glue and pin part J to the side of part A so that its upper surface is flush with the top edge of part A (*see* Fig 11.4). When the above assembly is completely dry glue and pin the remaining side A into position. The assembly is shown in Fig 11.7.

Take the two K parts that will form the dome. Apply a little glue to the edges of a notch and then slide the notches together to form the dome. The dome sits on top of the boot house as shown in Fig 11.5.

Cut to length eleven pieces of ¼in (6mm) wood dowel. The length of the dowels should be 5⁹⁄₁₆in (140mm). Sand the dowels lightly. Each dowel will be placed into a pair of holes that face across from each other, one hole in each A part. Place a little glue into a pair of ¼in (6mm) holes. Then insert a dowel so that it protrudes slightly out the end of each hole. Glue the rest of the dowels, one by one, in the same way. Then set aside the boot house until the glue has dried. When dry, the sand the protruding ends flush with the boot sides.

FINAL PAINTING

Complete the painting to your choice of colours. All the boot house needs now is some furnishings and a tenant!

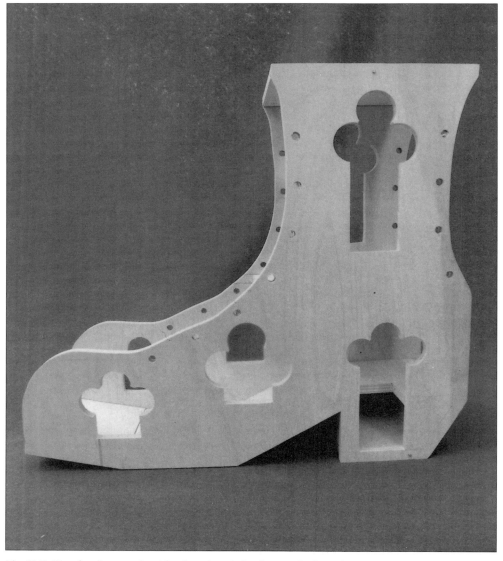

Fig 11.7 But for the wooden 'shoelaces' and the dome, the boot house is completely assembled.

Carpet Sweeper

This toy is a sturdy little carpet sweeper with a difference. When the handle is pulled back the top flips up to reveal two monkeys holding bells. The bells ring as the sweeper is pushed and pulled around the carpet.

The monkey sweeper is a favourite with visiting children (and keeps them out of trouble in my workshop!). Had I known it was going to be so popular I'd have fitted the sweeper with a real revolving brush, then there would be less sawdust around here.

MATERIALS

- birch ply 27 x 25 x $^3/_8$in (670 x 635 x 9mm)
- (4) wheels; diameter: 3$^1/_4$in (82mm)*
- (3) axles; length: 9$^7/_8$in (250mm); diameter: $^1/_4$in (6mm)*
- (6) $^1/_4$in (6mm) starlock washers and caps*
- (36) $^3/_4$in (18mm) No 4 countersunk brass screws*
- (4) brass bells*
- cord
- lightweight drawing paper such as newsprint
- carbon paper
- pencil
- panel pins
- wood glue
- sandpaper (coarse, medium and fine)
- wood filler
- masking tape
- primer
- paints

*see list of suppliers on page 181

TOOLS

- straight edge
- square
- coping saw or fret saw (or power fret saw if available)
- drill
- (3) drill bits: $^1/_4$in (6mm), $^1/_8$in (3mm) and $^1/_{16}$in (1.5mm)
- file
- light hammer
- punch
- pliers
- screwdriver
- brushes

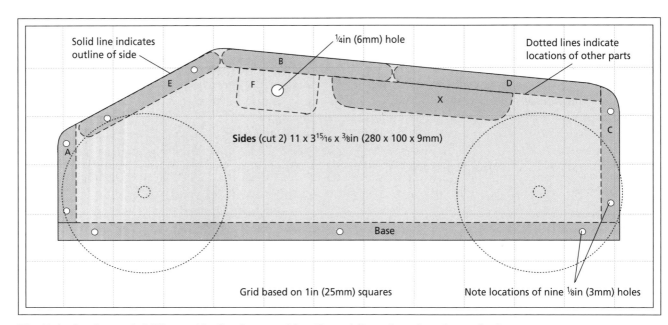

Solid line indicates outline of side

¼in (6mm) hole

Dotted lines indicate locations of other parts

E   B   F   D   X   C   A

Sides (cut 2) 11 x 3¹⁵/₁₆ x ³/₈in (280 x 100 x 9mm)

Base

Grid based on 1in (25mm) squares

Note locations of nine ¹/₈in (3mm) holes

Fig 12.1 Cutting and drilling guide for the two sides. Dotted lines show locations of other parts.

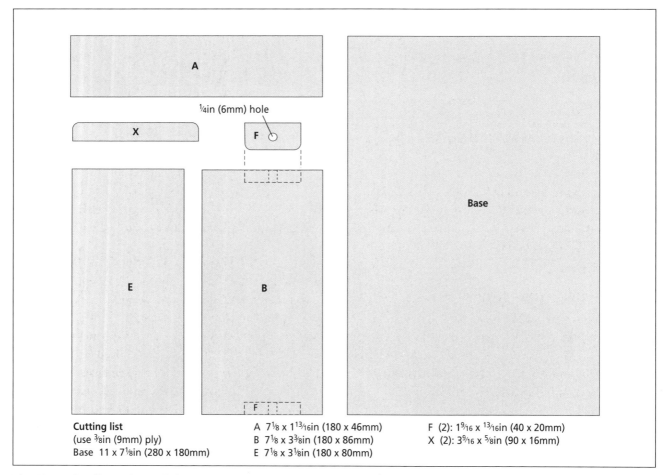

A

¼in (6mm) hole

X   F

E   B

Base

F

Cutting list
(use ³/₈in (9mm) ply)
Base 11 x 7¹/₈in (280 x 180mm)

A 7¹/₈ x 1¹³/₁₆in (180 x 46mm)
B 7¹/₈ x 3³/₈in (180 x 86mm)
E 7¹/₈ x 3¹/₈in (180 x 80mm)

F (2): 1⁹/₁₆ x ¹³/₁₆in (40 x 20mm)
X (2): 3⁹/₁₆ x ⁵/₈in (90 x 16mm)

Fig 12.2 The dimensions of the base, A, B, E, F and X. Note the ¼in (6mm) hole in F.

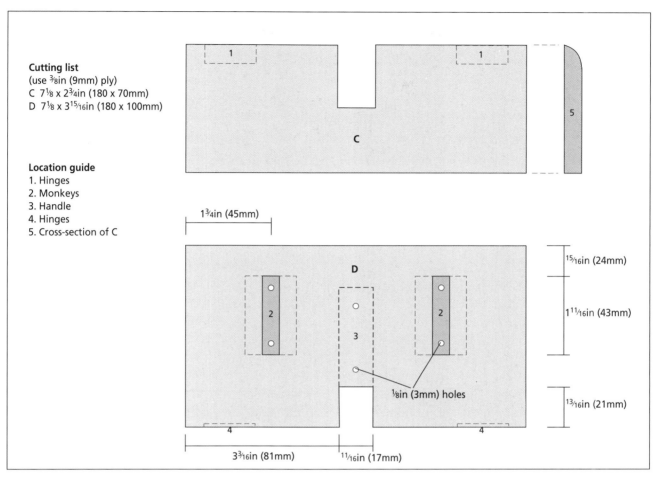

Cutting list
(use ³⁄₈in (9mm) ply)
C 7¹⁄₈ x 2³⁄₄in (180 x 70mm)
D 7¹⁄₈ x 3¹⁵⁄₁₆in (180 x 100mm)

Location guide
1. Hinges
2. Monkeys
3. Handle
4. Hinges
5. Cross-section of C

Fig 12.3 The dimensions of C and D. Dotted lines on D show where the handle (G) and the monkeys' bodies (H) are mounted on D.

Familiarize yourself with Figs 12.1–12.4. The carpet sweeper is made up of thirteen shapes. The parts are labelled A–J, side, base and X. Seven of the shapes will be duplicated (side, F, G, H, I, J and X) for a total of twenty parts.

LAYING OUT THE DIMENSIONS

Make a grid with 1in (25mm) squares. Draw a side and shapes G, H, I and J onto the grid following the plans at Figs 12.1 and 12.4. Trace the shapes onto the plywood. You will be sawing out the shapes in duplicate, so you will only need to trace each shape once.

The dimensions of the remaining parts (*see* Fig 12.2 and 12.3) can easily be marked out on the plywood using a straight edge and a square. Label each part lightly with a pencil before cutting.

Mark on the side the position of the three ¼ (6mm) and the nine ¹⁄₈in (3mm) holes to be drilled. Mark on F the position of the ¼in (6mm) hole to be drilled.

CUTTING OUT THE SHAPES

The sides, as well as F, G, H, I, J and X, will be sawed out in duplicate. With a light hammer and a supply of panel pins, pin together the two pieces of ply that will form each part. Leave the ends of the panel pins protruding so that they may be removed later with pliers. Since parts G will not be taken apart, the pieces of ply that will form G should be glued before pinning, and the heads of the panel pins should be countersunk. Set aside the glued and pinned G assembly until the glue has dried. Then, with a coping or fret saw, cut out the parts from each stack.

Saw the rest of the parts from the ply. Notice in

Fig 12.1 that the cross-sectional views of A, B, C and E show angled edges. These angles will be shaped with a file at a later stage and may be ignored for now. Do not attempt to cut the wood at a slant but simply cut with the saw blade at the usual straight up–and–down angle.

DRILLING

Drill the three ¼ (6mm) and the nine ⅛in (3mm) holes in the sides while the parts are still in a stack. Drill the ¼ (6mm) hole in the F stack as well.

FINISHING THE EDGES OF THE STACKS

While your seven stacks (the sides, F, G, H, I, J and X) are still pinned, take up the file and go over the edges of all the stacked shapes. Your goal here is to remove any bumps and irregularities left by the saw blade. Follow the filing with sanding in order to remove the marks of the file and to further smooth the edges. Use coarse, then medium sandpaper; follow with fine sandpaper. Remove the panel pins and take apart the stacks (except, of course, for the permanently glued G). The two parts from each stack will be identical.

Round all the edges of G with a file. Follow the filing with sanding.

FILING THE REST OF THE PARTS

Go over the edges of the rest of the parts (the base and A–E) with the file to remove the irregularities left by the saw blade. Follow the filing with sanding in order to remove the marks of the file and to further smooth the edges.

FILLING AND SANDING

The parts that were cut in a stack will have holes left from the panel pins. Fill all holes with wood filler. Check over all the other parts and fill any blemishes with wood filler. When the filler has dried, sand it level with the surface of the wood.

BEGINNING CONSTRUCTION

Trace from your grid the positions on the sides of A, B, C, D, E, X and the base line (for reference when assembling). Figs 12.1 and 12.5 show the locations of these parts on the side. Make sure that the two surfaces on which you have chosen to mark the locations face each other.

Refer to Fig 12.5. Glue and pin one X to each side in the position shown. Then glue and pin the base to the side as shown in Fig 12.6. Glue and pin the remaining side to the base. (The base fits between the two sides.)

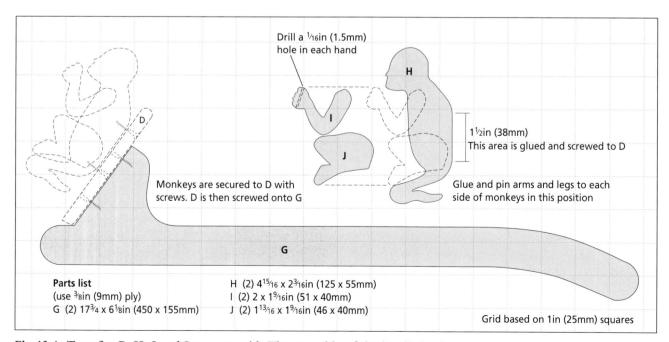

Fig 12.4 Transfer G, H, I and J to your grid. The assembly of the handle is also shown.

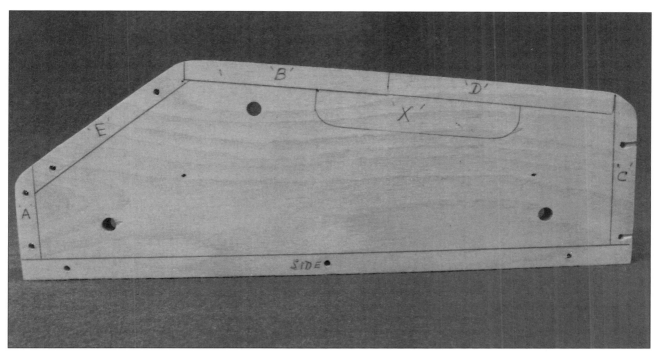

Fig 12.5 Draw the locations of the base, A, B, C, D and E onto both of the sides. Note the three ¼in (6mm) and nine ⅛in (3mm) holes.

Glue A to the sides in the position you have marked. Secure A in position by screwing the four screws (two on each side) through the holes in the sides and into A. Set aside until the glue has dried. Then shape the upper edge of A with a file. Your goal here is to make A match the curve of the sides. Sand the areas you have filed with coarse, then medium sandpaper to remove the marks of the file. Then sand the same areas with fine sandpaper to until smooth.

File the edges of E to the section shown at Fig 12.1. Remove the marks of the file with coarse, then medium sandpaper. Then sand the same areas with fine sandpaper until smooth. Glue E to the assembly in the position you have marked on the sides. Secure E in position by screwing the four screws (two on each side) through the holes in the sides and into A. Set aside until the glue has dried.

The rounded edges of E should fit snugly up to A and should allow B (constructed at the next stage) to pivot freely. Fig 12.8 shows these parts assembled.

Round off the edges of B to the profile shown at Fig 12.1 with a file. Remove the marks of the file with coarse, then medium sandpaper. Then sand the same areas with fine sandpaper until smooth.

Glue the two pivot brackets (F) in position, one on each end of part B (see Fig 12.7). The positions of F on B are shown on the plan at Fig 12.2. It is important to keep these two brackets parallel because they have to pivot freely on one of the metal rods. Once both parts F have been glued in position, place a metal rod through the holes in parts F until the glue has thoroughly dry. Fig 12.8 shows how B will fit into the assembly via the metal rod that passes through the holes in both brackets (F) and the sides.

Fig 12.6 Part X is mounted on a side, and the side is mounted on the base.

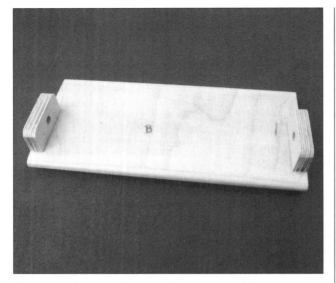

Fig 12.7 The two pivot brackets (F) glued into place on B.

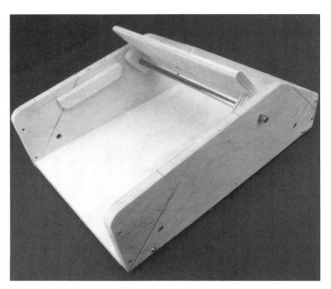

Fig 12.8 The B assembly pivots freely on the metal rod.

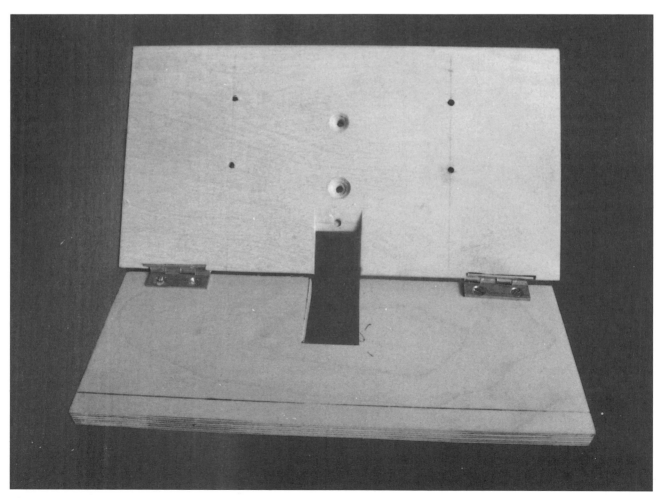

Fig 12.9 The countersunk holes in the centre are for the screws that secure D to the handle (G).

CONSTRUCTING THE HANDLE

Drill and countersink the six ⅛in (3mm) holes in part D (*see* Fig 12.3). Note that the two holes in the centre through which the handle is affixed are countersunk from the underside (*see* Fig 12.9). The other four holes, through which the monkeys are fixed, are countersunk on the upper side (*see* Fig 12.10).

Two hinges will attach D and C. Mark the positions for the hinges on D and C as shown at Fig 12.3. File notches in the edge of D so that the hinge flaps are flush with the top edge. Part C does not have to be notched, the flaps are simply screwed to the flat surface. Screw the hinges into place as shown at Figs 12.9 and 12.10.

Glue and screw (from the underside) the handle (G) to D as shown at Figs 12.4 and 12.11.

Drill a ¹⁄₁₆in (1.5mm) hole in each hand of the two monkeys (*see* Fig 12.4). The cord that the bells are attached to passes through these holes. With a file, round the edges of I, H and J. Follow the filing with sanding, first with coarse, then medium and finally with fine sandpaper.

Assemble the monkeys by gluing and pinning the limbs to the body as shown at Fig 12.4. When the glue has dried, glue and attach each monkey to the underside of D using screws that pass through the holes in D.

Fig 12.10 The four countersunk holes are for attaching the monkeys.

TRIAL ASSEMBLY

Fit the handle assembly to the sides by positioning C against the sides as shown in Fig 12.1 and screwing in the four screws partway. Raise and lower the handle to check that the movement is free. If, for instance, D is too tight against the sides when the handle is up, you may take out the handle assembly and remove some wood from the edges of D until it fits against the sides without scraping in the least. Remember that the sides and the edges of D will receive both primer and paint, so take this into account when filing the pieces to fit.

Fit the B assembly in place between the sides by passing the metal rod through the holes in the sides and brackets (F). Again check for free movement. Remove excess wood from the edges of B and the sides of F until the B assembly fits freely against the sides.

When the parts fit satisfactorily, disassemble the parts for painting.

PAINTING

Check over all the parts for sharp edges that need to be sanded and blemishes that need to be filled. Countersink the heads of any protruding panel pins. Fill any holes with wood filler. When the filler has dried, sand it level. You have already sanded some surfaces to a fine finish. Check over all parts and sand any remaining rough surfaces, first with medium, then fine sandpaper until perfectly smooth. Toys meant for children should have no sharp edges or points. Examine the toy thoroughly and sand all edges and corners so that they are slightly rounded.

Mask off with masking tape the surfaces on C and the corresponding areas on the two sides that will abut C when assembled. Prime all parts twice, sanding lightly between coats. Make sure all surfaces are clean, then paint all parts to whatever colour scheme you wish. Remove the masking tape before the paint sets. Set aside all parts until the paint has thoroughly dried.

FINAL ASSEMBLY

Glue and screw C of the handle assembly into place between the two sides. Set aside the assembly until the glue has dried.

Pass one of the metal rods through the sides and the brackets (F) as shown in Fig 12.8. Pass the two remaining metal rods through the lower holes in the sides and place a wheel on each end. Secure the wheels in position by pressing a starlock washer and cap over the end of each axle.

Attach a bell to the hand of each monkey with a short length of coloured cord.

Fig 12.11 Parts C and D are hinged together. The handle (G) is screwed onto D.

Storage Chest Toys

The storage of children's toys can sometimes be a problem. I have designed these projects to serve a dual purpose: the projects themselves can be played with as toys, and within each project is a compartment that can be used for storing small toys.

The first toy in this section, as you will notice, is an extension of the idea used for the panda in the first section, Animals with Young, and will serve to illustrate how ideas can be drawn from previous projects. In the following section, Rock-and-Ride Toys, you will see a further development of the idea in the Rocking Panda. I think that with a little ingenuity the penguin and kangaroo, also from Animals with Young, could be used to design this type of storage toy. Or you might want to design a storage toy based on the ever-popular dinosaur. It isn't necessary to make all the toys you design, but it is good practice to develop ideas with sketches and notes to form a library of rough designs that may later be developed and made into toys.

Panda Seat

*The panda seat is a chair that children will enjoy
sitting in. Lift up the seat and you have a large storage area for toys.*

MATERIALS

- birch ply 71¼ x 28 x ⅜in (1810 x 720 x 9mm)
- two-by-one softwood batten 107in (2.7m)
- 12¹¹⁄₁₆ x 1in (322 x 25mm) hardwood dowel
- piano hinge; length: 10in (254mm)
- (12) 1in (25mm) No 4 countersink screws*
- (50) ¾in (18mm) No 8 countersink screws*
- (12) screw cups*
- ¾in (18mm) panel pins
- primer
- paints
- wood glue
- sandpaper (coarse, medium and fine)
- woodfiller

*see list of suppliers on page 181

TOOLS

- lightweight drawing paper such as newsprint
- carbon paper
- pencil
- masking tape
- brushes
- straight edge
- square
- coping saw or fret saw (or power fret saw if available)
- drill
- drill bits: ⅛in (3mm)
- rasp
- file
- light hammer
- pliers

NOTE: Identify areas that would be better painted
before assembly. Before painting, mask off those areas
that will be glued.

Begin by scaling up the plans and transferring the parts
to ⅜in (9mm) plywood. The two-by-one battens are
cut to size from the dimensions shown on the plan.

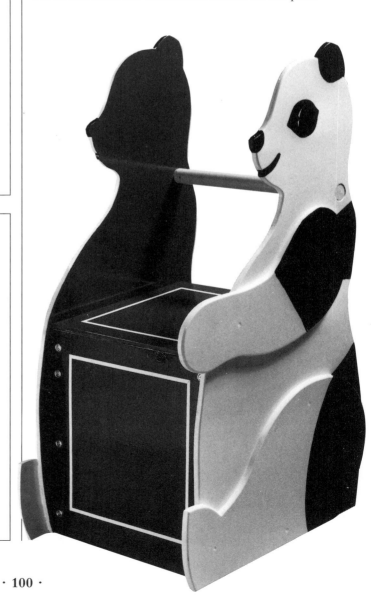

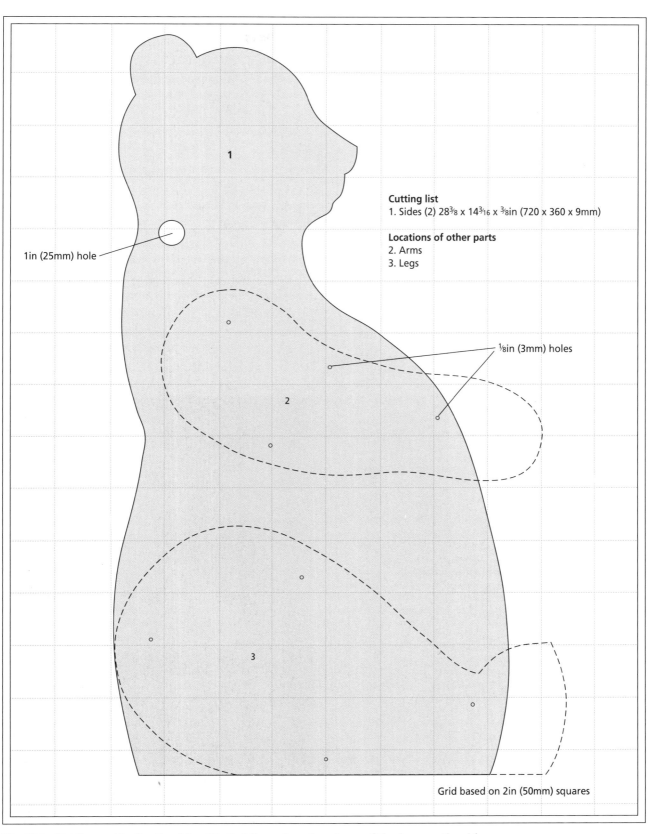

1

Cutting list
1. Sides (2) 28⅜ x 14³⁄₁₆ x ⅜in (720 x 360 x 9mm)

Locations of other parts
2. Arms
3. Legs

1in (25mm) hole

⅛in (3mm) holes

2

3

Grid based on 2in (50mm) squares

Fig 13.1 Cutting guide for the sides. Dotted lines show locations of the legs on the sides.

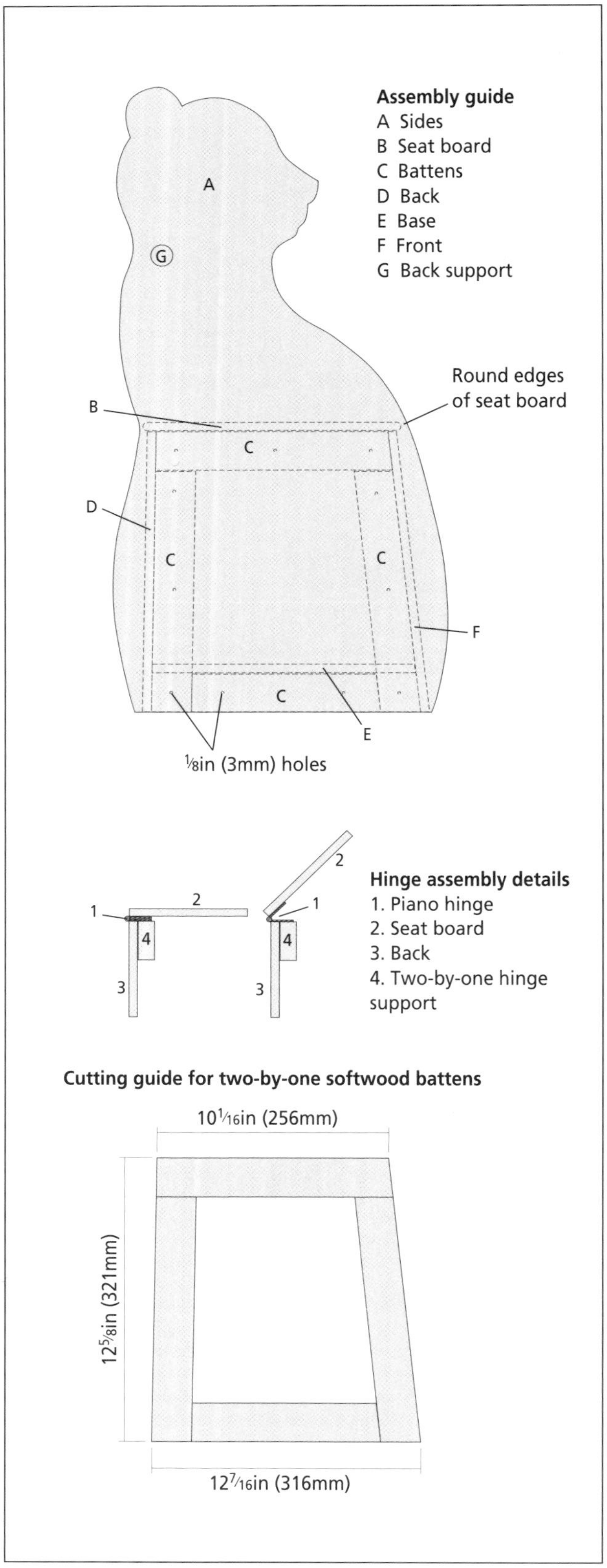

Fig 13.2 Cutting and assembly guides.

Assembly guide
A Sides
B Seat board
C Battens
D Back
E Base
F Front
G Back support

Round edges of seat board

⅛in (3mm) holes

Hinge assembly details
1. Piano hinge
2. Seat board
3. Back
4. Two-by-one hinge support

Cutting guide for two-by-one softwood battens

10¹⁄₁₆in (256mm)

12⅝in (321mm)

12⁷⁄₁₆in (316mm)

SIDES AND BATTENS

Cut to shape the two body sides (*see* Fig 13.1). These are better pinned together and cut in duplicate for accuracy. If you are cutting them by hand, you can pin the two pieces together later and shape and refine the edges so that both sides come out identical.

With the two pieces temporarily pinned together, drill the 1in (25mm) hole for the back rest support (which will be fitted at a later stage) and the screw holes for attaching the two-by-one battens. Separate the two body sides and countersink the screw holes on the outer faces of the sides. Now mark out the positions (from Fig 13.2) of the battens on the inner face of each body side. Cut the battens to shape. Then glue and pin the battens in place. While the pins hold the battens in position, fix them securely by screwing through the holes on the outer faces of the sides. Make sure that the screw heads are below the surface of the ply as these will be filled with wood filler at a later stage. Fig 13.3 shows the two-by-one battens glued and screwed to the body side.

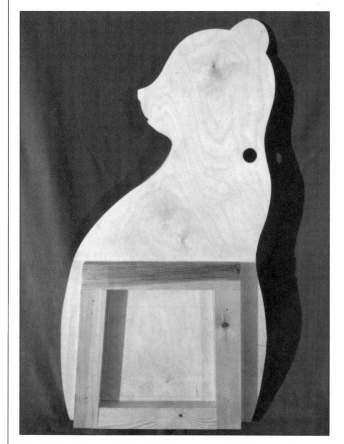

Fig 13.3 Glue and pin the battens to the inner sides.

ASSEMBLING THE BOX STRUCTURE

Mark the screw hole positions on the back (*see* Fig 13.4). Drill the screw holes but do not countersink these holes as they would be difficult to fill and sand after assembly. Screw cups will be fitted under the screw heads.

Now mark and drill the screw holes for fixing the hinge support to the top inner face of the back. Countersink these holes on the outer face.

Glue and screw the two-by-one hinge support in position on the back as shown in Fig 13.4. Then glue and screw the back to the two-by-one battens on the body sides as shown in the assembly guide in Fig 13.2. Fit screw cups underneath the screw heads when assembling, as shown in Fig 13.5.

Mark and drill the screw holes on the front (*see* Fig 13.4). Glue and screw the front to the two-by-one battens on the body sides as shown on the plan.

Cut out the notches in the base (*see* Fig 13.4) and glue in position (this part does not require screwing as it bears no weight) to the lower two-by-one battens on the body sides. The notches fit round the front and rear upright battens on the body sides. Fig 13.6 (with the front omitted for clarity) makes this clear.

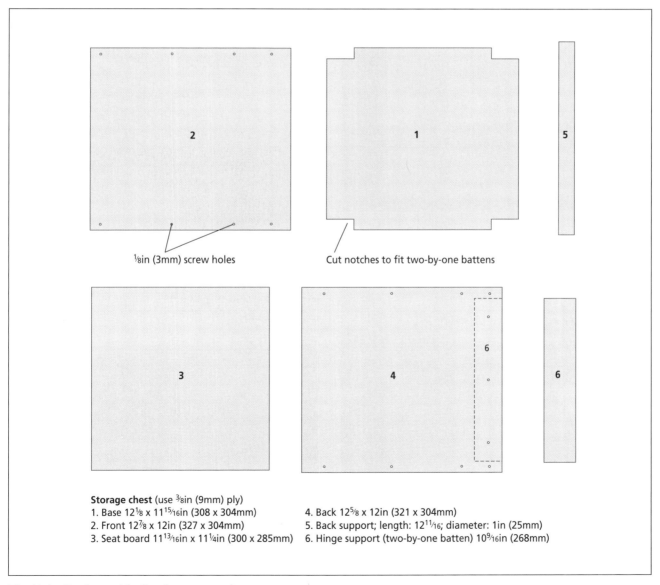

⅛in (3mm) screw holes

Cut notches to fit two-by-one battens

Storage chest (use ⅜in (9mm) ply)
1. Base 12⅛ x 11¹⁵⁄₁₆in (308 x 304mm)
2. Front 12⅞ x 12in (327 x 304mm)
3. Seat board 11¹³⁄₁₆in x 11¼in (300 x 285mm)
4. Back 12⅝ x 12in (321 x 304mm)
5. Back support; length: 12¹¹⁄₁₆; diameter: 1in (25mm)
6. Hinge support (two-by-one batten) 10⁹⁄₁₆in (268mm)

Fig 13.4 Cutting guide for the storage chest parts.

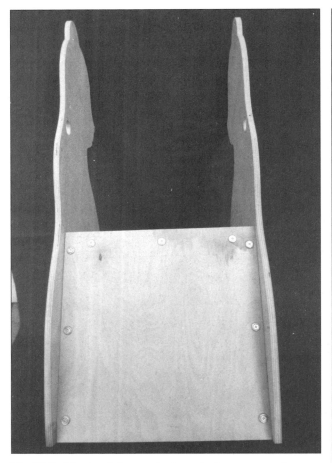

Fig 13.5 The back is attached to the battens on the sides with screws and screw cups.

Fig 13.6 The notches in the base fit neatly round the battens.

THE BACK SUPPORT

Glue the 1in (25mm) diameter back support into the 1in (25mm) holes in the body sides and fix securely by screwing through the edge of the body sides and into the dowel. This detail is shown in Fig 13.7.

With a file and sandpaper, round over the two sides and front edge of the seat board as shown in Fig 13.2.

FITTING THE HINGE

Cut the piano hinge to length and screw to the back underside edge of the seat board as shown in Fig 13.2. When this is done, screw the hinge to the top edge of the back as shown in Fig 13.8.

Check that when the seat board is lifted it does not bind on the body sides; if it does, unscrew the seat board from the hinge and file and sand the edges until a smooth fit is obtained.

THE LEGS

Enlarge and transfer the shapes of the front and rear legs (*see* Fig 13.9) to the ³⁄₈in (9mm) ply and cut to shape. Round over the edges of the four legs and drill and countersink the screw holes for attaching them to the body sides. Glue and screw the legs in the positions marked from Fig 13.9.

FINISHING

Fill all exposed screw heads with wood filler and sand smooth and level with the surface of the ply. Complete the priming and painting of the toy to your choice of colour scheme.

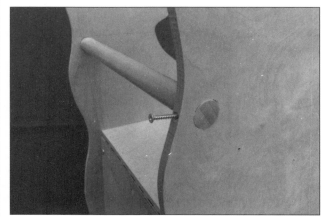

Fig 13.7 The back-support dowel is securely attached to the sides both with glue and screws.

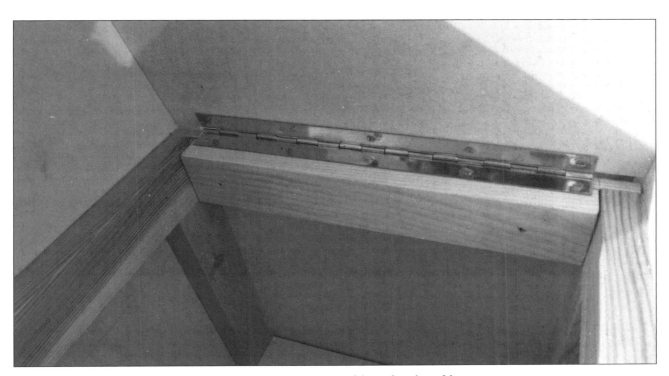

Fig 13.8 The seat board and hinge-support batten are screwed into the piano hinge.

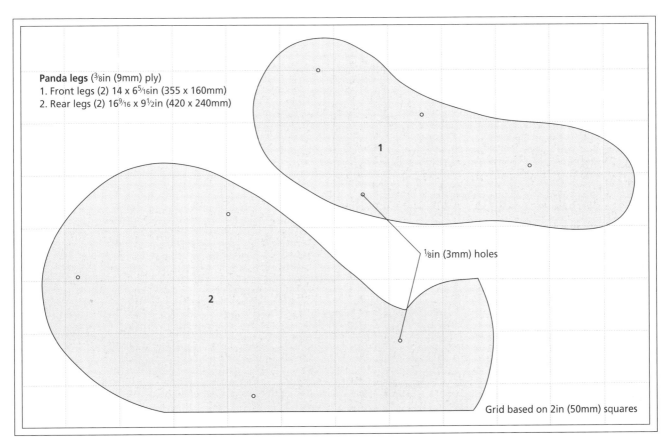

Panda legs (³⁄₈in (9mm) ply)
1. Front legs (2) 14 x 6⁵⁄₁₆in (355 x 160mm)
2. Rear legs (2) 16⁹⁄₁₆ x 9½in (420 x 240mm)

1

2

¹⁄₈in (3mm) holes

Grid based on 2in (50mm) squares

Fig 13.9 Cutting and drilling guide for the legs.

Noah's Ark

The ark is obviously not a new concept for a toy. But with its dual-purpose design
(toy and storage chest) and with the addition of a set of wheels, this project provides an example
of how you may breathe new life into an old idea.
The hull is made with a lift-off hatch for access to the storage area. The cabin, which
fits neatly over the hatch, lifts off the deck and can be played with as a separate toy.
Wheels make the ark a pull-along toy.

MATERIALS

- birch ply 45 x 32 x ³⁄₈in (1120 x 800 x 9mm)
- triangular softwood fillet 14in (355mm)
- (2) steel axle rod 9¹³⁄₁₆ x ¼in (250 x 6mm)*
- (4) 3in (75mm) diameter wheels*
- (4) ¼in (6mm) starlock washers and caps*
- (26) ³⁄₄in (18mm) No 4 countersunk screws
- ³⁄₄in (18mm) panel pins
- primer
- paints
- wood glue
- sandpaper (coarse, medium and fine)
- wood filler
- cord

*see list of suppliers on page 181

TOOLS

- lightweight drawing paper such as newsprint
- carbon paper
- pencil
- masking tape
- compass
- brushes
- straight edge
- square
- coping saw or fret saw (or power fret saw if available)
- drill
- drill bits: ¹⁄₈in (3mm), ¼in (6mm) and 1³⁄₁₆in (30mm)
- rasp
- file
- light hammer
- pliers
- G-cramps

NOTE: Certain parts of the toy are easier to paint as you progress, identify these as you proceed with the construction. Mask off areas that are to be glued before painting. Sand each piece thoroughly and remove sharp edges before assembling.

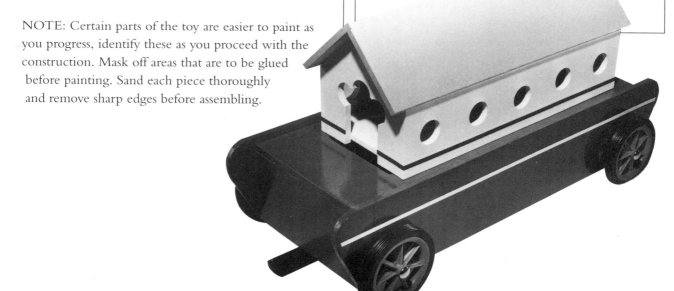

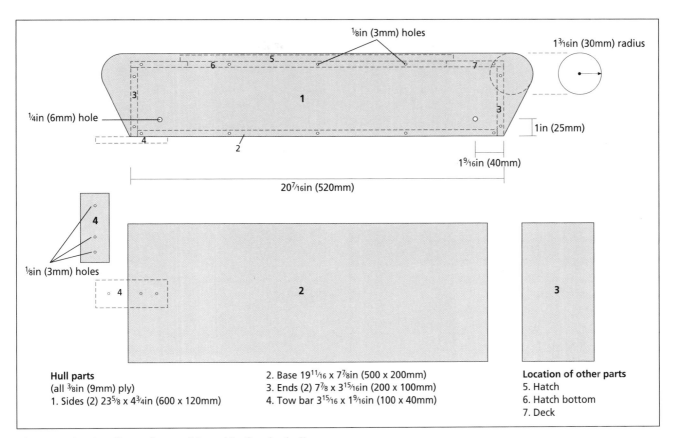

Hull parts
(all ³⁄₈in (9mm) ply)
1. Sides (2) 23⁵⁄₈ x 4³⁄₄in (600 x 120mm)

2. Base 19¹¹⁄₁₆ x 7⁷⁄₈in (500 x 200mm)
3. Ends (2) 7⁷⁄₈ x 3¹⁵⁄₁₆in (200 x 100mm)
4. Tow bar 3¹⁵⁄₁₆ x 1⁹⁄₁₆in (100 x 40mm)

Location of other parts
5. Hatch
6. Hatch bottom
7. Deck

Fig 14.1 Cutting list and assembly guide for the hull.

Enlarge the designs from Figs 14.1, 14.4, 14.7 and 14.8 and transfer them to the ply.

HULL

Temporarily pin together the two pieces of ply from which the hull sides are cut (*see* Fig 14.1). Mark out the design of the shaped ends of the hull sides and then cut to shape. With the sides still pinned together, mark the positions of the screw and axle holes. Drill and countersink (from the outer faces) the screw holes. Drill but do not countersink the ¼in (6mm) diameter axle holes. Fig 14.2 shows one end of the hull with the proper screw holes countersunk.

Separate the hull sides and from the plan mark the positions of the identical hull ends on the inner and outer faces of the hull sides. This will help position the parts when screwing them together. Smear a little glue on the two outer edges of the hull ends and position them between the hull sides as shown in Fig 14.1. Hold them together temporarily with large elastic bands or cramps. You might try wedging the base temporarily

between the hull ends to keep the ends square while fitting the hull sides.

Drill a small pilot hole (through the previously drilled holes in the hull sides) into the edges of the hull ends. Screw the parts together using the No 4 brass countersunk screws. This type of screw is used throughout the construction. The elastic bands or cramps can then be removed.

The hull bottom should now fit snugly between the hull sides and ends. Check for fit, then glue and screw the hull bottom to the hull sides and ends in the position shown in Fig 14.1. The position of the hull parts can also be clearly seen in Fig 14.3.

Saw out the deck (*see* Fig 14.4). Then, from the interior of the deck, saw out the hatch bottom, as shown in Fig 14.4. The hatch bottom will be fitted to the underside of the hatch at a later stage. File and sand smooth the sawn edges of the deck. Check that the deck fits snugly between the hull sides and sits squarely on the hull ends. Then glue and screw the deck in position (*see* Figs 14.1 and 14.5).

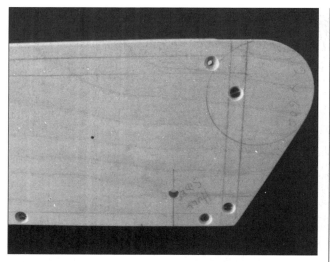

Fig 14.2 Countersink all screw holes on the hull side except the hole for the axle.

Fig 14.3 The hull sides, ends and base are fastened together.

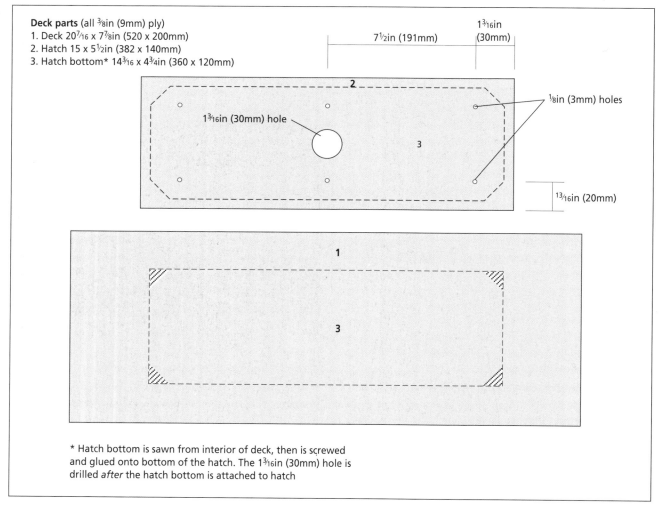

Deck parts (all ³⁄₈in (9mm) ply)
1. Deck 20⁷⁄₁₆ x 7⁷⁄₈in (520 x 200mm)
2. Hatch 15 x 5½in (382 x 140mm)
3. Hatch bottom* 14³⁄₁₆ x 4¾in (360 x 120mm)

7½in (191mm)

1³⁄₁₆in (30mm)

1³⁄₁₆in (30mm) hole

⅛in (3mm) holes

13⁄₁₆in (20mm)

* Hatch bottom is sawn from interior of deck, then is screwed and glued onto bottom of the hatch. The 1³⁄₁₆in (30mm) hole is drilled *after* the hatch bottom is attached to hatch

Fig 14.4 Dimensions for the deck, hatch and hatch bottom.

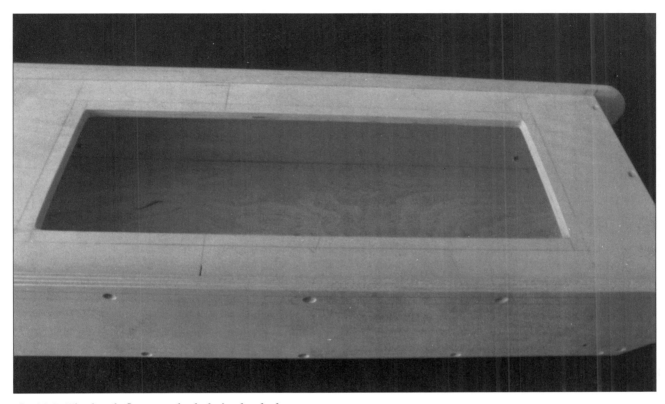

Fig 14.5 The hatch fits over the hole in the deck.

HATCH

From the details shown in Fig 14.4 mark the position of the hatch bottom on the underside of the hatch. Cut off the corners of the hatch bottom as shown in Fig 14.1. Sand the edges smooth. Glue and screw the hatch bottom to the underside of the hatch in the previously marked position (*see* Fig 14.6). From the detail shown on the plan, mark and drill the $1\frac{3}{16}$in (30mm) hole. This hole makes it easy to remove the hatch when it is fitted in the deck. The assembled hatch fits into the cutout in the deck as shown in Fig 14.1.

CABIN

Saw the cabin sides to shape (*see* Fig 14.7). Temporarily pin together the cabin sides and drill the $1\frac{3}{16}$in (30mm) holes (portholes) in the positions marked from Fig 14.7. Then drill and countersink the screw holes at each end for fixing to the cabin ends.

Saw the cabin ends to shape (*see* Fig 14.8). Drill and saw out the shaped doorways in the cabin ends to the details shown on the plan. These parts are identical and can be drilled and sawn in duplicate for accuracy.

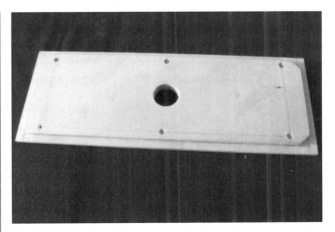

Fig 14.6 The hatch bottom is glued and screwed to the hatch, then the $1\frac{3}{16}$ (30mm) hole is drilled.

Mark on the roof pieces the position of the cabin ends and drill and countersink the screw holes for assembling these parts (*see* Fig 14.7). Glue and screw the two roof sides together to form a 90° angle. Note that one side is $\frac{3}{8}$in (9mm) wider than the other. The wider piece is glued and screwed to the edge of the narrower piece (*see* Fig 14.8).

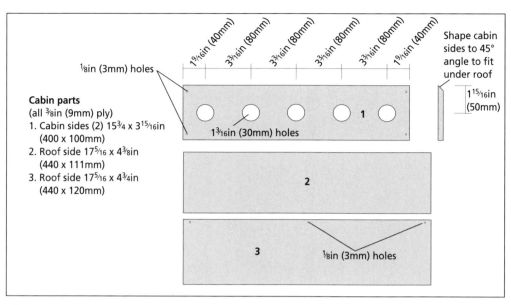

Cabin parts
(all ³⁄₈in (9mm) ply)
1. Cabin sides (2) 15³⁄₄ x 3¹⁵⁄₁₆in
   (400 x 100mm)
2. Roof side 17⁵⁄₁₆ x 4³⁄₈in
   (440 x 111mm)
3. Roof side 17⁵⁄₁₆ x 4³⁄₄in
   (440 x 120mm)

¹⁄₈in (3mm) holes

1⁹⁄₁₆in (40mm) 3³⁄₁₆in (80mm) 3³⁄₁₆in (80mm) 3³⁄₁₆in (80mm) 3³⁄₁₆in (80mm) 1⁹⁄₁₆in (40mm)

Shape cabin sides to 45° angle to fit under roof

1¹⁵⁄₁₆in (50mm)

1³⁄₁₆in (30mm) holes

¹⁄₈in (3mm) holes

Fig 14.7 Cutting list and drilling locations for the cabin.

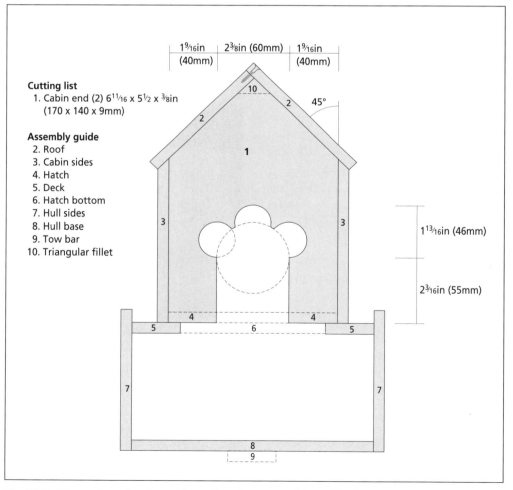

1⁹⁄₁₆in (40mm)   2³⁄₈in (60mm)   1⁹⁄₁₆in (40mm)

Cutting list
1. Cabin end (2) 6¹¹⁄₁₆ x 5¹⁄₂ x ³⁄₈in
   (170 x 140 x 9mm)

Assembly guide
2. Roof
3. Cabin sides
4. Hatch
5. Deck
6. Hatch bottom
7. Hull sides
8. Hull base
9. Tow bar
10. Triangular fillet

45°

1¹³⁄₁₆in (46mm)

2³⁄₁₆in (55mm)

Fig 14.8 Dimensions for the cabin end and an assembly guide for the whole toy.

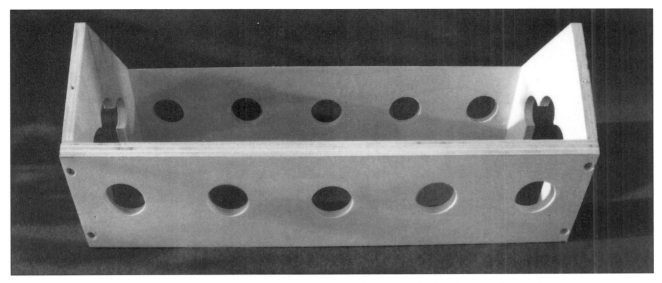

Fig 14.9 The top edge of each cabin side is shaped to a 45° angle to match the slope of the roof.

The top edges of the cabin sides will now have to be filed and sanded to the angle shown in Fig 14.7 to fit neatly against the inner face of the roof sides. When this is achieved glue and screw the cabin sides to the cabin sides as shown in Figs 14.9.

Cut to length the triangular fillet piece and glue it into the inner angle formed by the roof sides to strengthen the construction. See Fig 14.8 for an illustration of this. Then glue and screw the assembled roof to the cabin ends and sides. The assembled cabin should fit snugly over the hatch in the deck (*see* Fig 14.10).

TOW BAR

Saw to shape the tow bar (*see* Fig 14.1) and drill and countersink the two screw holes for attaching it to the underside of the hull bottom. Also drill the $\frac{1}{8}$in (3mm) hole for the cord used for pulling the toy. (The cord is not shown; any good quality cord may be used.)

Glue and screw the tow bar to the underside of the front of the hull floor. Then attach the pull cord by passing it through the $\frac{1}{8}$in (3mm) hole and knotting the cord so that it won't slip back through the hole.

WHEEL ASSEMBLY

Insert the $\frac{1}{4}$in (6mm) diameter axles through the previously drilled axle holes in the hull sides and fit a $\frac{1}{4}$in (6mm) brass washer over each end of the axles. Fit the 3in (75mm) diameter wheels (*see* the finished

toy on page 106) onto the axles. Do not secure with starlock washers and caps yet. When you are sure everything fits, remove the wheels and axles. You may then prime and paint to an imaginative colour scheme.

Fig 14.10 The cabin fits snugly over the hatch in the deck. The tow bar may be seen protruding from beneath the base.

Circus Wagon

In my younger days I was always excited at the prospect of visiting the circus, but I cannot remember ever seeing a cage or circus wagon on these visits, so I have designed this toy from illustrations used in advertising the events.
In an early stage of design the project was to be a simple cage for storing a child's soft toys, but with a little more thought I decided that the toy could have a dual purpose. In its latest form the cage detaches and can be used for play, while the base of the toy converts into a steerable truck — an ideal toy for two children to play with together (in theory!).

MATERIALS

- birch ply 33^{7}⁄$_{16}$ x 24 x ^{3}⁄$_{8}$in (850 x 610 x 9mm)
- birch ply 17^{3}⁄$_{4}$ x 4^{15}⁄$_{16}$ x 1in (450 x 125 x 12mm)
- birch ply 24 x 12^{3}⁄$_{16}$ x ^{1}⁄$_{4}$in (610 x 310 x 6mm)
- triangular softwood fillet 70in (1,768mm)
- two-by-one softwood batten 66in (1,676mm)
- ^{1}⁄$_{2}$in (12mm) diameter wood dowel 32.5ft (10m)
- 1^{3}⁄$_{16}$in (30mm) diameter hardwood dowel 9^{13}⁄$_{16}$in (250mm)
- (2) steel rod; length: 2^{3}⁄$_{8}$in (60mm); diameter: ^{1}⁄$_{4}$in (6mm)*
- steel rod; length: 12^{5}⁄$_{8}$in (320mm); diameter: ^{1}⁄$_{4}$in (6mm)*
- (4) 3in (75mm) diameter wheels; internal diameter: ^{1}⁄$_{4}$in (6mm)*
- (4) ^{1}⁄$_{4}$in (6mm) starlock washers and caps*
- (26) ^{3}⁄$_{4}$in (18mm) No 8 countersink screws
- steel bolt; length: 1^{3}⁄$_{8}$in (35mm); diameter: ^{1}⁄$_{4}$in (6mm)
- (2) metal washers; internal diameter: ^{1}⁄$_{4}$in (6mm)
- ^{3}⁄$_{4}$in (18mm) panel pins
- primer
- paints
- wood glue
- sandpaper (coarse, medium and fine)
- wood filler

*see list of suppliers on page 181

TOOLS

- lightweight drawing paper such as newsprint
- carbon paper
- pencil
- masking tape
- brushes
- straight edge
- square
- coping saw or fret saw (or power fret saw if available)
- drill
- drill bits: ^{1}⁄$_{8}$in (3mm), ^{1}⁄$_{4}$in (6mm), ^{1}⁄$_{2}$in (12mm) and 1^{3}⁄$_{16}$in (30mm)
- rasp
- file
- light hammer
- pliers

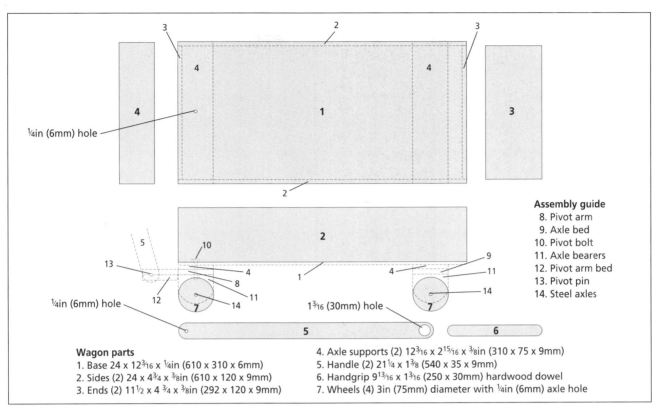

¼in (6mm) hole

Assembly guide
8. Pivot arm
9. Axle bed
10. Pivot bolt
11. Axle bearers
12. Pivot arm bed
13. Pivot pin
14. Steel axles

¼in (6mm) hole

1³⁄₁₆ (30mm) hole

Wagon parts
1. Base 24 x 12³⁄₁₆ x ¼in (610 x 310 x 6mm)
2. Sides (2) 24 x 4¾ x ³⁄₈in (610 x 120 x 9mm)
3. Ends (2) 11½ x 4¾ x ³⁄₈in (292 x 120 x 9mm)

4. Axle supports (2) 12³⁄₁₆ x 2¹⁵⁄₁₆ x ³⁄₈in (310 x 75 x 9mm)
5. Handle (2) 21¼ x 1³⁄₈ (540 x 35 x 9mm)
6. Handgrip 9¹³⁄₁₆ x 1³⁄₁₆ (250 x 30mm) hardwood dowel
7. Wheels (4) 3in (75mm) diameter with ¼in (6mm) axle hole

Fig 15.1 Cutting list and assembly guide for the wagon.

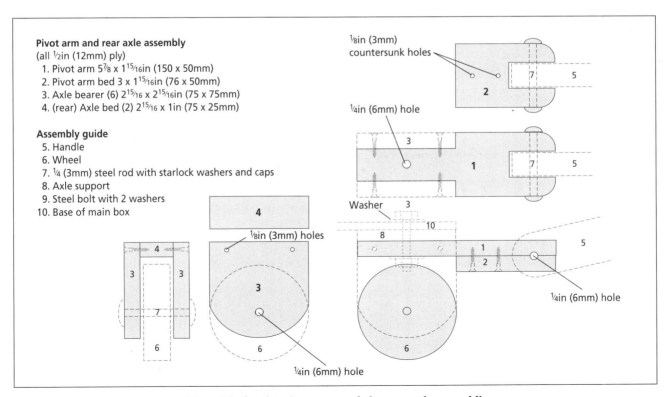

Pivot arm and rear axle assembly
(all ½in (12mm) ply)
1. Pivot arm 5⅞ x 1¹⁵⁄₁₆in (150 x 50mm)
2. Pivot arm bed 3 x 1¹⁵⁄₁₆in (76 x 50mm)
3. Axle bearer (6) 2¹⁵⁄₁₆ x 2¹⁵⁄₁₆in (75 x 75mm)
4. (rear) Axle bed (2) 2¹⁵⁄₁₆ x 1in (75 x 25mm)

Assembly guide
5. Handle
6. Wheel
7. ¼ (3mm) steel rod with starlock washers and caps
8. Axle support
9. Steel bolt with 2 washers
10. Base of main box

⅛in (3mm) countersunk holes

¼in (6mm) hole

¼in (6mm) hole

Washer

¼in (6mm) hole

⅛in (3mm) holes

¼in (6mm) hole

Fig 15.2 Cutting list and assembly guide for the pivot arm and the rear axle assemblies.

THE BASIC BOX

The box that forms the base of the cage and the body of the pull–along truck is a simple construction and is made up as follows. Cut out the two sides, two ends and the base to the sizes shown in Fig 15.1. Glue and pin the base to the sides as detailed in Fig 15.1 and then glue and pin the ends between the sides and to the base to form an open box.

THE PIVOT AND AXLE ASSEMBLIES

Cut to shape the two axle supports and drill and countersink the screw holes in each to attach them to the underside of the box.

Now saw to shape the six axle bearers (*see* Fig 15.2) and drill the ¼in (6mm) axle hole in each. Also drill and countersink the screw holes for attaching the axle bearers to the (rear) axle beds and (front) pivot arm. These are better cut and drilled in pairs for accuracy (if you have the facility of a powered fret saw).

The two rear axle beds and the two parts (pivot arm and pivot arm bed) that form the pivot arm are now cut to shape (*see* Fig 15.2). Drill and countersink the two screw holes in the pivot arm bed. Then glue and screw the pivot arm bed to the underside of the pivot arm.

Mark and drill the ¼in (6mm) hole at the rear of the pivot arm for the pivot bolt (fitted at a later stage) and the ¼in (6mm) hole drilled (horizontally) through the front of the pivot arm for attaching the handle by means of a steel dowel. All these details can be clearly seen in Figs 15.1 and 15.2.

Glue and screw the axle supports to the underside of the box in the positions shown in Fig 15.1. Drill the ¼in (6mm) hole for the pivot bolt through both the front axle support and base. The rear axle support is fixed in the same manner but is positioned 1⁹⁄₁₆in (40mm) in from the end of the base.

Drill and countersink the two screw holes in each of the rear axle beds (for attaching to the axle supports). Glue and screw an axle bearer to each side of the axle beds. Keep the bases level. Glue and screw these assemblies (through the holes previously drilled in the axle beds) to the ends of the rear axle supports as shown in Fig 15.1. Fig 15.3 shows how the rear axle assemblies are attached to the base of the box using countersunk screws.

Fig 15.3 A back wheel assembled. Note the countersunk screws.

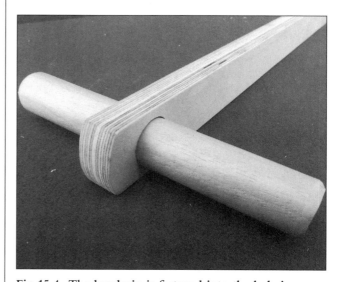

Fig 15.4 The handgrip is fastened into the hole in the handle.

Fig 15.5 The combined pivot arm and front wheel axle assemblies.

THE HANDLE

Cut the two parts of the handle from $\frac{3}{8}$in (9mm) ply (*see* Fig 15.1). Then glue and pin them together. When dry, sand smooth and round over the edges to remove sharp corners. Then mark and drill the $1\frac{3}{16}$in (30mm) hole for the handgrip and the $\frac{1}{4}$in (6mm) hole for attaching the handle to the pivot arm (by means of a $\frac{1}{4}$in (6mm) diameter steel dowel). Shape the ends of the handgrips to the rounded profile shown on the plan. Then glue and screw the handgrips into the $1\frac{3}{16}$in (30mm) hole in the handle as shown in Fig 15.4.

Insert the lower end of the handle into the slot in the pivot arm and pass the $\frac{1}{4}$in (6mm) steel dowel through the hole in the pivot arm and the $\frac{1}{4}$in (6mm) hole in the handle (*see* Fig 15.5). Secure the handle by fitting a starlock washer and cap to each end of the steel dowel. (Fit the starlock washers and caps only after finishing and painting the whole toy.)

Glue and screw the two remaining axle bearers to the pivot arm in the position shown in Figs 15.2 and 15.5, again ensuring that the bases of each are level.

Pass a washer onto the $1\frac{3}{8}$ x $\frac{1}{4}$in (35 x 6mm) bolt. Then pass the bolt through the hole (from the top) in the base and axle support and place the pivot arm assembly over the protruding bolt. Now place a $\frac{1}{4}$in (6mm) washer over the end of the bolt and screw on the nut to secure the pivot arm assembly. Adjust the nut to allow the pivot arm to move freely on the pivot bolt. Secure the nut with a little epoxy resin to prevent

Fig 15.6 The front wheel assembly in place on the wagon.

it coming loose in play. The assembly is shown in Figs 15.2 and 15.6.

THE WHEELS

The 3in (75mm) diameter wheels can now be fitted. Insert a $\frac{1}{4}$in (6mm) diameter axle a little way into a rear axle bearer. Place a wheel between the two axle bearers and pass through the wheel and the next axle bearer. Slide the axle along and into the opposite axle bearer and repeat the process. Secure the wheels on the axles with starlock washers and caps. Fig 15.3 shows a back wheel assembled.

The front wheels are fitted on the outside of the axle bearers. Insert the axle through the axle bearers and place a wheel on each end. Secure with starlock washers and caps. Figs 15.5 and 15.6 show the front wheels assembled.

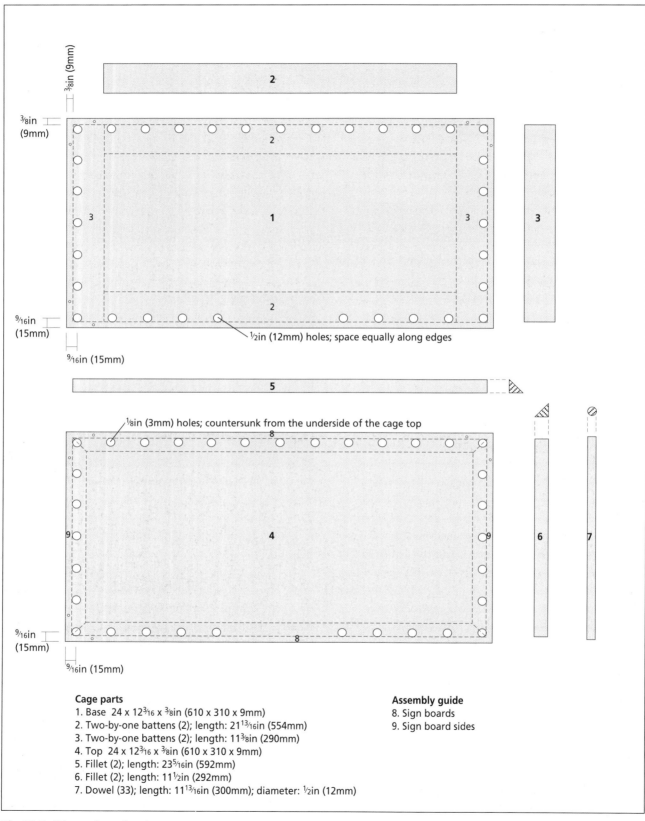

³⁄₈in (9mm)

³⁄₈in
(9mm)

2

2

3   1   3

3

⁹⁄₁₆in
(15mm)

2

½in (12mm) holes; space equally along edges

⁹⁄₁₆in (15mm)

5

⅛in (3mm) holes; countersunk from the underside of the cage top

8

9   4   9

6

7

8

⁹⁄₁₆in
(15mm)

8

⁹⁄₁₆in (15mm)

Cage parts
1. Base 24 x 12³⁄₁₆ x ³⁄₈in (610 x 310 x 9mm)
2. Two-by-one battens (2); length: 21¹³⁄₁₆in (554mm)
3. Two-by-one battens (2); length: 11³⁄₈in (290mm)
4. Top 24 x 12³⁄₁₆ x ³⁄₈in (610 x 310 x 9mm)
5. Fillet (2); length: 23⁵⁄₁₆in (592mm)
6. Fillet (2); length: 11½in (292mm)
7. Dowel (33); length: 11¹³⁄₁₆in (300mm); diameter: ½in (12mm)

Assembly guide
8. Sign boards
9. Sign board sides

Fig 15.7 Dimensions for the cage.

THE CAGE

Cut the cage top and cage floor to the dimensions shown in Fig 15.7. Temporarily pin the two pieces together, making sure all edges are square. Carefully mark the positions of the thirty-three $\frac{1}{2}$in (12mm) diameter holes around the edge of the top. Then drill the holes through both parts, keeping the drill vertical and at right angles to the ply. These details are shown on the plan. Mark the two pieces on one edge with a pencil before separating so that identification of their position is easy when assembling.

Separate the two pieces and mark, drill and countersink the $\frac{1}{8}$in (3mm) screw holes (on the underside of the cage top only) for attaching the sign boards.

Measure and cut the four pieces of two-by-one batten (*see* Fig 15.7). Mark the positions of the pieces on the underside of the cage floor then glue and pin in position. The battens can be seen in position in Fig 15.8.

Saw the thirty-three pieces of dowel to length, making sure the cuts are square. Place the cage base on a level worktop with the battens on the underside and the thirty-three holes facing up. Smear a little glue on

the end of a dowel and insert as far as it will go into one of the corner holes in the cage floor. Repeat this until the four corner dowels are in position. Now smear a little glue into each of the corner holes in the cage top. Make sure the cage top is in correct alignment with the cage floor, then place the top onto the upper ends of the four dowels. Check that the tops of the dowels are level with the top surface of the cage, then allow the assembly to dry.

When dry, glue the remaining dowels in position. The easiest way to do this is to insert a dowel partway through a hole in the cage top, smear a little glue on both ends of the dowel, then fit into the holes in the top and bottom of the cage. Wipe away any excess glue with a damp cloth. Fig 15.8 shows the dowels in position and shows the two-by-one battens on the underside of the cage base.

During assembly you will have noticed that an opening has been left in the front of the cage for access. You may wish to fit a barred gate, which should be interesting to design.

Fill any defects and sand the top of the cage smooth.

Fig 15.8 The assembled cage. The battens are in place on the bottom.

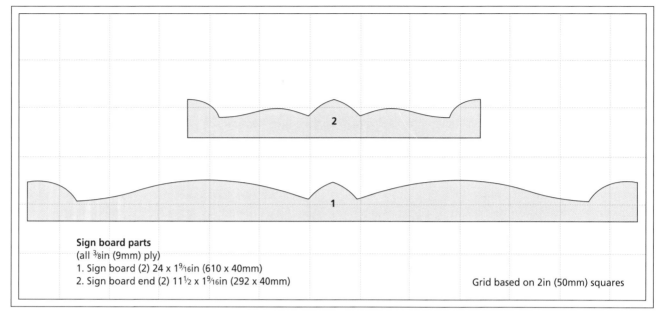

Sign board parts
(all ⅜in (9mm) ply)
1. Sign board (2) 24 x 1⁹⁄₁₆in (610 x 40mm)
2. Sign board end (2) 11½ x 1⁹⁄₁₆in (292 x 40mm)

Grid based on 2in (50mm) squares

Fig 15.9 Plans for the sign boards.

THE SIGN BOARDS

Saw the sign boards to the shape shown in Fig 15.9. Then glue and screw the sign boards to the cage top in the positions marked in Fig 15.7. Cut the triangular fillet to size (*see* Fig 15.7) and mitre the corners to 45°. Glue to the back of the sign boards and the cage top to strengthen these parts (*see* Fig 15.10).

THE FINISHED CIRCUS WAGON

When completed, the two-by-one battens on the base of the cage slot neatly into the box of the truck. The completed construction may be seen on page 112.

Finally, prime and paint the toy to your own satisfaction.

DESIGN NOTE: This toy could be an interesting one for the reader to play around with. For instance, the cage could be based on a circular pattern and the base on an octagonal pattern, or all the wheels could be made to swivel.

Fig 15.10 The top of the cage. The mitred triangular support fillets are being glued in place.

Sausage Dog

The Dachshund, or 'sausage dog' as it is fondly termed, makes a good subject
for a storage toy. The elongated body is fitted with hinged lids to give access to a storage area.
But it's not just a storage toy. A handle and wheels make it a ride-along toy, too.
This project also incorporates a woodworking technique not found in the other projects. You will
be bending and fixing thin plywood to form a curved surface.

MATERIALS

- birch ply 55 x 39 x ⅜in (1382 x 980 x 9mm)
- birch ply 23 x 17 x ⅛in (575 x 410 x 3mm)
- two-by-one softwood batten 10ft (3m)
- 9¹³⁄₁₆ x 1³⁄₁₆in (250 x 30mm) hardwood dowel
- four-by-two 26in (660mm)
- (2) piano hinges; length: 7³⁄₁₆in (182mm)
- (16) 1in (25mm) No 4 countersink screws
- ¾in (18mm) panel pins
- (2) 1in (24mm) plastic eyes*
- primer
- paints
- wood glue
- epoxy resin
- sandpaper (coarse, medium and fine)
- wood filler

*see list of suppliers on page 181

TOOLS

- lightweight drawing paper such as newsprint
- carbon paper
- pencil
- drawing compass
- masking tape
- brushes
- straight edge
- square
- coping saw or fret saw (or power fret saw if available)
- drill
- drill bits: ⅛in (3mm), ¼in (6mm) and 1³⁄₁₆in (30mm)
- rasp
- file
- light hammer
- pliers
- screwdriver

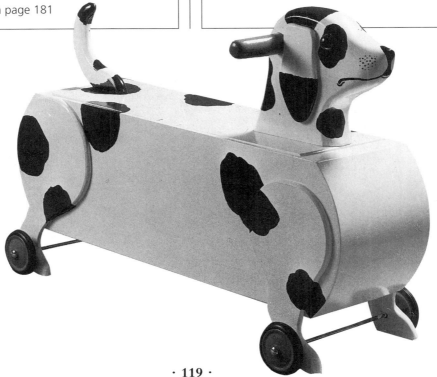

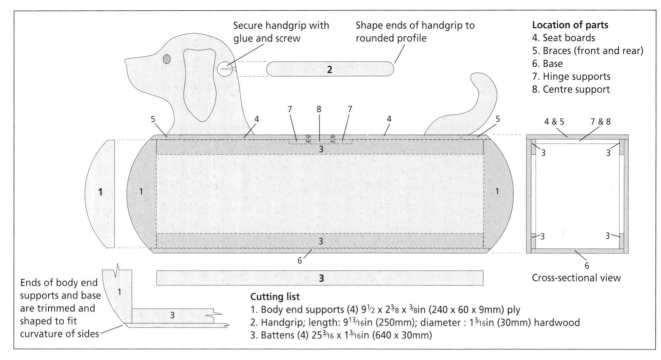

Secure handgrip with glue and screw

Shape ends of handgrip to rounded profile

Location of parts
4. Seat boards
5. Braces (front and rear)
6. Base
7. Hinge supports
8. Centre support

Cross-sectional view

Ends of body end supports and base are trimmed and shaped to fit curvature of sides

Cutting list
1. Body end supports (4) 9½ x 2⅜ x ⅜in (240 x 60 x 9mm) ply
2. Handgrip; length: 9¹³⁄₁₆in (250mm); diameter : 1³⁄₁₆in (30mm) hardwood
3. Battens (4) 25³⁄₁₆ x 1³⁄₁₆in (640 x 30mm)

Fig 16.1 Dimensions for the body end supports, handgrip and battens. Assembly guide for the storage chest parts.

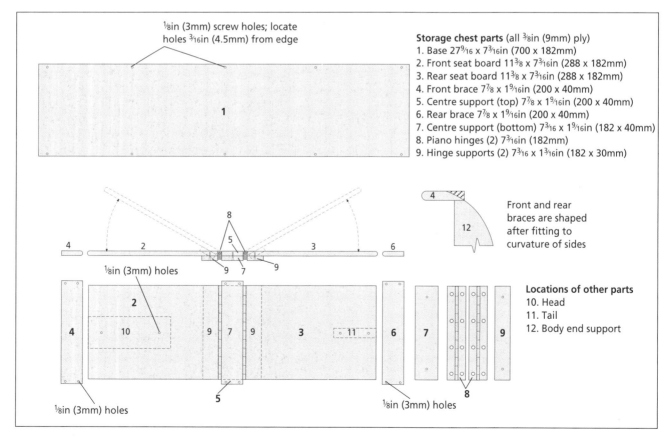

⅛in (3mm) screw holes; locate holes ³⁄₁₆in (4.5mm) from edge

Storage chest parts (all ⅜in (9mm) ply)
1. Base 27⁹⁄₁₆ x 7³⁄₁₆in (700 x 182mm)
2. Front seat board 11⅜ x 7³⁄₁₆in (288 x 182mm)
3. Rear seat board 11⅜ x 7³⁄₁₆in (288 x 182mm)
4. Front brace 7⅞ x 1⁹⁄₁₆in (200 x 40mm)
5. Centre support (top) 7⅞ x 1⁹⁄₁₆in (200 x 40mm)
6. Rear brace 7⅞ x 1⁹⁄₁₆in (200 x 40mm)
7. Centre support (bottom) 7³⁄₁₆ x 1⁹⁄₁₆in (182 x 40mm)
8. Piano hinges (2) 7³⁄₁₆in (182mm)
9. Hinge supports (2) 7³⁄₁₆ x 1³⁄₁₆in (182 x 30mm)

Front and rear braces are shaped after fitting to curvature of sides

⅛in (3mm) holes

Locations of other parts
10. Head
11. Tail
12. Body end support

⅛in (3mm) holes

⅛in (3mm) holes

Fig 16.2 Cutting list and assembly guide for the top of the storage chest.

Enlarge the plans and transfer all parts from Figs 16.1, 16.2, 16.5 and 16.7 to the correct thickness of ply. Cut out all parts.

Note from the plan that the ⅛in (3mm) ply end pieces are slightly larger than required. These pieces are fixed in position and then trimmed to size. This will become clear as the construction progresses. Note that it is important that the grain of the wood runs horizontally on these pieces to allow it to be bent round the curved sides of the body. This detail is made clear on the plan and can be seen in the photo illustrations.

Once again, study which parts would be better painted before assembly and mask off areas to be glued before painting.

BATTENS AND END SUPPORTS

Mark on the inner face of both body sides the positions of the battens and the body end supports (*see* Fig 16.1).

Drill and countersink the screw holes in these parts. Then glue and screw the battens and end supports in the positions marked on the inner faces of the body sides, making sure the rounded parts of the end supports are level with the rounded edge of the body sides. Before the glue starts to dry, cut away the ends of the body end supports level with the battens and wipe away the residue of glue with a damp cloth. This detail is shown in Fig 16.1.

THE BASE

Mark from the plan the position of the screw holes in the base (*see* Fig 16.2) for attaching to the battens on the body sides. Then drill and countersink the holes. These holes will be filled and sanded smooth at a later stage, so make sure the screw heads are below the surface of the ply. Glue and screw the base to the battens on the inner body sides in the position marked on the plan.

The ends of the base will protrude slightly past the curved shape of the body sides. File and sand the ends of the base to match the contour of the body sides. Fig 16.1 shows this detail.

Fig 16.3 Countersunk screws hold the rear brace to the top battens. The protruding edge will be filed down.

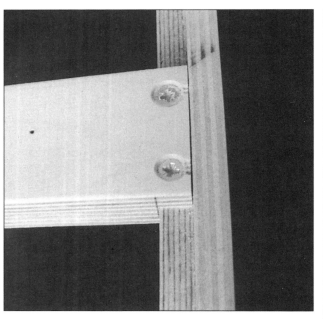

Fig 16.4 Countersunk screws hold the centre support to the top battens.

FRONT AND REAR BRACES

Drill and countersink the screw holes in the front and rear braces (*see* Fig 16.2). Round over the back edge of each brace with a file and sandpaper to the profile marked on the plan. Then glue and screw the braces in position on top of the battens at the front and rear of the body. You will note that these pieces also protrude past the curved ends of the body sides and must now be shaped to the contour of the body sides in the same manner as the base. Again, make sure that the screw holes in these parts are sufficiently countersunk to be filled completely at a later stage. Fig 16.3 shows a rear brace secured in place. The protruding edge has not yet been filed down.

CENTRE SUPPORT PIECES

The centre support is made up of a top and bottom piece as shown in Fig 16.2. Mark from the plan, then drill and countersink the screw holes in both parts.

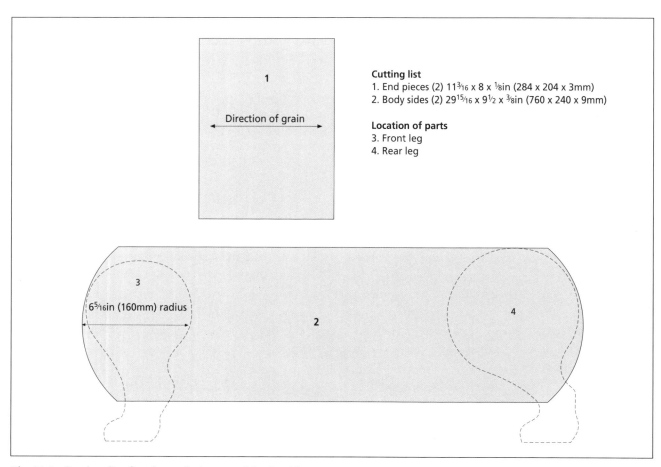

Cutting list
1. End pieces (2) 11³⁄₁₆ x 8 x ¹⁄₈in (284 x 204 x 3mm)
2. Body sides (2) 29¹⁵⁄₁₆ x 9¹⁄₂ x ³⁄₈in (760 x 240 x 9mm)

Location of parts
3. Front leg
4. Rear leg

Direction of grain

6⁵⁄₁₆in (160mm) radius

Fig 16.5 Cutting list for the end pieces and body sides.

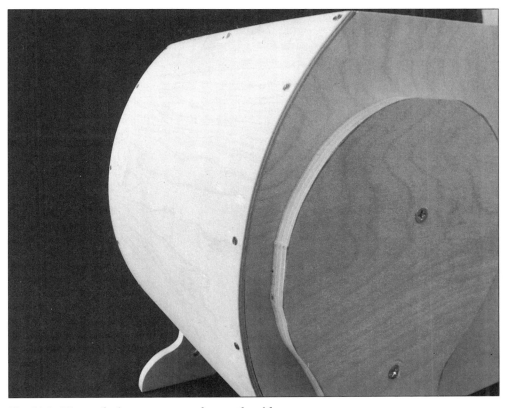

Fig 16.6 The end pieces are curved over the sides.

Then glue and screw the bottom piece to the underside of the top piece as shown in Fig 16.2. Glue and screw this assembly to the battens at the top centre of the body as shown on the plan and in Fig 16.4.

CURVING THE PLYWOOD

The $\frac{1}{8}$in (3mm) ply end pieces (*see* Fig 16.5) are now fitted as follows. Smear a little glue along the top inner edge of the end piece and along $1\frac{3}{16}$in (30mm) or so of the inner edges. Then, with one hand, hold the end piece against the front edges of the body sides, keeping the top level with the top edge of the brace. Drill a small pilot hole in the top corner of the end piece and into the body side and screw in position.

Continue drilling and fastening screws along the top edge. Then work down the sides (don't be concerned that the screw heads are proud of the ply surface; the screws are taken out and the holes filled and sanded smooth at a later stage), adding a little glue to the sides as you progress. Once you pass the halfway point the ply gets a little difficult to hold, and unless you have a strong grip you may need a helping hand.

When one end is completed, repeat the process with the opposite end. When the glue is completely dry, trim the edges neatly, flush with the body sides, base and top. This is just a matter of filing and sanding smooth. Fig 16.6 shows an end piece attached to the sides.

THE SEAT BOARDS

Mark, drill and countersink the screw holes for attaching the head in the front seat board (*see* Fig 16.2). Similarly, drill the screw holes in the rear seat board for attaching the tail. Countersink these holes from the underside of the seat boards.

Glue and pin the hinge supports (*see* Fig 16.2) to the underside of each seat board in the position shown on the plan.

THE TAIL

Glue and pin together the two parts of the tail (*see* Fig 16.7) and shape with rasp and file to a rounded cross-section. Sand to a smooth finish and glue and screw the tail to the rear seat board (from the underside) through the previously drilled holes (*see* Fig 16.2).

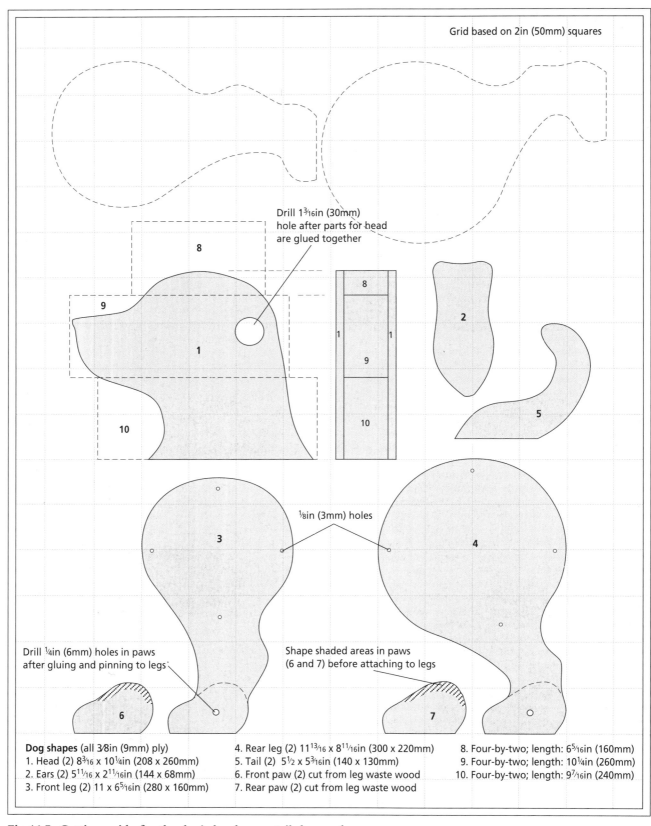

Grid based on 2in (50mm) squares

Drill 1³⁄₁₆in (30mm) hole after parts for head are glued together

8

9

1

10

8

1   1

9

10

2

5

3   ⅛in (3mm) holes   4

Drill ¼in (6mm) holes in paws after gluing and pinning to legs

Shape shaded areas in paws (6 and 7) before attaching to legs

6

7

Dog shapes (all 3⁄8in (9mm) ply)
1. Head (2) 8³⁄₁₆ x 10¼in (208 x 260mm)
2. Ears (2) 5¹¹⁄₁₆ x 2¹¹⁄₁₆in (144 x 68mm)
3. Front leg (2) 11 x 6⁵⁄₁₆in (280 x 160mm)

4. Rear leg (2) 11¹³⁄₁₆ x 8¹¹⁄₁₆in (300 x 220mm)
5. Tail (2) 5½ x 5³⁄₁₆in (140 x 130mm)
6. Front paw (2) cut from leg waste wood
7. Rear paw (2) cut from leg waste wood

8. Four-by-two; length: 6⁵⁄₁₆in (160mm)
9. Four-by-two; length: 10¼in (260mm)
10. Four-by-two; length: 9⁷⁄₁₆in (240mm)

Fig 16.7 Cutting guide for the dog's head, ears, tail, legs and paws.

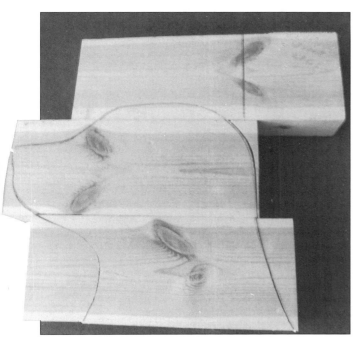

Fig 16.8 Trace the shape of the dog's head onto the four-by-twos.

THE HEAD

The head is made from two outer parts cut from ³⁄₈in (9mm) ply and three inner parts cut from offcuts of four-by-two (usually obtainable cheap or free from your local timber merchant).

Refer to Fig 16.7. Place the three pieces of four-by-two flat on the workbench and then place a head side on top of these, keeping the straight edge at the bottom of the head level with the straight edge of the lower piece of four-by-two. Trace round the outline of the head onto the four-by-two (*see* Fig 16.8). Then saw to shape. Use a coarse blade in your fret saw and keep the blade vertical while cutting.

Now lay an outer head side flat on the workbench and spread glue over the surface. Lay the three pieces of four-by-two on top of this keeping the edges level (remember to glue between the joints). Then glue and pin the remaining outer head side to this assembly. Turn the assembly over carefully and pin the lower head side in position.

Fig 16.9 The contours of the head are shaped and rounded with a rasp, file and sandpaper.

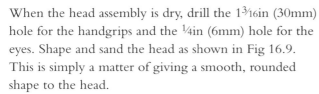

HANDGRIP

Cut the 1³⁄₁₆in (30mm) diameter hardwood dowel to size (*see* Fig 16.1). Shape the ends to a rounded profile. If you have the facility of a lathe, the handgrips can be turned to a more ornate shape.

EARS

Cut the ears to shape and round over the edges.

EYES

When the head assembly is dry, drill the 1³⁄₁₆in (30mm) hole for the handgrips and the ¼in (6mm) hole for the eyes. Shape and sand the head as shown in Fig 16.9. This is simply a matter of giving a smooth, rounded shape to the head.

Glue and screw the handgrip into the 1³⁄₁₆in (30mm) hole in the head and glue and pin the ears in the positions shown on the plan (*see* Fig 16.1). Finally, glue the eyes into the ¼in (6mm) holes with a little epoxy resin.

Glue and screw the head to the front seat board through the drilled holes (*see* Fig 16.9).

ATTACHING THE SEAT BOARDS

Cut to length two pieces of piano hinge and screw one to the rear edge of the front seat board and one to the front edge of the rear seat board. Then screw both to the centre support. These details are made clear in Fig 16.2.

THE LEGS

Round off the edges of the four legs and drill and countersink the screw holes in each for attaching to the body (*see* Fig 16.7). Shape the areas of the foot pieces shown shaded on the plan. Then glue and pin the foot pieces to the outer parts of each leg. When the glue has dried on these parts, drill the ¼in (6mm) hole for the axle through the combined leg and foot pieces (*see* Fig 16.10). Then glue and screw the legs to the body sides in the positions shown in Fig 16.5.

THE WHEELS AND AXLES

Pass the steel axle through the holes in the paws and fit a 4in (100mm) diameter wheel over each end of the axles. Secure the wheels in position (after you have finished painting the toy!) with the starlock washers and caps.

FINISHING

The completed construction is shown on page 119. All that remains to do is to prime and paint to your choice of colours.

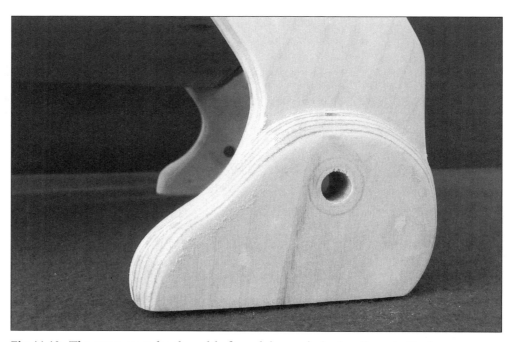

Fig 16.10 The paws must be shaped before gluing and pinning them to the legs.

Rock-and-Ride Toys

Rocking toys are always a great favourite with children. Indeed, adults' recollections of childhood will often reveal that a rocking toy, usually a horse, was their most treasured toy.

All of the toys in this section are based on a similar basic rocking frame. The rocker sides are all the same size. The only difference is that the upper edge is shaped in the dog and panda designs. I am sure the reader will visualize designs involving other animals that could be incorporated into the basic rocker frame.

If you wish to develop further designs based on these principles, remember that the toy must be balanced. That is, the seat board should be horizontal and parallel to the floor when completed. If the heavy weight on the head is too far forward, then the rocker will tilt towards the floor and the rider will tend to slide forward and be unable to rock and, worse, might fall over the front of the rocker! So you may have to juggle with the positions of the various parts during construction to achieve the proper balance.

Rocking Panda

Study the plans and photographs carefully before commencing construction. Make any alterations or adaptations where you want to include your own ideas. Some parts are described as painted before final assembly; for the purpose of photographing the parts in various stages of construction, they were left completely unpainted. Consider which parts would be better painted before gluing and screwing, and remember to mask off the areas to be glued before painting.

MATERIALS

▌ birch ply 47 x 56 x $\frac{3}{8}$in (1180 x 1400 x 9mm)
▌ two-by-one softwood batten 6ft (1.7m)
▌ $9\frac{7}{8}$ x $1\frac{3}{16}$in (250 x 30mm) hardwood dowel
▌ (50) $\frac{3}{4}$in (18mm) No 8 countersink screws
▌ (12) screw cups
▌ (2) 1in (25mm) plastic eyes*
▌ $\frac{3}{4}$in (18mm) panel pins
▌ primer
▌ paints
▌ wood glue
▌ epoxy resin
▌ sandpaper (coarse, medium and fine)
▌ wood filler

*see list of suppliers on page 181

TOOLS

▌ lightweight drawing paper such as newsprint
▌ carbon paper
▌ pencil
▌ masking tape
▌ brushes
▌ drawing compass
▌ straight edge
▌ square
▌ coping saw or fret saw (or power fret saw if available)
▌ drill
▌ drill bits: $\frac{1}{8}$in (3mm), $\frac{1}{4}$in (6mm), $1\frac{3}{16}$in (30mm)
▌ file
▌ light hammer
▌ pliers

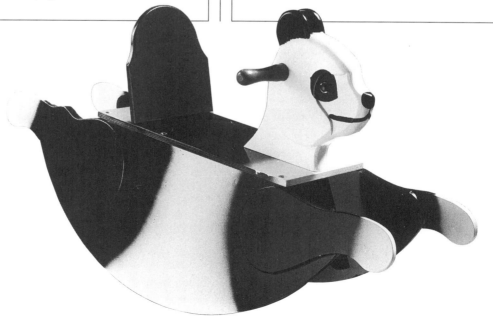

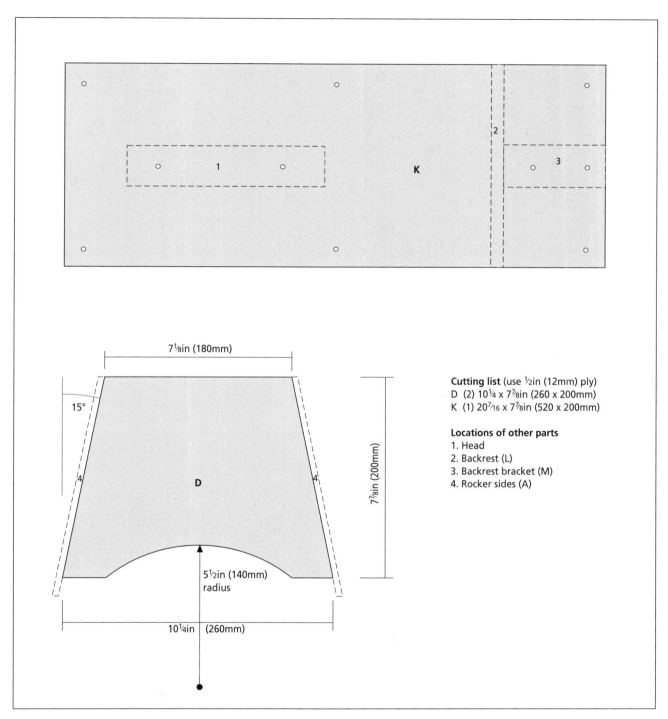

Cutting list (use ½in (12mm) ply)
D (2) 10¼ x 7⅞in (260 x 200mm)
K (1) 20⁷⁄₁₆ x 7⅞in (520 x 200mm)

Locations of other parts
1. Head
2. Backrest (L)
3. Backrest bracket (M)
4. Rocker sides (A)

Fig 17.1 The dimensions for D and K. Positions of other parts are indicated by dotted lines.

TRANSFERRING THE DIMENSIONS

Begin by scaling up all the parts shown on the plans (*see* Figs 17.1–17.4) to full size and then transfer the designs onto the correct thickness of ply. Mark the location of all the screw holes as well.

THE ROCKER

The rocker consists of two rocker sides (A), two-by-one (36mm x 18mm) battens (B and C) and two rocker end pieces (D). These parts form the basic frame, which is common to all the toys in this section.

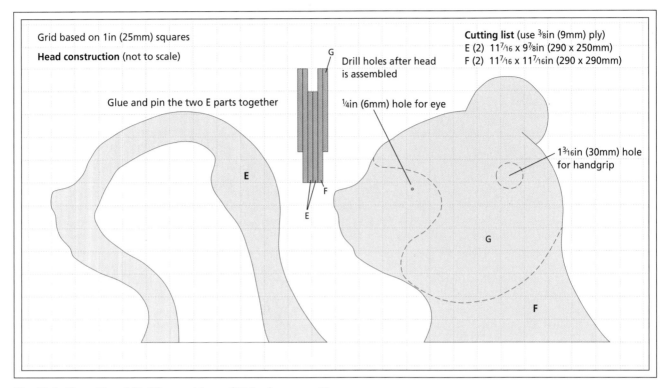

Grid based on 1in (25mm) squares

Head construction (not to scale)

Glue and pin the two E parts together

Drill holes after head is assembled

¼in (6mm) hole for eye

1³⁄₁₆in (30mm) hole for handgrip

Cutting list (use ³⁄₈in (9mm) ply)
E (2) 11⁷⁄₁₆ x 9⁷⁄₈in (290 x 250mm)
F (2) 11⁷⁄₁₆ x 11⁷⁄₁₆in (290 x 290mm)

Fig 17.2 Parts E and F. The position of G is shown on F.

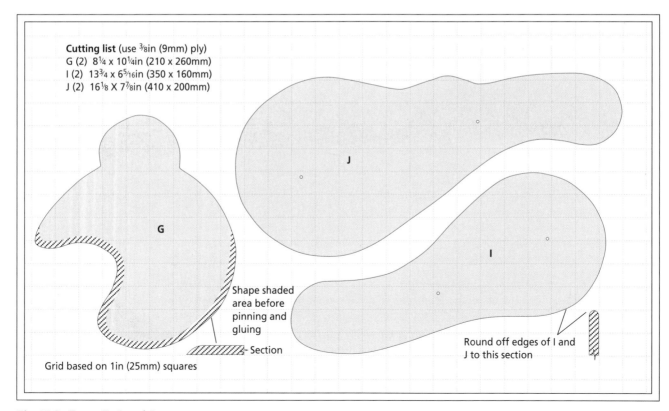

Cutting list (use ³⁄₈in (9mm) ply)
G (2) 8¼ x 10¼in (210 x 260mm)
I (2) 13¾ x 6⁵⁄₁₆in (350 x 160mm)
J (2) 16⅛ X 7⁷⁄₈in (410 x 200mm)

Shape shaded area before pinning and gluing

Section

Round off edges of I and J to this section

Grid based on 1in (25mm) squares

Fig 17.3 Parts G, I and J.

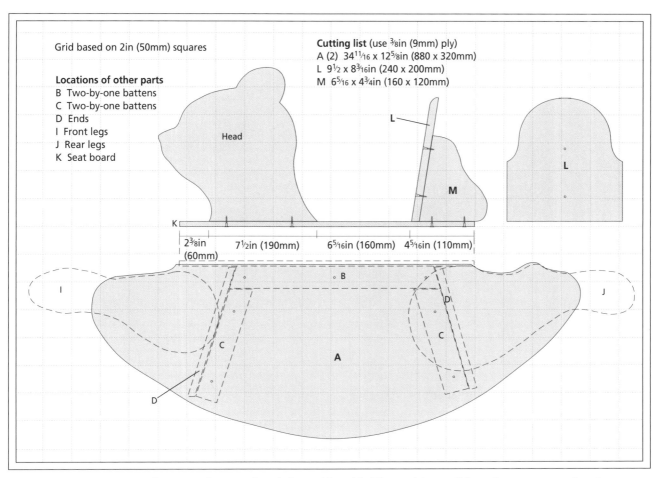

Grid based on 2in (50mm) squares

Locations of other parts
B Two-by-one battens
C Two-by-one battens
D Ends
I Front legs
J Rear legs
K Seat board

Cutting list (use ⅜in (9mm) ply)
A (2) 34¹¹⁄₁₆ x 12⅝in (880 x 320mm)
L 9½ x 8³⁄₁₆in (240 x 200mm)
M 6⁵⁄₁₆ x 4¾in (160 x 120mm)

Head

2³⁄₈in (60mm)   7½in (190mm)   6⁵⁄₁₆in (160mm)   4⁵⁄₁₆in (110mm)

Fig 17.4 The dimensions for A can be transferred from this grid. The positions of the other parts are also shown.

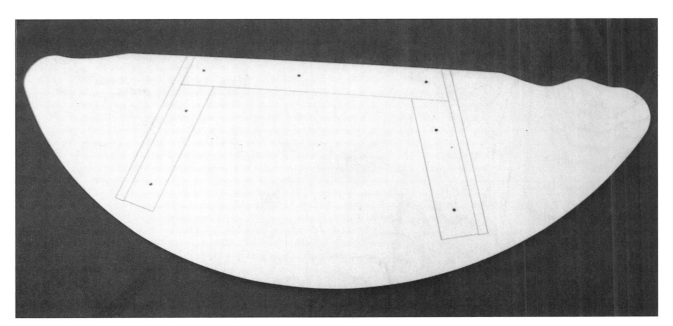

Fig 17.5 Draw the positions of B and C on A, as well as the positions of the drill holes.

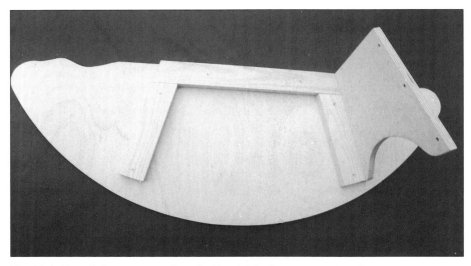

Fig 17.6 B and C are screwed to A. Part D is then screwed to C.

Temporarily pin together the two pieces of ply for the rocker sides (A) and cut them out two in duplicate. Drill all the holes marked from the plan and countersink the holes on the outer surface of the sides so that the screw heads will be well below the surface of the wood. The countersunk areas will be filled at a later stage and sanded smooth for painting.

Cut two parts B and four parts C from the two-by-one batten material. Separate the two sides (A) and mark the positions for parts B and C (*see* Fig 17.5). Glue and pin parts B and C in position on the inner faces of A. The pins are to hold the battens in position while they are screwed through the holes in A. As the screws are tightened, excess glue will be forced out from beneath the battens. Wipe away the excess glue with a damp cloth.

Saw the two rocker end pieces (D) to shape with a fret saw and drill the screw holes in each piece. These holes are not countersunk as they would be difficult to fill and sand when fitted. Screw cups are fitted underneath the heads of the screws instead. Fig 17.6 shows B and C glued and screwed in position and an end piece (D) temporarily screwed into place.

THE HEAD

Cut out two of each part E, F and G. These parts form the head. Parts E have the interior cut out to reduce the weight of the head. Glue and pin together the two E parts and glue and pin one part G to each side of this assembly, keeping the edges in alignment.

While this assembly is drying, shape the areas on the cheek pieces (G) as shown shaded on the plan and sand to a smooth finish. Now glue and pin a G part to each side of the head. Countersink the panel pins and fill the holes with wood filler. When the filler has dried, sand it level.

When the assembly is dry, drill the hole for the eyes and the hole for the handgrips completely through the head. The hole positions are shown in Fig 17.2. Finally, round and smooth all edges of the head (except the base) with a file. Then sand the completed head as shown in Fig 17.7.

The handgrips (H) can be made in two styles. The simplest method is to purchase a length of 1³⁄₁₆in (30mm) diameter hardwood dowel and shape the ends to a rounded section. If you have a lathe, a much more attractive handgrip can be turned from a suitable hardwood such as beech or sycamore. Fig 17.8 shows designs for both types.

When completed, the handgrip is fixed centrally into the 1³⁄₁₆in (30mm) hole in the head with wood glue. Then glue the eyes in position with epoxy resin. The photograph of the finished toy shows the eyes and handgrip secured to the head. The head can now be primed and painted in your intended colour scheme.

THE LEGS

Saw the front (I) and rear (J) legs (*see* Fig 17.3) to shape and round the edges with sandpaper to remove sharp

Fig 17.7 **Parts E, F, and G form the head. Holes have been drilled for the plastic eyes and the handgrip. Edges have been rounded and smoothed with the file and sandpaper.**

corners. Drill and countersink the two screw holes in each leg. Set them aside for now.

THE SEAT BOARD

Cut the seat board (K) to the size shown in Fig 17.1, and drill the screw holes for attaching the head and the back rest. Countersink these holes from the underside of K. Drill the screw holes along each edge of K. These holes are for attaching K to the rocker assembly. Countersink these holes from the top surface. With a file, followed by sandpaper, round the edge of K to a quarter-round section. The dotted lines on K in Fig 17.1 show the positions of the head and tail assemblies.

THE BACK REST

Saw the back rest (L) and the two M parts to shape (*see* Fig 17.4). Drill the two holes shown on the plan and countersink. Glue and pin the two M parts together, keeping the edges level. With a file, round the upper edge of L. Follow with sandpaper to remove sharp edges and corners. Do the same for the combined M parts.

Glue and screw L to M as shown in Fig 17.4, keeping the base of each piece level. Fill the screw holes with wood filler and sand smooth. Prime and paint the completed assembly.

ASSEMBLY

Smear glue on the base of the head assembly and position it on top of the seat board (K), then screw from the underside as shown in Fig 17.4. Wipe away excess glue with a damp cloth. Glue and screw the back-rest assembly in position (*see* Fig 17.4) at the rear of the seat board.

Prime and paint the inner parts of the two A parts, first masking the areas of C to which the rocker end pieces (D) are glued. Prime and paint the outer sides of D as well. When the paint is completely dry, glue and screw both D parts to C. Use screw cups beneath the screw heads for a neat appearance.

Glue and screw the seat-board assembly to B on both sides of the rocker assembly.

Finally, glue and screw the four legs in the position marked on the plan (*see* Fig 17.4) onto the rocker sides (A).

FINISHING

Fill all screw holes in the seat board, rocker sides and legs and sand smooth and level with the surface of the ply. Prime and paint according to your colour scheme to complete the toy.

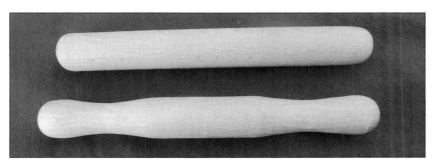

Fig 17.8 **Two styles of handgrip.**

Rocking Dolphin

This is my favourite of all the rocking toys, perhaps because the curved shape of the rocker matches the shape of the dolphin so well. Also, I think the rocking motion of the toy in play resembles movements dolphins really make. To my way of thinking a dolphin is just as natural a subject for a rocking toy as a horse.

MATERIALS

▌ birch ply 52 x 37 x ³/₈in (1300 x 920 x 9mm)
▌ birch ply 10¼ x 9⅛ x ½in (260 x 229 x 12mm)
▌ two-by-one softwood batten 107in (2.7m)
▌ four-by-two 56in (1422mm)
▌ hardwood dowel 10in x 1³/₁₆in (255 x 30mm)
▌ (60) ¾in (18mm) No 8 countersunk screws
▌ (12) screw cups
▌ (2) 25mm plastic eyes*
▌ ¾in (18mm) panel pins
▌ primer
▌ paints
▌ wood glue
▌ epoxy resin
▌ sandpaper (coarse, medium and fine)
▌ wood filler

*see list of suppliers on page 181

TOOLS

▌ lightweight drawing paper such as newsprint
▌ carbon paper
▌ pencil
▌ masking tape
▌ brushes
▌ straight edge
▌ square
▌ coping saw or fret saw (or power fret saw if available)
▌ drill
▌ drill bits: ⅛in (3mm), ¼in (6mm), 1³/₁₆in (30mm)
▌ file
▌ light hammer
▌ pliers

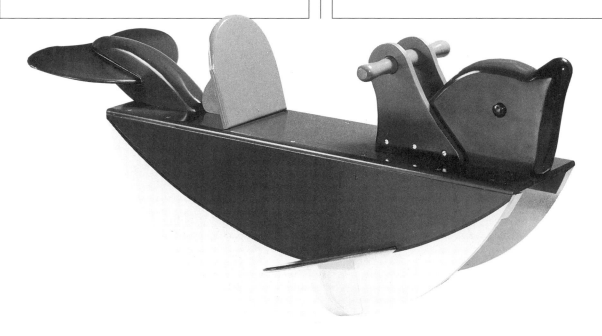

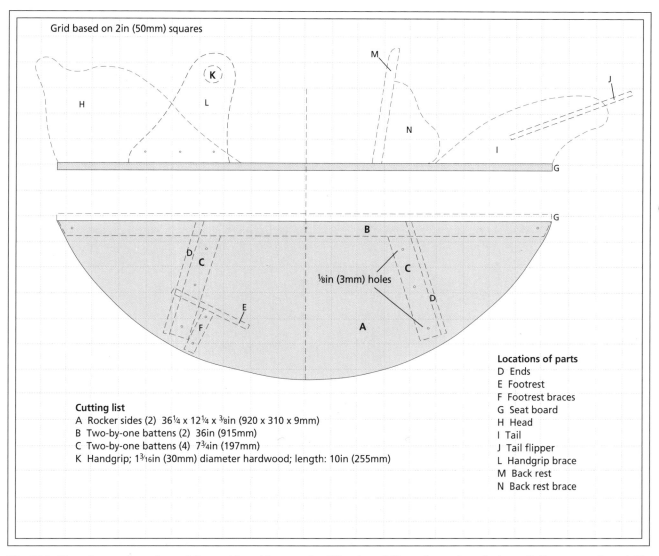

Grid based on 2in (50mm) squares

M
K
J
H
L
N
I
G
G
B
D
C
C
⅛in (3mm) holes
D
E
F
A

Cutting list
A Rocker sides (2) 36¼ x 12¼ x ⅜in (920 x 310 x 9mm)
B Two-by-one battens (2) 36in (915mm)
C Two-by-one battens (4) 7¾in (197mm)
K Handgrip; 1³⁄₁₆in (30mm) diameter hardwood; length: 10in (255mm)

Locations of parts
D Ends
E Footrest
F Footrest braces
G Seat board
H Head
I Tail
J Tail flipper
L Handgrip brace
M Back rest
N Back rest brace

Fig 18.1 Part A may be enlarged from this grid onto ply. The dotted lines show the relation of all parts to A and G.

TRANSFERRING THE DIMENSIONS

Enlarge all the parts shown in Figs 18.1–18.5 and transfer the shapes onto the correct thickness of ply. Mark the locations of all the screw holes as well.

THE ROCKER

Temporarily pin together the two pieces of ply for parts A and cut them out in duplicate. Drill and countersink the screw holes that will be used for fixing the battens (B and C). Drill on both A parts the screw holes through which part F of the footrest assemblies will be attached.

Separate the two A parts and mark out the positions of B and C on the inner surfaces of each A (*see* Fig 18.6).

Countersink the holes for the footrest assemblies on the inner faces of A.

Cut B and C to the dimensions you have marked on A. Then glue and pin B and C in position on A. Fix B and C firmly by screwing through the holes previously drilled in the rocker sides. Wipe away excess glue from around the edges of the battens with a damp cloth. Fig 18.7 shows B and C glued and screwed in the previously marked positions on A.

Cut G to size (*see* Fig 18.2) and mark the positions for the head (H), tail (I) and back rest (N) assembly as shown in Figs 18.2 and 18.8. Drill the screw holes in G and countersink them from the underside. Shape the edges of G to a quarter-round section. Fig 18.8 shows G

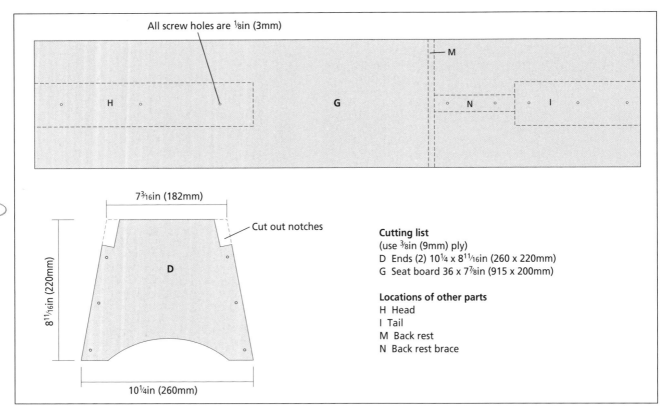

All screw holes are ⅛in (3mm)

M

H   G   N   I

7³⁄₁₆in (182mm)

Cut out notches

8¹¹⁄₁₆in (220mm)

D

10¼in (260mm)

Cutting list
(use ⅜in (9mm) ply)
D Ends (2) 10¼ x 8¹¹⁄₁₆in (260 x 220mm)
G Seat board 36 x 7⅞in (915 x 200mm)

Locations of other parts
H Head
I Tail
M Back rest
N Back rest brace

Fig 18.2 The dimensions for parts D and G. The plan for G shows the position of the head, backrest and tail assemblies.

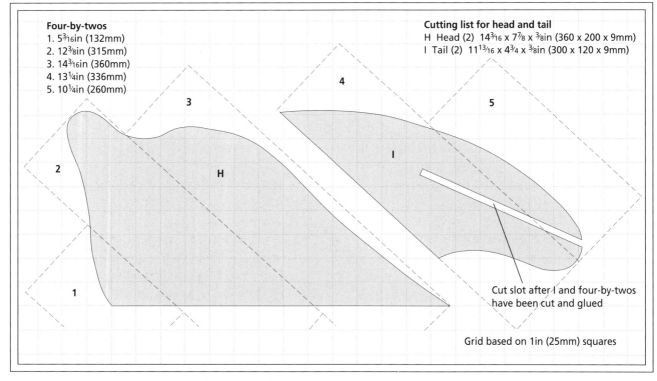

Four-by-twos
1. 5³⁄₁₆in (132mm)
2. 12⅜in (315mm)
3. 14³⁄₁₆in (360mm)
4. 13¼in (336mm)
5. 10¼in (260mm)

Cutting list for head and tail
H Head (2) 14³⁄₁₆ x 7⅞ x ⅜in (360 x 200 x 9mm)
I Tail (2) 11¹³⁄₁₆ x 4¾ x ⅜in (300 x 120 x 9mm)

3

4

5

2

H

I

1

Cut slot after I and four-by-twos
have been cut and glued

Grid based on 1in (25mm) squares

Fig 18.3 Dotted lines show the position of the four-by-twos.

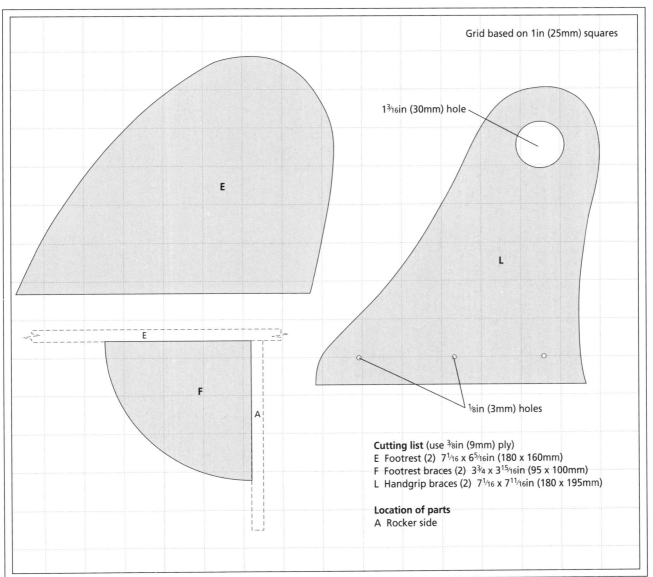

Grid based on 1in (25mm) squares

E

1³⁄₁₆in (30mm) hole

L

E

F

A

⅛in (3mm) holes

Cutting list (use ³⁄₈in (9mm) ply)
E Footrest (2) 7¹⁄₁₆ x 6⁵⁄₁₆in (180 x 160mm)
F Footrest braces (2) 3¾ x 3¹⁵⁄₁₆in (95 x 100mm)
L Handgrip braces (2) 7¹⁄₁₆ x 7¹¹⁄₁₆in (180 x 195mm)

Location of parts
A Rocker side

Fig 18.4 Enlarge E, F and L from the grid. Part F is shown in relation to A and E.

cut to size with the screw holes drilled and the positions marked for the head, tail and back-rest assemblies.

Saw the two D parts to shape (*see* Fig 18.2). You will note that these parts have notches cut out of the upper corners. The notches enable D to fit around the B parts that are attached to the top edge of A. Fig 18.9 shows D screwed into place.

THE HEAD

Saw the two H parts to shape and then cut to length three pieces of four-by-two. Lay the three pieces of four-by-two flat on the worktop (*see* Fig 18.3) and

position an H part on top of them. Draw round the outline of the head onto the four-by-twos and then saw out the profile.

Assemble the head by gluing together the edges of the four-by-twos. Then pin and glue one H to each side of the four-by-twos, like a four-by-two sandwich (*see* Fig 18.10). When the glue is dry, drill the ¼in (6mm) hole for the eyes. Then, with a rasp followed by sandpaper, shape the contours of the head to a smooth round section. The bottom of the head should be left flat. Glue the plastic eyes into the ¼in (6mm) holes in the head with epoxy resin.

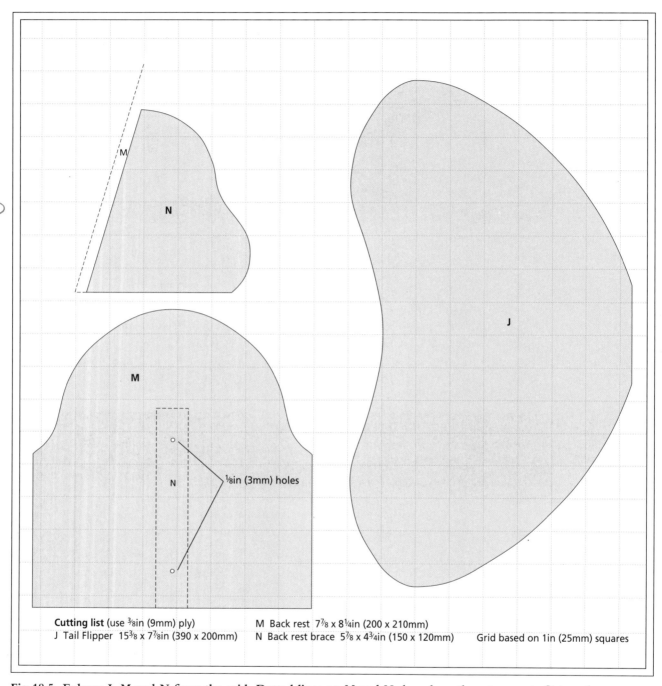

Cutting list (use ⅜in (9mm) ply)
J Tail Flipper 15⅜ x 7⅞in (390 x 200mm)

M Back rest 7⅞ x 8¼in (200 x 210mm)
N Back rest brace 5⅞ x 4¾in (150 x 120mm)

Grid based on 1in (25mm) squares

⅛in (3mm) holes

Fig 18.5 Enlarge J, M and N from the grid. Dotted lines on M and N show how these two parts fit together.

THE TAIL

The tail section of the dolphin is constructed in the same manner as the head, but do not cut the slot for the tail fin (*see* Fig 18.3) until the glue in the four-by-two sandwich of I parts and four-by-twos is dry. After cutting the slot, shape the contours of the I sandwich with a rasp and sandpaper to a smooth round section.

THE HANDGRIP

Using panel pins and a hammer, temporarily pin together the two pieces of ply for L. Then saw to shape (*see* Fig 18.4). Drill the 1³⁄₁₆in (30mm) hole through both pieces. Also drill and countersink the three screw holes for attaching the L parts of the handgrip assembly to the head.

Fig 18.6 Part A with the positions of D and the battens (B and C) marked in pencil.

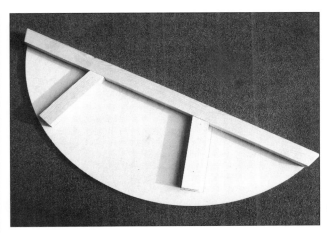

Fig 18.7 Part A with the battens (B and C) glued and screwed into place.

Separate the two L parts and sand the edges to a small radius to remove the sharp corners. Glue and screw the two L parts to the head in the position shown in Fig 18.1. The handgrips (K) are formed exactly as described in the Rocking Panda project (*see* page 132). Glue K into the holes in L.

THE TAIL FIN

Saw to shape the tail fin (J) and shape the edges to a smooth rounded profile (*see* Fig 18.5). Then glue J into position in the slot in the tail section (*see* Fig 18.1). The photograph of the finished toy on page 134 shows the tail assembly attached to the seat board (G).

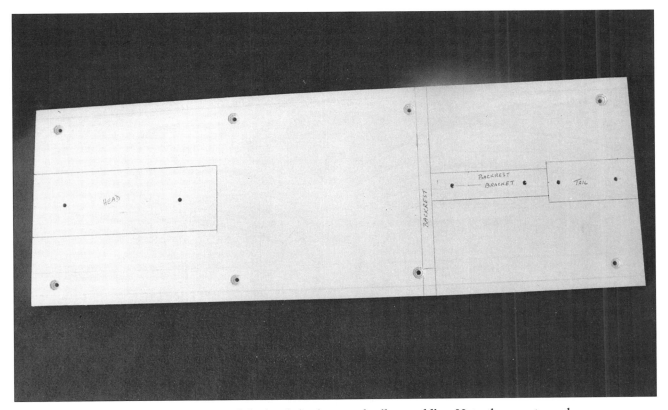

Fig 18.8 Part G showing the positions of the head, backrest and tail assemblies. Note the countersunk screw holes for attaching G to the two A parts.

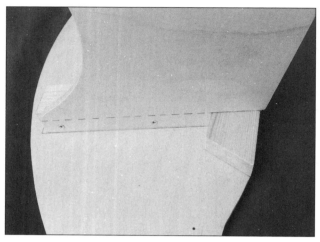

Fig 18.9 The notch in D fits around B. Screws attach D to C.

PAINTING THE HEAD AND TAIL

Examine the head and tail assemblies carefully. Punch any stray protruding panel pins below the surface of the wood. Fill all holes and blemishes with wood filler, then sand level. Prime and paint the head and tail assemblies.

THE BACK REST

Saw to shape the back rest (M) and the two back rest braces (N). Fig 18.5 shows the shapes of these parts. Shape the edge of M to a smooth rounded profile. Glue and pin the two N parts together and, when dry, round over the sharp edges. Drill and countersink the two holes in M and glue and screw M to N. When the glue has dried, fill the screw holes with wood filler and sand smooth and level with the surface of the ply. Prime and paint the completed assembly.

BEGINNING ASSEMBLY

Glue and screw the head, back rest and tail sections to the seat board (G) in the positions shown in Fig 18.1. Note that all these assemblies are screwed from the underside of the seat board.

THE FOOTRESTS

Referring to Fig 18.4, saw the two fin footrests (E) to shape. Saw the four pieces that form the footrest brackets (F) as well. Glue and pin together two parts F. Repeat the gluing and pinning with the remaining two F parts. Shape and sand the edges of the two E parts,

except the edges that will abut A. Drill and countersink two holes in each E part for attaching each E to a pair of F parts. The photograph of the finished project shows E screwed onto F.

Sand the edges of both F parts to a small radius and glue and screw an E part to each F. Unscrew the rocker end pieces (D) from the rocker sides (A), and glue and screw a completed fin footrest assembly to each A through the previously drilled holes.

PAINTING THE INTERIOR

Prime and paint the inner parts of A (mask off with masking tape the areas on A to which the D parts will be glued). Prime and paint the D parts as well.

FINAL ASSEMBLY

When the paint is completely dry, glue and screw both D parts in position using screw cups beneath the screw heads.

Glue and screw G (with head, back rest and tail assemblies attached) to the A parts.

FINAL PAINTING

Fill all screw holes and any blemishes with wood filler. When the filler has dried, sand flush with the surface of the ply. Prime and paint the rocker sides and seat board to complete the toy.

NOTE: Remember that paint will not cover blemishes, pin holes and scratches on the wood surface. Always check that these are filled and sanded smooth before painting.

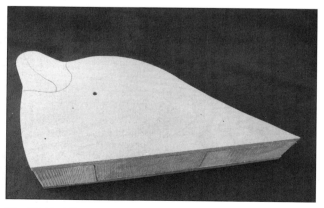

Fig 18.10 The two H parts (top and bottom) sandwich the three pieces of four-by-two.

See-Saw

The see-saw was a favourite ride in playgrounds and parks when I was a child, so I decided to include it among these rock-and-ride toys. The one I made was tested vigorously by my neighbours' children before being painted, and I'm happy to report that the construction methods are sound. However, it took hours to sand away the grubby hand marks. The patterns for the rocker sides are the same as for the previous toy (Rocking Dolphin) except that the battens on the top edges of the sides are longer and extend past the rocker sides to support the seat board.

MATERIALS

- birch ply 8ft x 32 x ³⁄₈in (2390 x 810 x 9mm)
- two-by-one softwood batten 15ft (4.5m)
- 9¹³⁄₁₆ x 1³⁄₁₆in (250 x 30mm) hardwood dowel
- (55) ¾in (18mm) No 8 countersink screws
- 12 screw cups
- ¾in (18mm) panel pins
- primer
- paints
- wood glue
- sandpaper (coarse, medium and fine)
- wood filler

TOOLS

- lightweight drawing paper such as newsprint
- carbon paper
- pencil
- masking tape
- brushes
- drawing compass
- straight edge
- square
- coping saw or fret saw (or power fret saw if available)
- drill
- drill bits: ¹⁄₈in (3mm), 1³⁄₁₆in (30mm)
- file
- light hammer
- pliers
- G-cramps

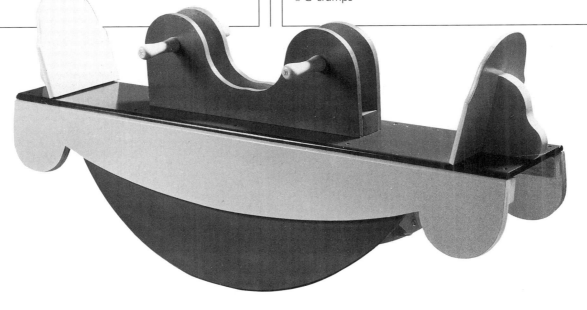

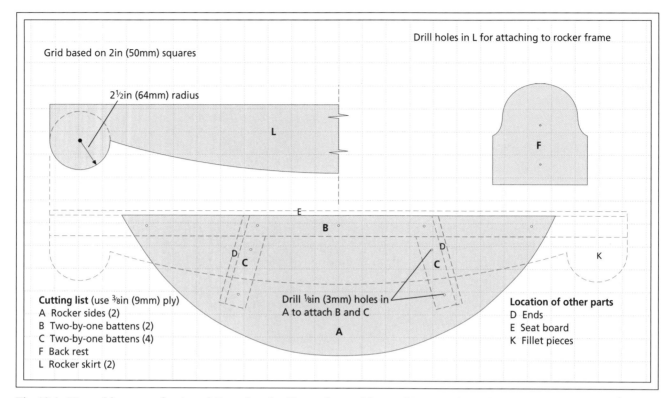

Fig 19.1 Use grid to transfer A and F to the ply. Draw the positions of B, C and D (shown by dotted lines) on the inner faces of A.

Grid based on 2in (50mm) squares

Drill holes in L for attaching to rocker frame

2½in (64mm) radius

L

F

E

B

D

C

D

C

K

A

Cutting list (use ⅜in (9mm) ply)
A Rocker sides (2)
B Two-by-one battens (2)
C Two-by-one battens (4)
F Back rest
L Rocker skirt (2)

Drill ⅛in (3mm) holes in A to attach B and C

Location of other parts
D Ends
E Seat board
K Fillet pieces

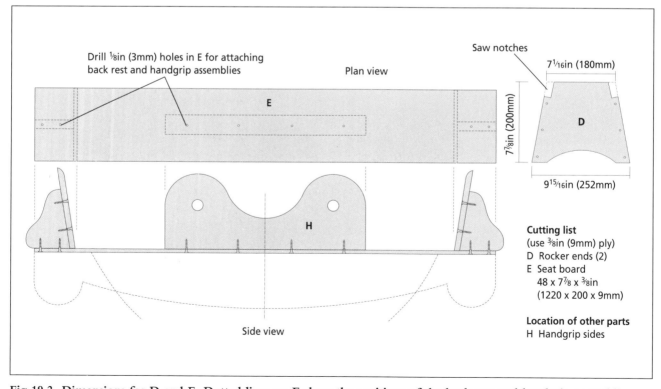

Fig 19.2 Dimensions for D and E. Dotted lines on E show the positions of the back rest and handgrip assemblies.

Drill ⅛in (3mm) holes in E for attaching back rest and handgrip assemblies

Plan view

Saw notches

7¹⁄₁₆in (180mm)

7⅞in (200mm)

9¹⁵⁄₁₆in (252mm)

E

D

H

Side view

Cutting list
(use ⅜in (9mm) ply)
D Rocker ends (2)
E Seat board
48 x 7⅞ x ⅜in
(1220 x 200 x 9mm)

Location of other parts
H Handgrip sides

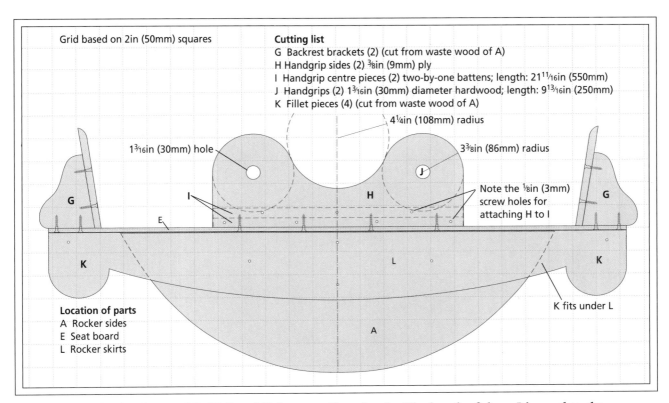

Grid based on 2in (50mm) squares

Cutting list
G Backrest brackets (2) (cut from waste wood of A)
H Handgrip sides (2) ³⁄₈in (9mm) ply
I Handgrip centre pieces (2) two-by-one battens; length: 21¹¹⁄₁₆in (550mm)
J Handgrips (2) 1³⁄₁₆in (30mm) diameter hardwood; length: 9¹³⁄₁₆in (250mm)
K Fillet pieces (4) (cut from waste wood of A)

4¼in (108mm) radius

1³⁄₁₆in (30mm) hole

3³⁄₈in (86mm) radius

Note the ⅛in (3mm)
screw holes for
attaching H to I

G

I

E

H

J

G

K

L

K

K fits under L

Location of parts
A Rocker sides
E Seat board
L Rocker skirts

A

Fig 19.3 Transfer the shapes of G, H, L and K from a grid to the ply. The length of shape I is equal to the length of H.

TRANSFERRING THE DIMENSIONS

Enlarge all the parts shown in Figs 19.1–19.3 onto a grid. Then transfer the shapes onto the correct thickness of ply. Mark the locations of all screw holes as well.

THE ROCKER

Temporarily pin together the two pieces of ply for parts A and cut them out in duplicate. Drill and countersink the screw holes that will be used for fixing the battens (B and C) to the A parts. Draw the positions of the battens on the inner faces of parts A. (An example of this step from the Rocking Dolphin project can be seen in Fig 18.6, page 139.)

Cut to size the two-by-one battens (B and C). It will be found useful to mark a centre line on the upper edge of B and on the outer face of both A parts to make alignment of these parts easier.

Glue and pin B and C onto A in the positions marked (making sure that the centre line matches B and A). Screw B and C firmly to A through the previously drilled holes.

Saw the two D parts to shape and cut out the notches on each piece. Drill (don't countersink) the screw holes for attaching D to C on A.

Screw D temporarily in position to C. Fig 19.4 shows how the notches in D fit round the two-by-one batten (B) on the top edge of A.

THE SEAT BOARD

Cut E to size (*see* Fig 19.2). Drill the screw holes for attaching the back rest and handgrip assemblies. Countersink these holes on the underside of E. Then shape the edges of E to a quarter-round section.

THE BACK RESTS

Saw to shape the two F parts and shape the edges to a smooth rounded section. Drill and countersink the two screw holes in each F.

Cut to shape the four G parts. These will form the back rest brackets. Glue and pin two of these parts together, and when dry shape the curved edge to a small radius to remove the sharp edges. Repeat this process with the remaining two pieces.

Fig 19.4 Part D is screwed onto C. The slot in D fits over B.

Fig 19.5 The two parts I are stacked together to form the base of the handgrip assembly.

Glue and screw each F to a bracket (G) through the previously drilled holes. Fill the screw holes with wood filler and sand smooth. Prime and paint to your choice of colour scheme.

THE HANDGRIP ASSEMBLY

The two handgrip sides (H) are now cut to shape and the 1³⁄₁₆in (30mm) holes drilled for the handgrips (J). Also drill and countersink the holes (marked from the plan) for attaching the H parts to the two I parts. Sand the top and side edges to a small radius.

Cut to length two pieces of two-by-one batten material and glue and pin together to form a block (*see* Fig 19.3). This will form the handgrip base. Glue and screw the two H parts (through the previously drilled holes) to the handgrip base, keeping the ends and bases level (*see* Fig 19.5).

Shape the handgrips (J) as described in the rocking panda project (*see* page 132). Glue a J part into each 1³⁄₁₆in (30mm) hole in H. Fill the screw holes with wood filler and sand smooth. Prime and paint the

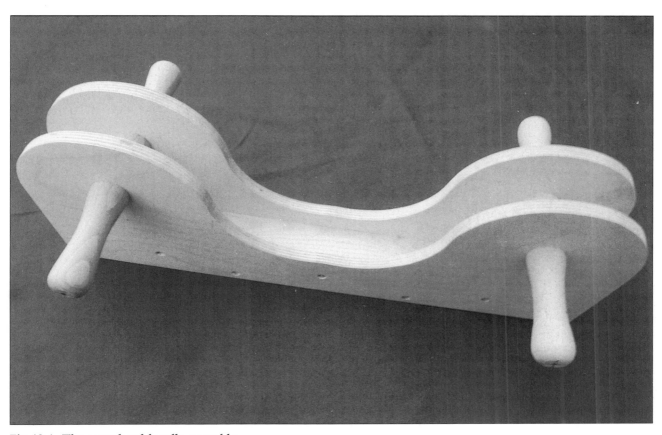

Fig 19.6 The completed handle assembly.

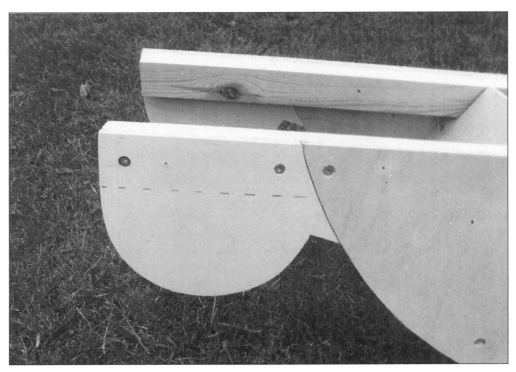

Fig 19.7 Part K is glued and screwed to B (position of B indicated by dotted line).

Fig 19.8 Part L fits into place on top of A and covers K.

handgrip assembly. Fig 19.6 shows the completed assembly.

THE ROCKER SKIRT

Now saw to shape the four K parts and drill and countersink the two holes in each part. Glue and screw one K to each A on the battens extending from A. The semicircular edge of K should fit snugly against the top of A (*see* Figs 19.4 and 19.7).

Saw the two L parts to shape and drill and countersink the holes for screwing L to A. Sand smooth the lower edges. (The rounded ends will be sanded at the next stage.) Glue and cramp the two L parts in position on A and put in the screws through the holes. When the glue has dried, shape the top edges of L to a quarter-round section. Fig 19.8 shows L glued and screwed to A.

Shape and sand the rounded ends of L to match the contours of K. Then shape and sand the top edge of L to a quarter-round section.

PAINTING THE INTERIOR

Unscrew rocker ends (D) from C. Prime and paint the inner sides of the rocker frame (mask off areas to be glued) and the outer faces of the D parts.

FINAL ASSEMBLY

When the paint is completely dry, glue and screw the D parts to C, fitting screw cups beneath the screw heads.

Glue and screw the handgrip and back-rest assemblies to E in the position shown in Fig 19.2. Then glue and screw E to the top of the rocker frame as shown in the photograph of the finished toy.

FINISHING

Punch any stray protruding panel pins below the surface of the wood. Fill all screw holes, pin holes and blemishes with wood filler. Finally, prime and paint the rocker to your choice of colour scheme.

Rocking Dog

The last toy in this section is a rocking dog, and to make it easy to name him I've covered him in spots!

MATERIALS

- birch ply 48 x 48 x ³⁄₈in (1180 x 1180 x 9mm)
- birch ply 8³⁄₈ x 3³⁄₄ x ¹⁄₂in (212 x 94 x 12mm)
- two-by-one softwood batten 52in (1.3m)
- 9¹³⁄₁₆ x 1³⁄₁₆in (250 x 30mm) hardwood dowel
- four-by-two 27in (690mm)
- (38) ³⁄₄in (18mm) No 8 countersink screws
- (12) screw cups
- ³⁄₄in (18mm) panel pins
- (2) 1in (25mm) plastic eyes*
- primer
- paints
- wood glue
- epoxy resin
- sandpaper (coarse, medium and fine)
- wood filler

*see list of suppliers on page 181

TOOLS

- lightweight drawing paper such as newsprint
- carbon paper
- pencil
- protractor
- masking tape
- brushes
- straight edge
- square
- coping saw or fret saw (or power fret saw if available)
- drill
- drill bits: ¹⁄₈in (3mm), ¹⁄₄in (6mm), 1³⁄₁₆in (30mm)
- rasp
- file
- light hammer
- pliers

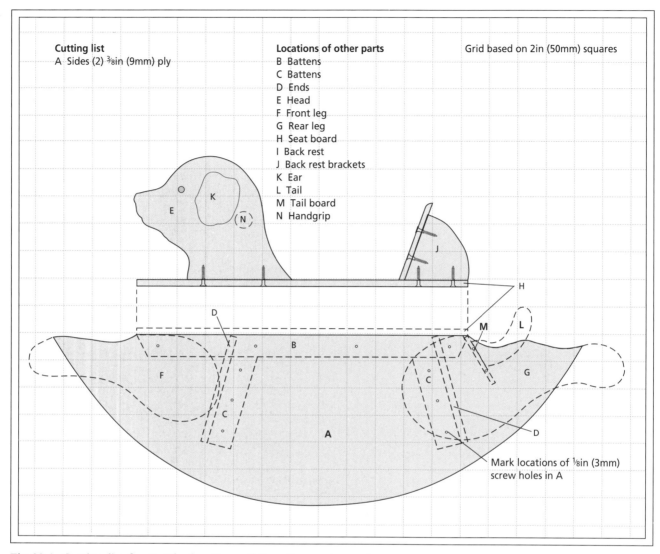

Fig 20.1 Cutting list for A. The locations of the other parts are shown.

TRANSFERRING THE DIMENSIONS

Enlarge the parts from Figs 20.1–20.4 and transfer the shapes to the correct thicknesses of ply. Mark the positions of all drill holes.

THE ROCKER

Saw to shape A, D, E, F, G, I and J. I find it quicker to saw all the parts for a given project first. It also enables me to remove the fret saw from the workbench, giving me more room for construction.

As usual, it is easier to saw and drill identical parts in duplicate if you have a suitable motorized fret saw and a pillar drill. Drill and countersink the screw holes in A for attaching the two-by-one battens (B and C). Mark

the positions for B and C on the inner surfaces of A as shown in Fig 20.1. An example of marking out B and C on the ply can be seen in Fig 18.6 of the Rocking Dolphin project (*see* page 139).

Drill the screw holes in D (do not countersink) for attaching D to C. Cut to shape B and C. Glue, pin and screw them to the previously marked positions on the inner faces of parts A. Temporarily screw the D parts to C.

THE SEAT BOARD

Saw the seat board (H) to the dimensions shown in Fig 20.2. Drill the screw holes for attaching the head and back-rest assemblies. Countersink these holes from the

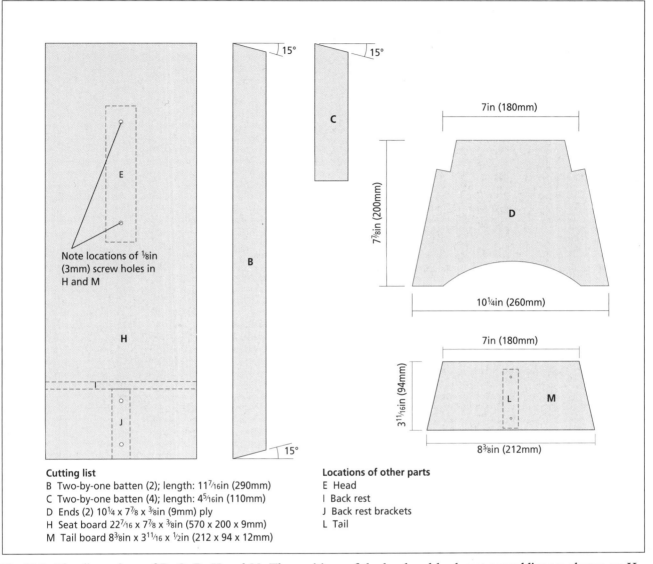

Cutting list
B Two-by-one batten (2); length: 11⁷⁄₁₆in (290mm)
C Two-by-one batten (4); length: 4⁵⁄₁₆in (110mm)
D Ends (2) 10¼ x 7⁷⁄₈ x ³⁄₈in (9mm) ply
H Seat board 22⁷⁄₁₆in x 7⁷⁄₈ x ³⁄₈in (570 x 200 x 9mm)
M Tail board 8³⁄₈in x 3¹¹⁄₁₆ x ½in (212 x 94 x 12mm)

Locations of other parts
E Head
I Back rest
J Back rest brackets
L Tail

Fig 20.2 The dimensions of B, C, D, H and M. The positions of the head and back rest assemblies are shown on H.

underside of H. Drill the screw holes for fixing H to B. Countersink these holes on the upper surface of H. Shape the edges of H to a quarter-round section to remove the sharp corners.

THE HEAD

The head is constructed in the same manner as the dolphin's head was in the rocking dolphin project. Please refer to the detailed explanations and illustrations for making the dolphin's head (*see* page 137) and apply them to this project.

The inner section of the head is made up of three pieces of four-by-two and sandwiched between two pieces of ply (E). Fig 20.3 shows the arrangement of the four-by-twos on a part E. Fig 20.5 shows the completed sandwich.

When the glue is dry, drill the 1³⁄₁₆in (30mm) hole to accept the handgrip and the ¼in (6mm) hole for fixing the eyes. Shape the head to a smooth rounded section. Glue the eyes into the ¼in (6mm) holes in the head with epoxy resin.

Saw the ears (K) to shape (*see* Fig 20.3). Round off the edges. Glue and pin the ears (K), one to each side of the head, in the positions shown in Fig 20.3. Fig 20.6 shows the head shaped and sanded and the eyes and ears fitted.

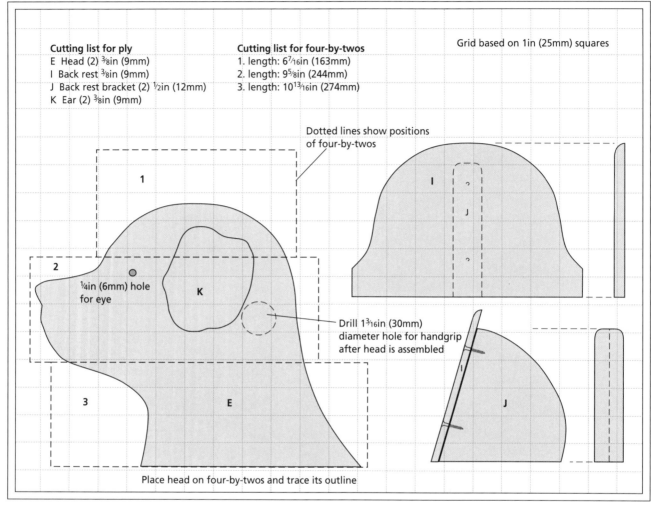

Fig 20.3 The dimensions of E, I, J and K.

Within the figure:

Cutting list for ply
E Head (2) $\frac{3}{8}$in (9mm)
I Back rest $\frac{3}{8}$in (9mm)
J Back rest bracket (2) $\frac{1}{2}$in (12mm)
K Ear (2) $\frac{3}{8}$in (9mm)

Cutting list for four-by-twos
1. length: $6\frac{7}{16}$in (163mm)
2. length: $9\frac{5}{8}$in (244mm)
3. length: $10\frac{13}{16}$in (274mm)

Grid based on 1in (25mm) squares

Dotted lines show positions of four-by-twos

$\frac{1}{4}$in (6mm) hole for eye

Drill $1\frac{3}{16}$in (30mm) diameter hole for handgrip after head is assembled

Place head on four-by-twos and trace its outline

THE TAIL

Cut to shape the three pieces of $\frac{1}{2}$in (12mm) ply that will form the tail (see Fig 20.4). Glue and pin the three pieces (L) together (see Fig 20.7). Saw M to the dimensions shown in Fig 20.2. Drill the two screw holes through which the tail will be attached to M. When the glue has dried on the L stack, shape and sand the tail to a rounded section (see Fig 20.8). Then glue and screw L to M. Fig 20.8 shows the completed tail assembly.

THE HANDGRIPS

The handgrips (N) are formed exactly as described in the Rocking Panda project (see page 132). Glue the handgrips into the $1\frac{3}{16}$in (30mm) hole previously drilled in the head.

THE BACK REST

Shape and sand the upper edge and sides of I to the section shown in Fig 20.3. Drill and countersink the two screw holes for attaching I to J. Glue and pin together the two J parts. When dry, sand the edges of the combined J part to a small radius to remove the sharp corners. Glue and screw I to J. Fill the screw holes with wood filler and sand smooth. Prime and paint the completed assembly.

PAINTING THE INTERIOR

Unscrew the rocker end pieces (D), and prime and paint the inner sides of A and D. (Mask off areas to be glued.) When the paint is completely dry, glue and screw the D parts in position between the A parts. Use screw cups under the heads of the screws.

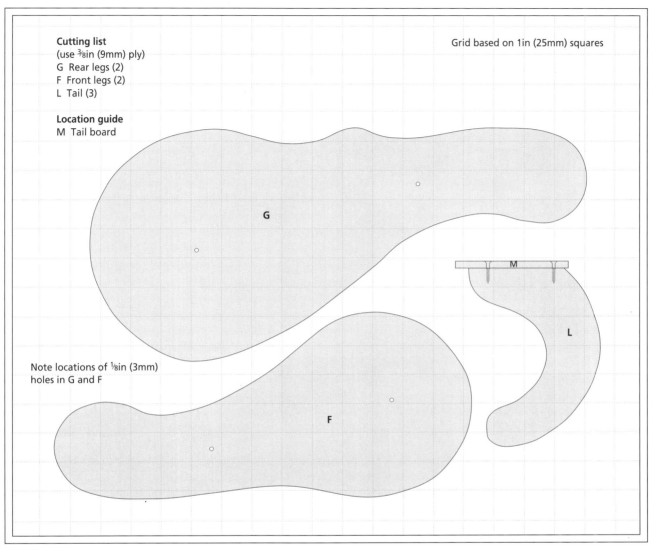

Cutting list
(use ³⁄₈in (9mm) ply)
G Rear legs (2)
F Front legs (2)
L Tail (3)

Location guide
M Tail board

Grid based on 1in (25mm) squares

G

M

L

Note locations of ¹⁄₈in (3mm)
holes in G and F

F

Fig 20.4 The dimensions of F, G and L. Part L is shown attached to M by two screws.

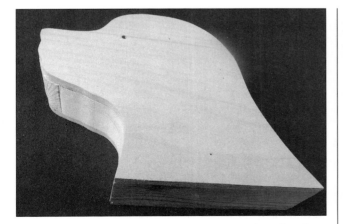

Fig 20.5 Three pieces of four-by-two are pinned and glued between two pieces of ply to make the head.

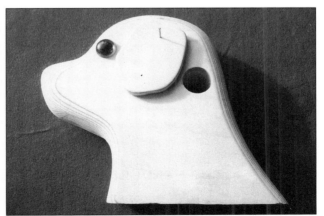

Fig 20.6 The contours of the head are rounded and smoothed with a rasp and sandpaper.

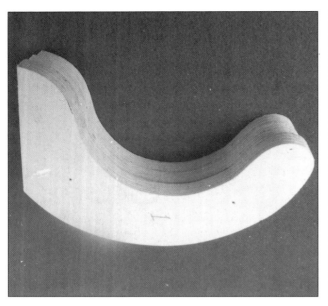

Fig 20.7 Three pieces of ply are pinned and glued together to make the tail.

ASSEMBLING THE TOY

Glue and screw (through the previously drilled holes) the tail assembly (L and M) in position between the A parts as shown in Fig 20.1.

Glue and screw the head (E) and back rest (I and J) assemblies to H. Glue and screw H to A.

Drill and countersink the two screw holes in F and G, and round off the edges of F and G to a smooth finish. Glue and screw F and G to the rocker sides (A) in the positions shown in Fig 20.1. The contoured upper edges of F and G align with the shaped top edges of A.

FINISHING

Fill all screw holes, pin holes and any other blemishes with wood filler and sand smooth and level with the surface of the ply. Then prime and paint to your choice of colours.

Fig 20.8 The tail mounted on M.

Animals With Young

4. Kangaroo and 'Joey'

2. Duck

1. Panda and Cub

3. Penguin and Chick

2. Duckling

Toys Based on Geometric Shapes

7. Skittles (Rectangle)

5. Clock (Circle)

6. Jigsaw Puzzle (Octagon)

8. Ball-in-a-Cube Game (Square)

Toys Based on Everyday Articles

12. Carpet Sweeper

11. Boot House

9. Pop-up Toaster

10. Teapot House

15. Circus Wagon

14. Noah's Ark

16. Sausage Dog

13. Panda Seat

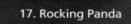

17. Rocking Panda

20. Rocking Dog

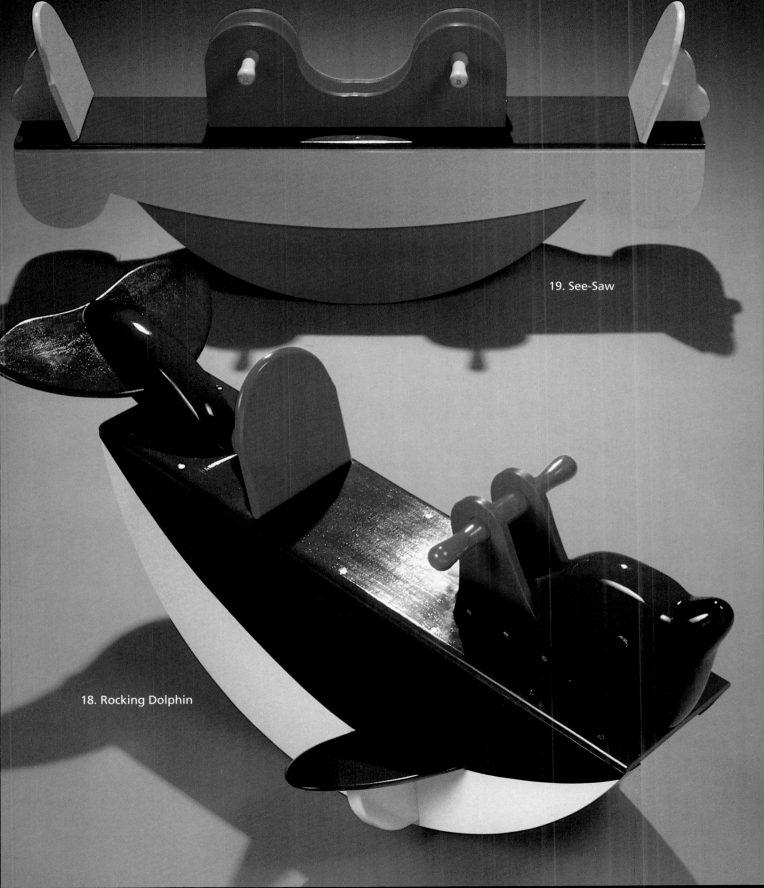

19. See-Saw

18. Rocking Dolphin

Sand-operated Toys

21. Diving Dolphins

22. Trapeze Artists

23. Men at Work

24. Windmill

Sand-operated Toys

Throughout the ages toys have been created with moving parts operated by a variety of ingenious devices. Water, sand, magnets and a range of sprung-wound and electrically driven forces have been used to provide toys with movement, with the illusion of life.

In this last section I have developed four toys that have moving parts operated by sand. Sand flows at a controlled rate from a hopper onto the paddles of a wheel (similar to a water wheel). The weight of the sand forces the wheel to turn. The wheel continues in motion until the supply of sand is exhausted. The sand falls from the paddles of the wheel into a collection tray (sandbox), which is emptied into the hopper to re-start the operation. The power of the turning wheel operates various devices which, in turn, animate the moving parts of each toy.

Ordinary builder's sand is not suitable for operating the toy. Silver sand is ideal for the purpose and can be purchased from your local garden centre. The sand may contain a little moisture when obtained and should be dried thoroughly before use.

Diving Dolphins

Draw all parts from the plans on the correct thickness of ply. Most of the parts can be transferred by measurement alone, but the fascia (waves) and dolphins will need enlarging from the grid. Mark the positions of all holes that need drilling.

MATERIALS

▊ birch ply 44 x 26 x $^3/_8$in (1110 x 650 x 9mm)
▊ birch ply 16 x 15 x $^1/_4$in (395 x 365 x 6mm)
▊ birch ply 10 x 8 x $^1/_{16}$in (240 x 200 x 1.5mm)
▊ triangular softwood fillet; length: $9^{13}/_{16}$in (250mm)
▊ hardwood dowel; length: $7^7/_8$in (200mm); diameter: $^3/_8$in (9mm)
▊ steel axle; length: $4^3/_8$in (112mm); diameter: $^1/_4$in (6mm)
▊ starlock washer and cap; internal diameter: $^1/_4$in (6mm)
▊ (4) steel washers; internal diameter: $^1/_4$in (6mm)
▊ (2) bronze bearings; internal diameter: $^1/_4$in (6mm)
▊ (19) $^3/_4$in (18mm) No 4 countersunk screws
▊ $^3/_4$in (18mm) panel pins
▊ primer
▊ paints
▊ wood glue
▊ sandpaper (coarse, medium and fine)
▊ wood filler
▊ epoxy resin
▊ 1lb (.5k) silver sand

TOOLS

▊ lightweight drawing paper such as newsprint
▊ carbon paper
▊ pencil
▊ masking tape
▊ brushes
▊ drawing compass
▊ straight edge
▊ square
▊ coping saw or fret saw (or power fret saw if available)
▊ drill
▊ drill bits: $^1/_8$in (3mm), $^1/_4$in (6mm) and $^3/_8$in (9mm)
▊ file
▊ light hammer
▊ pliers
▊ G-cramps

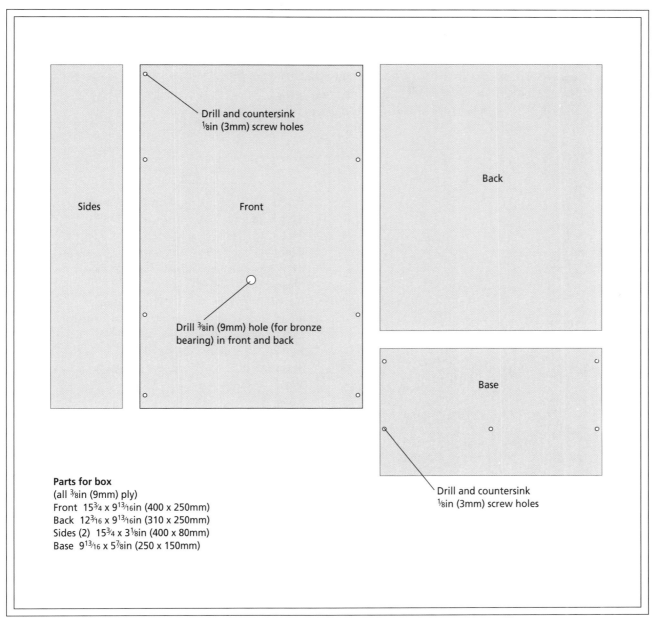

Parts for box
(all ⅜in (9mm) ply)
Front 15¾ x 9¹³/₁₆in (400 x 250mm)
Back 12³/₁₆ x 9¹³/₁₆in (310 x 250mm)
Sides (2) 15¾ x 3⅛in (400 x 80mm)
Base 9¹³/₁₆ x 5⅞in (250 x 150mm)

Fig 21.1 Dimensions for the front, back, sides and base.

THE BASIC BOX

Begin by sawing to size the front, back, two sides and the base from Fig 21.1. Drill and countersink the screw holes in these parts in the positions marked from the plan. All parts must be sanded to a good finish before construction. Identify those parts that require painting before assembly and be sure to paint them before gluing and assembling.

Glue and screw the front to the two sides. Fill the

screw holes with wood filler and sand smooth and flush with the surface of the ply.

Screw (do not glue) the back to the two sides as shown in Fig 21.2. The back is shorter than the front to allow space for the sandbox, which will be fitted at a later stage.

Now glue and screw the base to the bottom edges of the front and sides as shown in Fig 21.2. These screw holes do not need to be filled.

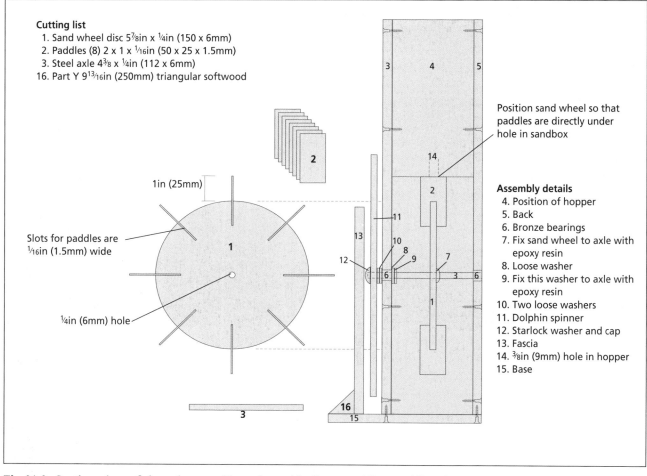

Cutting list
1. Sand wheel disc 5⅞in x ¼in (150 x 6mm)
2. Paddles (8) 2 x 1 x ¹⁄₁₆in (50 x 25 x 1.5mm)
3. Steel axle 4⅜ x ¼in (112 x 6mm)
16. Part Y 9¹³⁄₁₆in (250mm) triangular softwood

1in (25mm)

Slots for paddles are ¹⁄₁₆in (1.5mm) wide

¼in (6mm) hole

Position sand wheel so that paddles are directly under hole in sandbox

Assembly details
4. Position of hopper
5. Back
6. Bronze bearings
7. Fix sand wheel to axle with epoxy resin
8. Loose washer
9. Fix this washer to axle with epoxy resin
10. Two loose washers
11. Dolphin spinner
12. Starlock washer and cap
13. Fascia
14. ⅜in (9mm) hole in hopper
15. Base

Fig 21.2 Section view of the axle assembly and a guide for assembling paddle wheel.

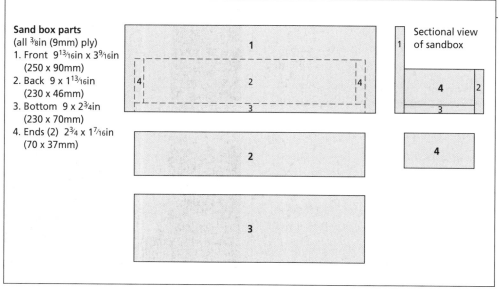

Sand box parts
(all ⅜in (9mm) ply)
1. Front 9¹³⁄₁₆in x 3⁹⁄₁₆in (250 x 90mm)
2. Back 9 x 1¹³⁄₁₆in (230 x 46mm)
3. Bottom 9 x 2¾in (230 x 70mm)
4. Ends (2) 2¾ x 1⁷⁄₁₆in (70 x 37mm)

Sectional view of sandbox

Fig 21.3 The parts for the sandbox.

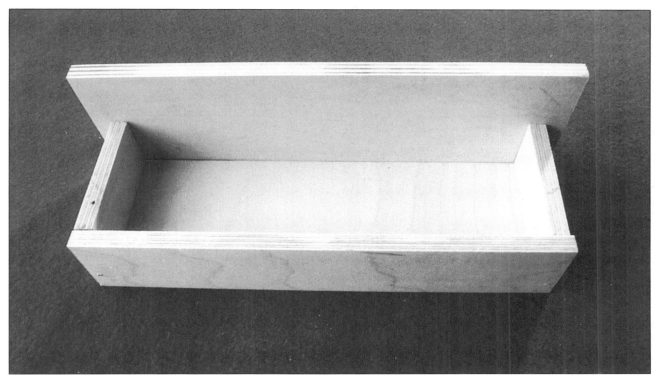

Fig 21.4 The assembled sandbox.

INSTALLING THE BEARINGS

Mark the position of the ³⁄₈in (10mm) hole for the
bronze bearings on the front and drill the hole
completely through front and back. (Put a piece of
scrap wood under the front and back before drilling.) I
found this method was more accurate than drilling the
front and back separately as the holes have to be perfectly
aligned for the axle to rotate freely in the bearings.

Unscrew and remove the back from the sides and
prime and paint these parts. When the paint is fully dry
insert a bronze bearing into the ³⁄₈in (10mm) holes in
the front and back. This is done by placing a piece of
scrap ply over the end of the bearing and tapping gently
with a hammer until the bearing is flush with the outer
face of each piece.

SANDBOX

Cut out the parts for the sandbox (*see* Fig 21.3) and
assemble by gluing and pinning together as shown in
the detail on the plan.

The assembled sandbox is shown in Fig 21.4. Fig
21.5 shows the sandbox fitted into the box. The
bearing can also be seen fitted into place.

**Fig 21.5 The sandbox in place in the main box. Also,
one of the bearings can be seen in place.**

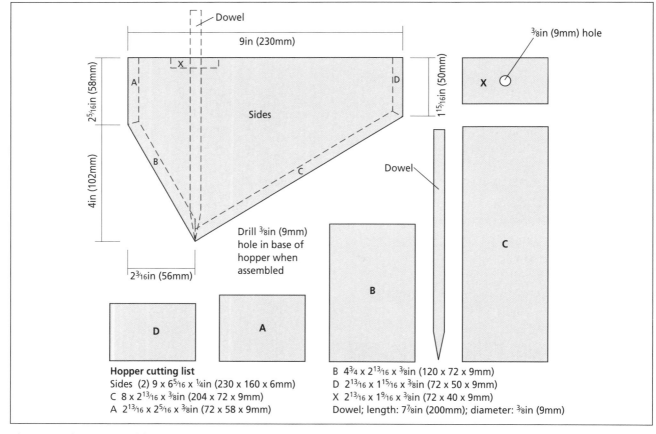

Fig 21.6 The parts and location guide for the hopper assembly.

Fig 21.7 File a flat area first, then drill the hole through which the sand pours.

HOPPER

Proceed by cutting out the parts that form the hopper (*see* Fig 21.6). The edges of parts A, B, C and D are filed and sanded to an angle (shown on the plan) so that these parts fit snugly together when assembled. Any small gaps may be filled with wood filler and sanded smooth.

The pointed base of the hopper is now drilled with a $^3/_8$in (9mm) hole to allow sand to flow from the hopper. Do this by turning the hopper upside down; file a flat area at the centre of the point and then drill the $^3/_8$in (9mm) hole as shown in Fig 21.7.

Now cut part X to size and drill a $^3/_8$in (9mm) hole at its centre (*see* Fig 21.6). Cut a length of $^3/_8$in (9mm) wooden dowel to size and shape one end to a point (*see* Fig 21.6).

Place part X between the hopper sides and above the hole in the base of the hopper and insert the dowel through the hole in part X and the pointed end into the hole in the hopper base. Align part X until the wooden dowel is vertical. Then glue part X in position between the hopper sides as shown in Fig 21.6. The flow of sand from the hopper is controlled by raising the pointed dowel from the hole in the base of the hopper. To stop the sand flowing the pointed dowel is pushed down into the hole.

Glue the hopper to the rear face of the front as shown in Fig 21.8. The hopper will have to be cramped in position while the glue dries.

SAND WHEEL

Referring to Fig 21.2, cut the circular disc and mark off and saw the eight slots into which the paddles are fitted. Drill the ¼in (6mm) hole at the centre of the disc for the ¼in (6mm) axle on which the sand wheel turns. Cut the eight paddles to size and glue them centrally into the slots in the disc. The finished sand wheel may be seen in Fig 21.8.

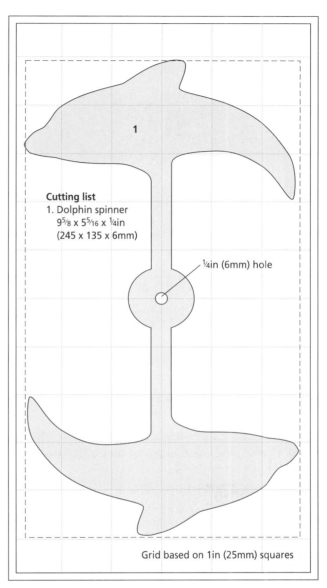

Cutting list
1. Dolphin spinner
   9⅝ x 5⁵⁄₁₆ x ¼in
   (245 x 135 x 6mm)

¼in (6mm) hole

Grid based on 1in (25mm) squares

Fig 21.9 The dolphin spinner.

Fig 21.8 The hopper and paddle wheel in place in the main box.

DOLPHIN SPINNER

Saw out the dolphin spinner to the shape shown in Fig 21.9. Drill the ¼in (6mm) hole for the axle at its centre. Fig 21.10 shows the spinner completed.

FASCIA

Cut out the fascia from the details shown in Fig 21.11. Cut to size the triangular section (Y), which is glued to the bottom of the fascia in the position shown in Fig 21.11. The triangular section is softwood and can be purchased from your local timber merchant or DIY shop. Prime and paint the fascia to obtain a sea effect.

Fig 21.10 The dolphin spinner mounted on the front.

ASSEMBLY OF SAND WHEEL TO AXLE

Cut to size the ¼in (6mm) steel axle and press a starlock washer and cap onto one end. Smear a little epoxy resin around the axle next to the starlock washer with a toothpick then insert the axle through the dolphin spinner. Press the spinner up to the starlock washer and cap and allow the epoxy resin to set.

When the epoxy resin is dry, place two ¼in (6mm) steel washers over the axle and against the spinner then insert the axle through the bronze bearing in the front. A detail of the assembly is shown in Fig 21.2.

Place another washer over the axle and against the rear face of the front. Now cut a piece of thin card and cut a ¼in (6mm) hole at the centre and place it over the axle and against the washer. (The card is to allow a little space for free movement of the axle when the next stage has been completed.) Now place another ¼in (6mm) washer over the axle and against the card and secure in place with epoxy resin. When the epoxy resin has dried, tear away the card.

Place the assembled sand wheel onto the axle by inserting the axle through the hole in the centre of the disc and position centrally so that the hole in the base of the hopper is directly above the centre of the paddles. Fix the sand wheel to the axle with epoxy resin. Again, refer to Fig 21.2 for a diagram showing the order of assembly. Fig 21.8 shows the sand wheel fixed in position.

Guide the end of the axle into the bronze bearing in the back and screw the back to the sides through the previously drilled holes in the back.

Smear glue along the bottom of the fascia assembly and glue to the front of the base to complete the assembly.

OPERATING THE TOY

To operate, fill the hopper with silver sand and adjust the pointed dowel to release a steady flow of sand. Help the sand wheel to gather momentum by giving the spinner a flick with the finger. The dolphins jump and dive as the spinner turns.

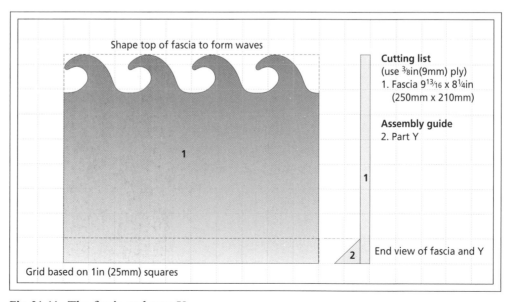

Fig 21.11 The fascia and part Y.

Trapeze Artists

*This and the following toy (Men at Work) in this section contain small parts
and short lengths of wire, making them more suitable as adult collector's toys. Young children
should not be allowed to play with them except under the supervision of an adult.*

MATERIALS

- birch ply 44 x 26 x $^3/_8$in (1110 x 650 x 9mm)
- birch ply 24 x 20 x $^1/_4$in (600 x 500 x 6mm)
- birch ply 7 x 3$^3/_{16}$ x $^1/_{16}$in (160 x 80 x 1.5mm)
- metal rod; length: 4$^3/_8$in (112mm); diameter: $^1/_4$in (6mm)*
- metal wire; length: 25in (635mm); diameter: $^1/_{16}$in ($^1/_5$mm)
- (2) wooden balls $^1/_2$in (12mm)*
- (4) steel washers
- starlock washer and cap $^1/_4$in (6mm)*
- (2) brass tube; length: $^5/_{16}$in (8mm); internal diameter: $^1/_8$in (3mm)
- (2) bronze bearings; length: $^3/_4$in (18mm); inside diameter: $^1/_4$in (6mm)*
- (19) $^3/_4$in (18mm) No 4 countersunk screws
- (1) brass round-head $^3/_4$in (18mm) No 8 screw
- $^3/_4$in (18mm) panel pins
- primer
- paints
- wood glue
- sandpaper (coarse, medium and fine)
- wood filler

*see list of suppliers on page 181

TOOLS

- lightweight drawing paper such as newsprint
- carbon paper
- pencil
- masking tape
- brushes
- straight edge
- square
- coping saw or fret saw (or power fret saw if available)
- drill
- drill bits: $^1/_8$in (3mm), $^1/_4$in (6mm) and $^3/_8$in (10mm)
- rasp
- file
- light hammer
- pliers
- punch

Much of the construction is the same or similar to the preceding toy (Diving Dolphins) in this section and reference may occasionally by made to instructions from that project.

Transfer all parts from the plans to the correct thickness of ply. Mark the locations of all drill holes.

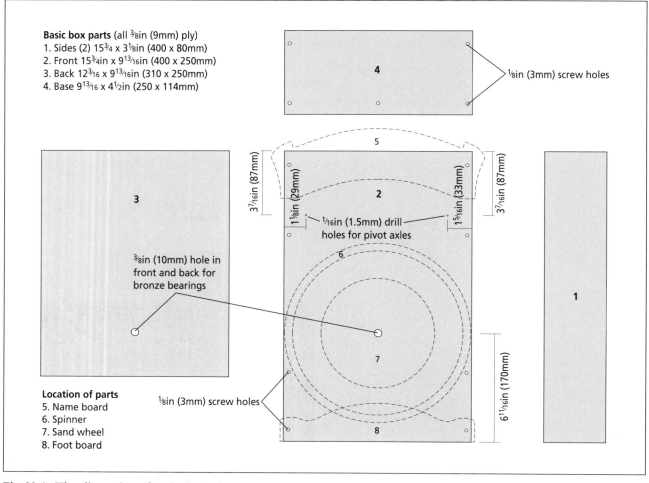

Basic box parts (all ⅜in (9mm) ply)
1. Sides (2) 15¾ x 3⅛in (400 x 80mm)
2. Front 15¾in x 9¹³⁄₁₆in (400 x 250mm)
3. Back 12³⁄₁₆ x 9¹³⁄₁₆in (310 x 250mm)
4. Base 9¹³⁄₁₆ x 4½in (250 x 114mm)

⅛in (3mm) screw holes

3⁷⁄₁₆in (87mm)

1⅛in (29mm)

1⁵⁄₁₆in (33mm)

3⁷⁄₁₆in (87mm)

¹⁄₁₆in (1.5mm) drill holes for pivot axles

⅜in (10mm) hole in front and back for bronze bearings

6¹¹⁄₁₆in (170mm)

Location of parts
5. Name board
6. Spinner
7. Sand wheel
8. Foot board

⅛in (3mm) screw holes

Fig 22.1 The dimensions for the basic box.

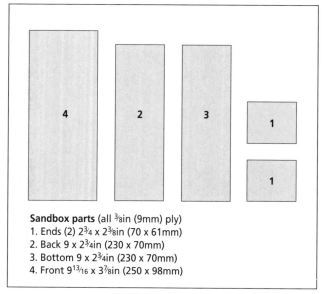

Sandbox parts (all ⅜in (9mm) ply)
1. Ends (2) 2¾ x 2⅜in (70 x 61mm)
2. Back 9 x 2¾in (230 x 70mm)
3. Bottom 9 x 2¾in (230 x 70mm)
4. Front 9¹³⁄₁₆ x 3⅞in (250 x 98mm)

Fig 22.2 The dimensions for the sandbox.

THE BASIC BOX

Cut to size the front, back, sides and base, and drill and countersink the screw holes as shown in Fig 22.1. Assemble the above parts into a box construction and drill the ⅜in (10mm) hole for the bronze bearings through the front and back as explained for the preceding toy (*see* page 157).

Unscrew and remove the back, and prime and paint all parts. When dry, fit the bronze bearings into the ⅜in (10mm) holes in the front and back as previously described (*see* page 157).

SANDBOX

Cut out the parts for the sandbox assembly (*see* Fig 22.2). Glue and pin the ends, back, bottom and front together just as you did with the sandbox in the Diving Dolphins project (*see* page 156 and 157).

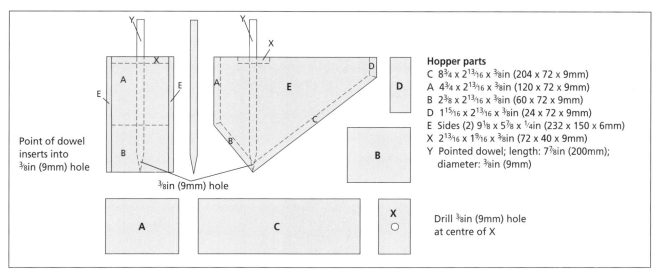

Hopper parts

C 8¾ x 2¹³⁄₁₆ x ⅜in (204 x 72 x 9mm)
A 4¾ x 2¹³⁄₁₆ x ⅜in (120 x 72 x 9mm)
B 2⅜ x 2¹³⁄₁₆ x ⅜in (60 x 72 x 9mm)
D 1¹⁵⁄₁₆ x 2¹³⁄₁₆ x ⅜in (24 x 72 x 9mm)
E Sides (2) 9⅛ x 5⅞ x ¼in (232 x 150 x 6mm)
X 2¹³⁄₁₆ x 1⁹⁄₁₆ x ⅜in (72 x 40 x 9mm)
Y Pointed dowel; length: 7⅞in (200mm); diameter: ⅜in (9mm)

Point of dowel inserts into ⅜in (9mm) hole

⅜in (9mm) hole

Drill ⅜in (9mm) hole at centre of X

Fig 22.3 The parts and assembly details for the hopper.

HOPPER

Now saw to shape the parts that will form the hopper (*see* Fig 22.3) and file and sand the bevels on parts A, B, C and D to the angles shown on the plan. Assemble by gluing and pinning the parts together as shown in Fig 22.3. An assembled hopper (already glued and pinned into place in the basic box, which is the next step) may be seen in Fig 22.4.

File a flat section on the pointed base of the hopper and drill a ⅜in (9mm) hole centrally (*see* Fig 21.7 of Diving Dolphins). Cut part X and the pointed dowel to size. Drill the hole in part X. Glue X between the hopper sides as shown in Fig 22.3. When the glue is dry, insert the pointed dowel through the hole in part X and into the ⅜in (9mm) hole in the base of the hopper. When construction of the hopper is complete, glue and cramp the hopper to the rear face of the front as shown in Fig 22.4. Remove the cramps when the glue is dry.

From Fig 22.1 mark and drill the ¹⁄₁₆in (1.5mm) holes in the front for the pivot axles, which will be fitted at a later stage. Note that these holes pass through the sides of the hopper and into the back.

SPINNER

Saw the spinner to the design shown in Fig 22.5 and drill the ¼in (6mm) centre hole and the ¹⁄₁₆in (2mm) pilot hole for a ¾in (18mm) No 6 brass round-head screw in the outer rim.

Fig 22.4 The hopper glued into place in the basic box.

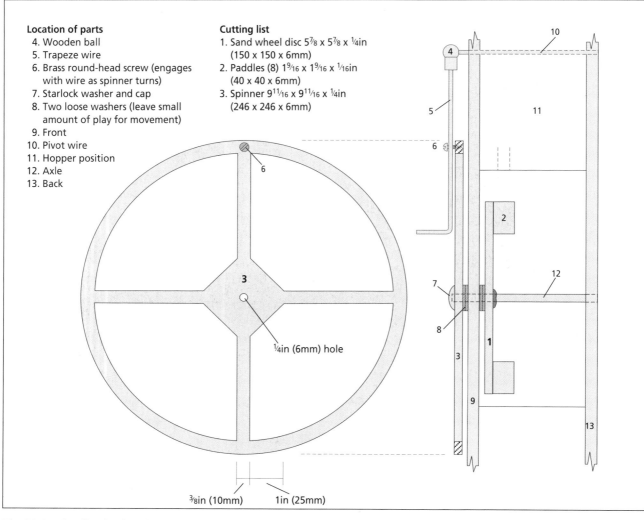

Location of parts

4. Wooden ball
5. Trapeze wire
6. Brass round-head screw (engages with wire as spinner turns)
7. Starlock washer and cap
8. Two loose washers (leave small amount of play for movement)
9. Front
10. Pivot wire
11. Hopper position
12. Axle
13. Back

Cutting list

1. Sand wheel disc $5\frac{7}{8}$ x $5\frac{7}{8}$ x $\frac{1}{4}$in (150 x 150 x 6mm)
2. Paddles (8) $1\frac{9}{16}$ x $1\frac{9}{16}$ x $\frac{1}{16}$in (40 x 40 x 6mm)
3. Spinner $9\frac{11}{16}$ x $9\frac{11}{16}$ x $\frac{1}{4}$in (246 x 246 x 6mm)

$\frac{1}{4}$in (6mm) hole

$\frac{3}{8}$in (10mm)   1in (25mm)

Fig 22.5   The flywheel and a detail of the assembly of the central axle and the pivot axles.

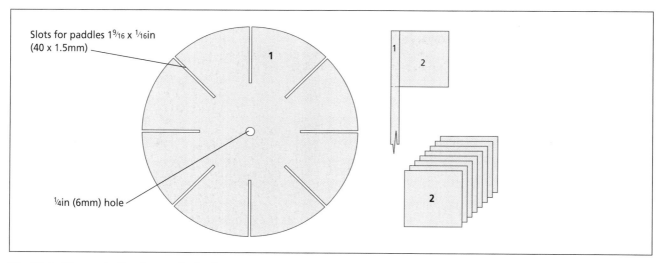

Slots for paddles $1\frac{9}{16}$ x $\frac{1}{16}$in (40 x 1.5mm)

$\frac{1}{4}$in (6mm) hole

Fig 22.6   The parts for the sand wheel.

Fig 22.7 The sand wheel in place on the central axle. The sandbox is also shown in place.

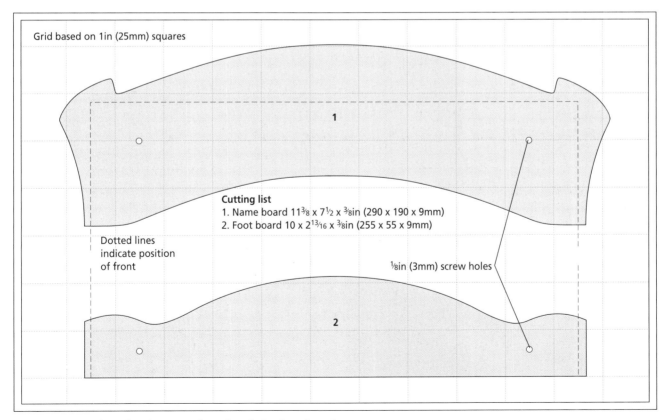

Grid based on 1in (25mm) squares

1

Cutting list
1. Name board 11³⁄₈ x 7½ x ³⁄₈in (290 x 190 x 9mm)
2. Foot board 10 x 2¹³⁄₁₆ x ³⁄₈in (255 x 55 x 9mm)

Dotted lines
indicate position
of front

¹⁄₈in (3mm) screw holes

2

Fig 22.8 The plans for the name board and the foot board.

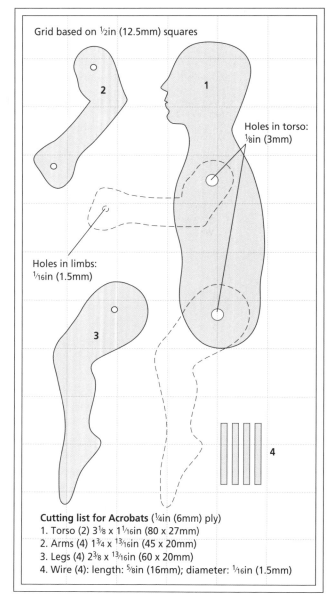

Grid based on ½in (12.5mm) squares

2

1

Holes in torso:
⅛in (3mm)

Holes in limbs:
1/16in (1.5mm)

3

4

Cutting list for Acrobats (¼in (6mm) ply)
1. Torso (2) 3⅛ x 1 1/16in (80 x 27mm)
2. Arms (4) 1¾ x 13/16in (45 x 20mm)
3. Legs (4) 2⅜ x 13/16in (60 x 20mm)
4. Wire (4): length: ⅝in (16mm); diameter: 1/16in (1.5mm)

Fig 22.9 Enlarge the shapes for the acrobats from the grid to the ply.

Fig 22.10 Epoxy glue is used to secure the wire into the hole in the arm.

Prime and paint the spinner. When dry, screw the brass round-head screw into the pilot hole in the rim so that the screw head projects from the rim approximately ½in (12mm). *See* Fig 22.5 for details. The screw in the spinner operates the movement of the acrobats by causing the trapeze wires to swing as the spinner rotates.

SAND WHEEL ASSEMBLY

The plywood disc is marked for the eight slots into which the paddles are glued and the ¼in (6mm) hole drilled at its centre (*see* Fig 22.6). The paddles for the sand wheel are now cut to shape. The sand wheel is constructed a little differently than that of the preceding toy in that the paddles do not protrude from the edge of the disc and are fitted to one side of the disc. Fig 22.7 shows the completed sand wheel in position.

Fit the sand wheel as follows. Cut to length a piece of ¼in (6mm) steel dowel for the axle (*see* Fig 22.5). Press a starlock washer and cap firmly onto one end of the steel axle. Smear a little epoxy resin around the axle next to the starlock washer and slide the spinner along the axle and against the starlock washer. Leave the assembly for the epoxy resin to dry.

Place two ¼in (6mm) washers on the axle and against the spinner, then insert the axle through the bronze bearing in the front. Place two ¼in (6mm) washers on the axle and against the rear face of the front. Now slide the assembled sand wheel onto the axle with the projecting paddles towards you.

Leave about a 1/16in (2mm) space between the back of the sand wheel and the washers. Then fix the sand wheel onto the axle with epoxy resin. Use a toothpick to build a bead of resin around the axle and against the sand wheel. The sand wheel may be seen in Fig 22.7.

THE NAME BOARD AND FOOT BOARD

Saw the name board to shape as shown in Fig 22.8. Drill and countersink the two screw holes in the name board and glue and screw the name board to the top of the front in the position shown in Fig 22.1. Fill the screw heads with wood filler and sand smooth.

Now cut the foot board to shape and glue and pin to the front edge of the base. The foot board may be seen in position in the photograph of the finished toy at the beginning of the project.

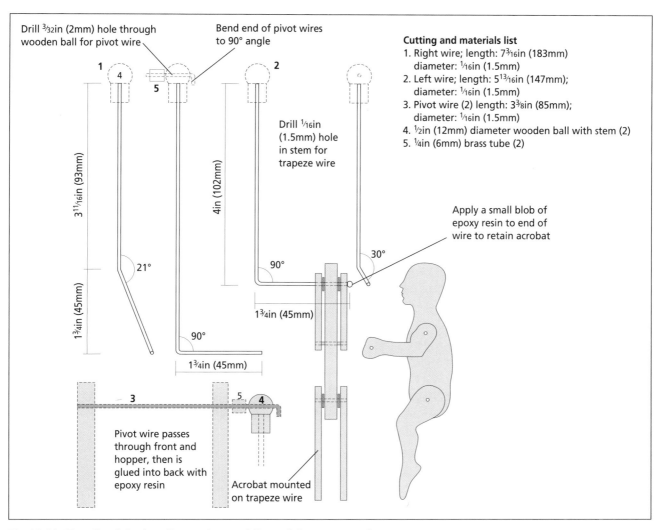

Drill ³⁄₃₂in (2mm) hole through wooden ball for pivot wire

Bend end of pivot wires to 90° angle

Drill ¹⁄₁₆in (1.5mm) hole in stem for trapeze wire

Apply a small blob of epoxy resin to end of wire to retain acrobat

Cutting and materials list
1. Right wire; length: 7³⁄₁₆in (183mm) diameter: ¹⁄₁₆in (1.5mm)
2. Left wire; length: 5¹³⁄₁₆in (147mm); diameter: ¹⁄₁₆in (1.5mm)
3. Pivot wire (2) length: 3³⁄₈in (85mm); diameter: ¹⁄₁₆in (1.5mm)
4. ½in (12mm) diameter wooden ball with stem (2)
5. ¼in (6mm) brass tube (2)

3¹¹⁄₁₆in (93mm)

4in (102mm)

1¾in (45mm)

21°

90°

90°

90°

30°

1¾in (45mm)

1¾in (45mm)

Pivot wire passes through front and hopper, then is glued into back with epoxy resin

Acrobat mounted on trapeze wire

Fig 22.11 Details of the bending and assembling of the trapeze wires.

TRAPEZE ARTISTS

Carefully saw out the parts of the two figures (the trapeze artists) and drill the ⅛in (3mm) holes in the torso and the ¹⁄₁₆in (1.5mm) holes in the arms and legs from the details shown in Fig 22.9. The two figures are identical.

Cut four pieces of ¹⁄₁₆in (1.5mm) wire to ⅝in (16mm) lengths as shown in Fig 22.9. These pieces of wire attach the arms and legs to the torso so that they swing freely. Prime and paint the figures before assembling the parts.

Attach the limbs to the torsos as follows. Apply a little epoxy resin to one end of the ¹⁄₁₆in (1.5mm) wire and insert into the ¹⁄₁₆in (1.5mm) hole in the arm. Repeat the process on the leg (do this with both

figures) and leave to dry. If a quick setting epoxy resin is used it will dry in approximately 15 minutes. Fig 22.10 shows a wire glued into the arm.

When these parts are dry, assemble the figures as follows. Place a ¹⁄₁₆in (1.5mm) washer over the end of the wire so that it rests flat on the limb, then pass the end of the wire through the torso (insert a thin piece of card between the washer and the torso to leave a little free movement). Place another ¹⁄₁₆in (1.5mm) washer over the wire. Then apply a little epoxy resin to the end of the wire and insert into the remaining limb. Remove the card when the epoxy resin has set.

Proceed in this manner until all limbs are fitted. File the ends of the wires flush with the surface of the limbs and retouch the paint.

THE TRAPEZE

Now cut and bend the two ¹⁄₁₆in (1.5mm) trapeze wires to length and bend to the shapes shown in Fig 22.11. Make sure these wires are positioned correctly in the following stages. Figs 22.11, 22.12 and 22.13 will make this clear.

Two ¹⁄₂in (12mm) diameter wooden balls with a ³⁄₈in (9mm) diameter dowel stem are required in the following assembly. A supplier of these components is listed at the back of the book (*see* Suppliers, page 181).

Drill a ³⁄₃₂in (2mm) hole horizontally through the centre of the wooden ball and a ¹⁄₁₆in (1.5mm) hole up the centre of the stem (details are made clear in Fig 22.11). Smear a little epoxy resin on the top of each trapeze wire and insert into the ¹⁄₁₆in (1.5mm) holes in the stems of the wooden balls, making sure that the wires are in the position shown on the plan.

Cut to length (sizes are shown in Fig 22.11) the two pieces of ¹⁄₁₆in (1.5mm) wire to form the pivot axles. With a pair of pliers bend one end of each to a 90° angle. Insert the straight end of each wire through the ³⁄₃₂in (2mm) holes in the wooden balls; cut a ³⁄₈in (9mm) length of ¹⁄₄in (6mm) diameter brass tube as a spacer and fit onto the pivot axle close to the wooden ball (but leaving a little space for free movement). Fig 22.12 shows a pivot axle assembled this far. Then pass the pivot axle through the front, sandbox, and back and glue in position with epoxy resin as shown in Fig 22.5.

Fig 22.13 An acrobat suspended from a trapeze wire.

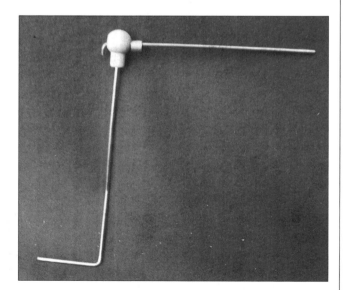

Fig 22.12 The trapeze wire that appears on the right in the photograph of the finished toy (see page 161).

Place a figure onto each of the trapeze wires as shown in Figs 22.13 and the photograph of the finished toy at the beginning of the project and smear a blob of epoxy resin onto the ends of the trapeze wires with a toothpick to prevent the figure slipping off. The photo of the finished toy shows both acrobats in place. All that remains is to prime and paint the toy to your colour scheme.

OPERATING THE TOY

To operate the toy fill the hopper with silver sand and raise the pointed dowel from the hole in the hopper until the spinner begins to turn. The screw in the outer rim of the rotating spinner causes the trapeze wires to swing as it touches them. While making these sand toys, sketch and keep notes of ideas to create your own original designs.

Men at Work

*On relaxing after completing this toy, your efforts will be rewarded by watching
the two men at work, one busy swinging his hammer and his mate trimming a board with his axe.*

MATERIALS

- birch ply 44 x 26 x $\frac{3}{8}$in (1110 x 650 x 9mm)
- birch ply 9 x 9 x $\frac{1}{4}$in (220 x 220 x 6mm)
- birch ply $8\frac{1}{16}$ x $1\frac{15}{16}$ x $\frac{1}{16}$in (205 x 50 x 1.5mm)
- triangular coping $9\frac{13}{16}$ x $\frac{3}{4}$ x $\frac{3}{4}$ x 1in (250 x 18 x 18 x 26mm)
- $7\frac{7}{8}$ x $1\frac{3}{16}$in (250 x 30mm) hardwood dowel
- steel axle; length; $4\frac{3}{8}$in (112mm); diameter: $\frac{1}{4}$in (6mm)*
- wire; length $6\frac{11}{16}$in (170mm); diameter: $\frac{1}{16}$in ($\frac{1}{5}$mm)
- (4) steel washers; internal diameter: $\frac{1}{4}$in (6mm)
- (2) starlock washers and caps; internal diameter: $\frac{1}{4}$in (6mm)*
- (2) bronze bearings; internal diameter: $\frac{1}{4}$in (6mm)*
- 1lb (.5k) silver sand
- (19) $\frac{3}{4}$in (18mm) No 4 countersunk screws
- $\frac{3}{4}$in (18mm) panel pins
- 1in (25mm) panel pins
- primer
- paints
- wood glue
- epoxy resin
- sandpaper (coarse, medium and fine)
- wood filler

*see list of suppliers on page 181

TOOLS

- lightweight drawing paper such as newsprint
- carbon paper
- pencil
- masking tape
- brushes
- straight edge
- square
- coping saw or fret saw (or power fret saw if available)
- drill
- drill bits: $\frac{1}{8}$in (3mm), $\frac{1}{4}$in (6mm) and $\frac{3}{8}$in (10mm)
- file
- light hammer
- pliers

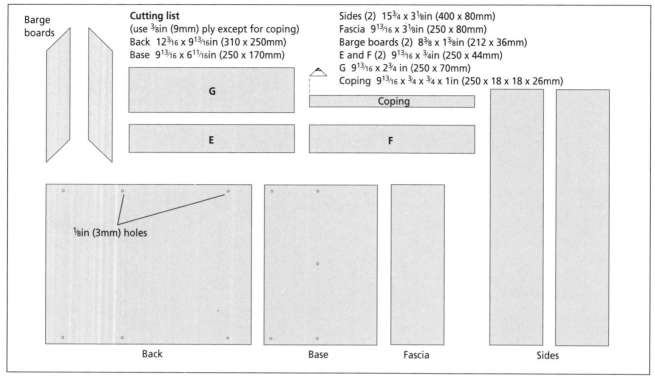

Fig 23.1 (a) The dimensions of the parts for the basic box.

Begin the construction by transferring the dimensions and shapes for all parts from the plans to the correct thickness of plywood. Mark the locations of all holes to be drilled.

THE BASIC BOX

Cut out the front, back, two ends and base as shown in Figs 23.1 (a) and (b). Drill and countersink the screw holes as shown on the plan.

Carefully mark then drill the $\frac{1}{8}$in (3mm) holes in the front through which the wires that operate the figures pass. Also mark and drill the $\frac{3}{8}$in (10mm) axle holes in the front and back. Insert the bronze bearings after first painting these parts. Refer to pages 155–157 of the Diving Dolphins project for a full explanation for constructing the basic box. Then construct the box.

THE WORKMEN

Saw to shape the parts for the two workmen as shown in Fig 23.2. Drill the $\frac{1}{16}$in (1.5mm) holes in the arms and the $\frac{1}{8}$in (3mm) holes in the bodies. Prime and paint these parts, but do not paint the back of the figures as these will be glued to the front at a later stage.

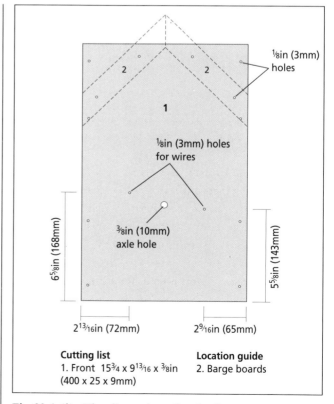

Fig 23.1 (b) The dimensions for the front.

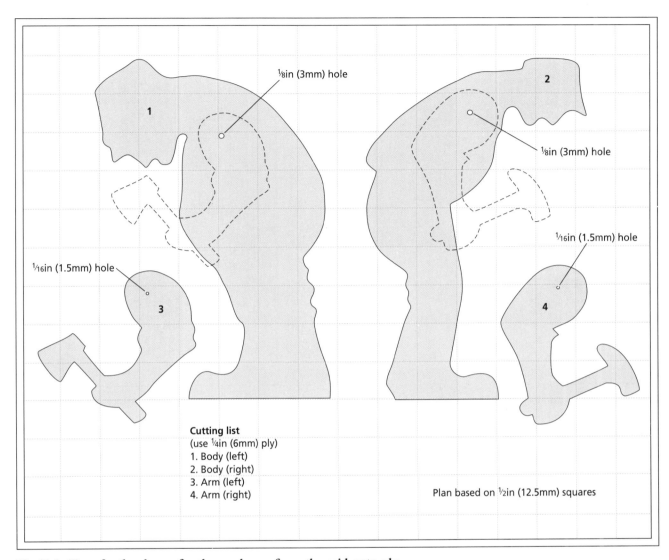

Fig 23.2 Transfer the shapes for the workmen from the grid onto ply.

Cut and bend to shape the operating wires as shown in Fig 23.3. The plan is life size, so the wires may be laid over the drawings to check for correct shape. Assemble the figures on the operating wires as follows. Glue the bodies to the front in their respective positions (*see* Fig 23.4), making sure the ⅛in (3mm) hole in the body and the ⅛in (3mm) hole in the front correspond. Place a small washer (fixed with epoxy resin to the operating wire at a later stage) over the end of the straight section of the operating wire. Then insert the end of the wire (from the rear face) through the front and body. The sectional drawing in Fig 23.3 shows the assembly in detail. Fig 23.5 shows the wires sticking out of the rear face of the front.

Place another small washer over the wire protruding from the body, then apply a little epoxy resin to the end of the wire and insert into the arm. Make sure the end of the wire is flush with the ply face so that no sharp edge is projecting. Note that the position of the arms in Fig 23.4 must correspond to the position of the bent operating wires in Fig 23.6. When the above assembly is complete, check that the arms swing freely, then attach the two washers (behind the rear face of the front) to the operating wires with epoxy resin. Leave a little space, about 1/16in (2mm), between the washers and the front to allow free movement. Fig 23.7 shows how the operating wire is assembled. The front has been omitted so that the order of assembly is clear.

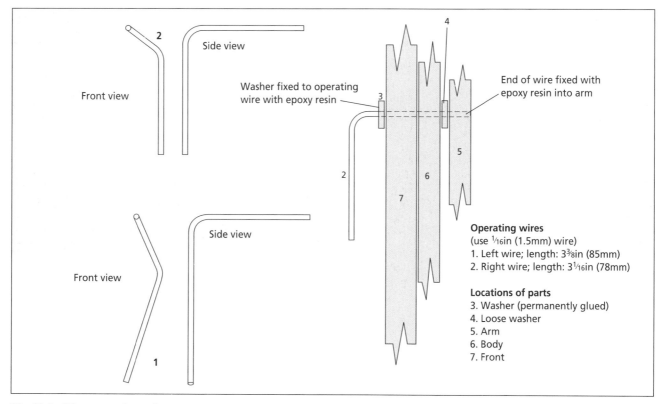

2

Front view

Side view

Washer fixed to operating
wire with epoxy resin

End of wire fixed with
epoxy resin into arm

3

4

2

7

6

5

Front view

Side view

1

Operating wires
(use $\frac{1}{16}$in (1.5mm) wire)
1. Left wire; length: $3\frac{3}{8}$in (85mm)
2. Right wire; length: $3\frac{1}{16}$in (78mm)

Locations of parts
3. Washer (permanently glued)
4. Loose washer
5. Arm
6. Body
7. Front

Fig 23.3 The operating wires.

**Fig 23.4 The bodies of the workmen are affixed to the
front, the arms are affixed to the operating wires.**

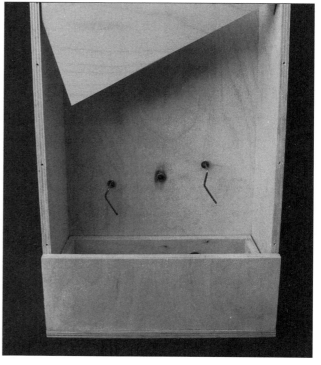

**Fig 23.5 The hopper, sandbox, axle and operating wires
in position.**

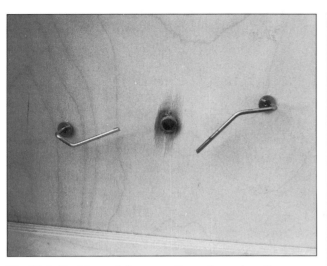

Fig 23.6 Position of the operating wires when the arms are in the position shown in Fig 23.4.

Fig 23.7 An operating–wire/workman assembly.

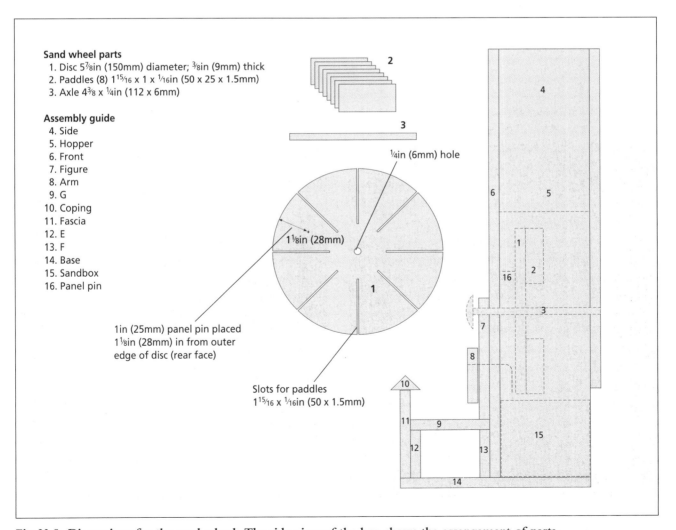

Sand wheel parts
1. Disc 5⅞in (150mm) diameter; ⅜in (9mm) thick
2. Paddles (8) 1¹⁵⁄₁₆ x 1 x ¹⁄₁₆in (50 x 25 x 1.5mm)
3. Axle 4⅜ x ¼in (112 x 6mm)

Assembly guide
4. Side
5. Hopper
6. Front
7. Figure
8. Arm
9. G
10. Coping
11. Fascia
12. E
13. F
14. Base
15. Sandbox
16. Panel pin

¼in (6mm) hole

1⅛in (28mm)

1in (25mm) panel pin placed 1⅛in (28mm) in from outer edge of disc (rear face)

Slots for paddles 1¹⁵⁄₁₆ x ¹⁄₁₆in (50 x 1.5mm)

Fig 23.8 Dimensions for the sand wheel. The side view of the box shows the arrangement of parts.

THE SAND WHEEL

Saw to shape the disc and cut the slots for the paddles. Tap a 1in (25mm) panel pin into the back of the disc in the position marked from the plan (*see* Fig 23.8). Cut the eight paddles to shape and assemble exactly as in the previous toy (*see* page 166). Fig 23.9 shows the panel pin in position. The protruding panel pin in the back of the sand wheel operates the movement of the arms of the workmen by engaging with the operating wires as the sand wheel rotates.

SANDBOX AND HOPPER

Cut to shape the parts for the sandbox (*see* Fig 23.10). Assemble as described in the Diving Dolphins project on page 157. The sandbox fits into the base of the main assembly as shown in Fig 23.5.

From Fig 23.10 cut the parts for the hopper, pointed dowel and part X and assemble exactly as explained on pages 157–159 of the Diving Dolphins project. When the glue has dried, glue the completed assembly to the rear face of the front in the position shown in Fig 23.5.

FITTING THE SAND WHEEL

Cut to length a piece of ¼in (6mm) diameter steel axle and press a starlock washer and cap firmly onto one end (*see* Fig 23.8). Place a ¼in (6mm) washer over the axle and against the starlock washer, then pass the axle through the bronze bearing in the front and place the sand wheel onto the axle from the rear.

Position the sand wheel on the axle so that the panel pin in the back of the sand wheel engages with the operating wires as it is turned. The arms of the workmen should move up and down as the sand wheel is turned by hand. When the operation is smooth, fix the sand wheel to the axle with epoxy resin.

The back is fitted by guiding the end of the axle through the bronze bearing in the back and then screwing the back to the sides through the previously drilled holes. Fit a starlock washer and cap to the end of the axle to prevent the axle moving when in operation.

FINAL CONSTRUCTION

Cut to shape parts E, F and G (*see* Fig 23.1 (*a*)). Glue in the positions shown in Figs 23.4 and 23.8. Saw the barge boards to shape (*see* Fig 23.1 (*a*)) and drill and countersink the two screw holes in each. Then glue

Fig 23.9 The rear face of the sand wheel disc. Note the location of the panel pin.

and screw the barge boards to the front as shown if Fig 23.1 (*b*). Fig 23.4 shows the barge boards glued and screwed to the front and part G glued to the top edges of parts E and F.

Cut the fascia and coping (*see* Fig 23.1 (*a*)) to size. Then glue and pin the coping to the top edge of the fascia. When the glue is dry, glue and pin the fascia to the front of part B. Figs 23.8 and the photo of the finished toy at the beginning of the project show these parts fitted.

Now cut to size the parts for the workmen's benches and the platform on which the smaller man is standing (*see* photos of finished toy on page 169 and in the colour section). These are simply glued and pinned together as shown on the plan.

Complete the priming and painting to your choice of colour scheme.

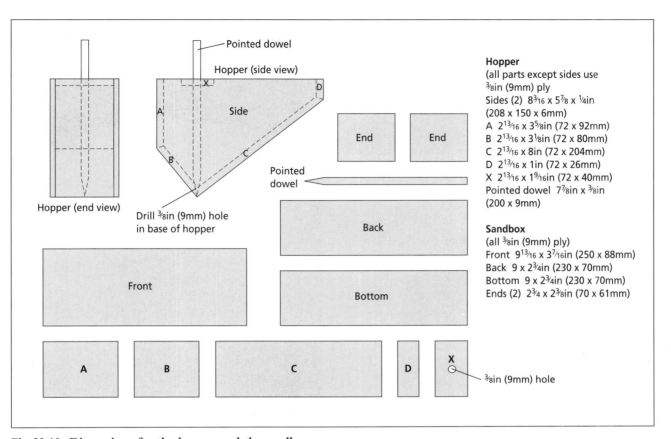

Hopper
(all parts except sides use
⅜in (9mm) ply)
Sides (2) 8³⁄₁₆ x 5⅞ x ¼in
(208 x 150 x 6mm)
A 2¹³⁄₁₆ x 3⅝in (72 x 92mm)
B 2¹³⁄₁₆ x 3⅛in (72 x 80mm)
C 2¹³⁄₁₆ x 8in (72 x 204mm)
D 2¹³⁄₁₆ x 1in (72 x 26mm)
X 2¹³⁄₁₆ x 1⁹⁄₁₆in (72 x 40mm)
Pointed dowel 7⅞in x ⅜in
(200 x 9mm)

Sandbox
(all ⅜in (9mm) ply)
Front 9¹³⁄₁₆ x 3⁷⁄₁₆in (250 x 88mm)
Back 9 x 2¾in (230 x 70mm)
Bottom 9 x 2¾in (230 x 70mm)
Ends (2) 2¾ x 2⅜in (70 x 61mm)

Fig 23.10 Dimensions for the hopper and the sandbox.

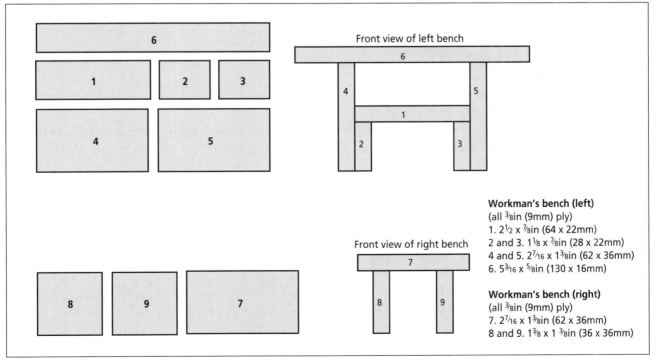

Workman's bench (left)
(all ⅜in (9mm) ply)
1. 2½ x ⅞in (64 x 22mm)
2 and 3. 1⅛ x ⅞in (28 x 22mm)
4 and 5. 2⁷⁄₁₆ x 1⅜in (62 x 36mm)
6. 5³⁄₁₆ x ⅝in (130 x 16mm)

Workman's bench (right)
(all ⅜in (9mm) ply)
7. 2⁷⁄₁₆ x 1⅜in (62 x 36mm)
8 and 9. 1⅜ x 1 ⅜in (36 x 36mm)

Fig 23.11 Dimensions for the workbenches.

Windmill

The last toy in this section is on a larger scale than the previous sand toys, although the construction and operation is based on the same principle.

MATERIALS

- birch ply 34 x 30 x $^3/_8$in (850 x 750 x 9mm)
- birch ply 7$^9/_{16}$ x 7$^1/_2$ x $^1/_4$in (192 x 190 x 6mm)
- birch ply 9$^1/_2$ x 7$^7/_8$ x $^1/_{16}$in (240 x 200 x 1.5mm)
- metal rod 1$^1/_2$ x $^1/_4$in (38 x 6mm)
- (4) steel washers
- (2) starlock washers and caps $^1/_4$in (6mm)*
- (2) bronze bearings; length: $^3/_4$in (18mm); inside diameter: $^1/_4$in (6mm)*
- (16) $^3/_4$in (18mm) No 8 countersunk screws
- $^3/_4$in (18mm) panel pins
- primer
- paints
- wood glue
- epoxy resin adhesive
- sandpaper (coarse, medium and fine)
- wood filler

*see list of suppliers on page 181

TOOLS

- lightweight drawing paper such as newsprint
- carbon paper
- pencil
- masking tape
- brushes
- straight edge
- square
- coping saw or fret saw (or power fret saw if available)
- drill
- drill bits: $^1/_8$in (3mm), $^1/_4$in (6mm) and $^3/_8$in (10mm)
- rasp
- file
- light hammer
- pliers

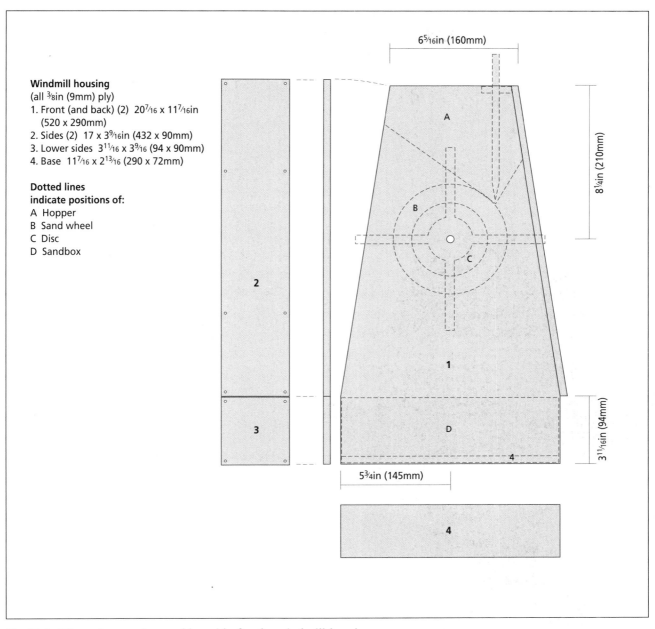

Windmill housing
(all ³⁄₈in (9mm) ply)
1. Front (and back) (2) 20⁷⁄₁₆ x 11⁷⁄₁₆in
   (520 x 290mm)
2. Sides (2) 17 x 3⁹⁄₁₆in (432 x 90mm)
3. Lower sides 3¹¹⁄₁₆ x 3⁹⁄₁₆ (94 x 90mm)
4. Base 11⁷⁄₁₆ x 2¹³⁄₁₆ (290 x 72mm)

Dotted lines
indicate positions of:
A Hopper
B Sand wheel
C Disc
D Sandbox

Fig 24.1 Dimensions and assembly guide for the windmill housing.

Begin by transferring all the parts from the plans to the correct thickness of ply. Saw all parts to shape, then sand them to a smooth finish before assembling.

WINDMILL HOUSING

Mark and drill the ³⁄₈in (10mm) axle hole in the front for the bronze bearing (*see* Fig 24.1). From the detail shown in Fig 24.1 mark, drill and countersink the screw holes in the two sides. Glue and screw the sides to the edges of the front as shown in Figs 24.1 and 24.6.

SAND WHEEL MECHANISM

Drill a ³⁄₈in (10mm) hole in the centre of the disc labelled '2' in Fig 24.2. Insert a bronze bearing into the hole. You will find that the bearing is a tight fit in the hole. The best way to fit the bearing is to place a piece of scrap ply over the top end of the bearing and tap gently with a light hammer until the bearing is flush with the face of the ply. The bronze bearing fitted into disc 2 will protrude from the disc by ³⁄₈in (9mm) as shown in Fig 24.3.

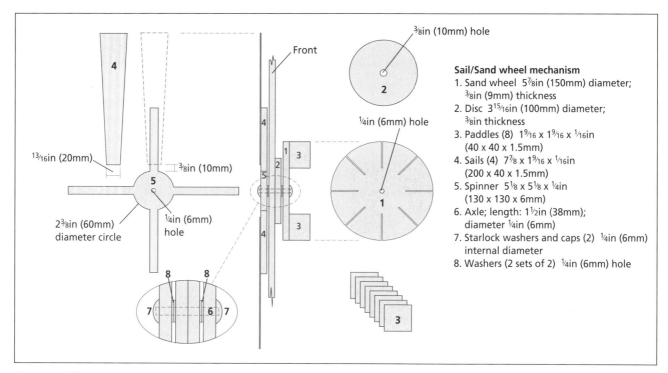

Sail/Sand wheel mechanism
1. Sand wheel 5⅞in (150mm) diameter; ⅜in (9mm) thickness
2. Disc 3¹⁵⁄₁₆in (100mm) diameter; ⅜in thickness
3. Paddles (8) 1⁹⁄₁₆ x 1⁹⁄₁₆ x ¹⁄₁₆in (40 x 40 x 1.5mm)
4. Sails (4) 7⅞ x 1⁹⁄₁₆ x ¹⁄₁₆in (200 x 40 x 1.5mm)
5. Spinner 5⅛ x 5⅛ x ¼in (130 x 130 x 6mm)
6. Axle; length: 1½in (38mm); diameter ¼in (6mm)
7. Starlock washers and caps (2) ¼in (6mm) internal diameter
8. Washers (2 sets of 2) ¼in (6mm) hole

Fig 24.2 Dimensions and assembly guide for the sail/sand wheel mechanism.

Fig 24.3 The bronze bearing protrudes from the disc.

Smear a little glue on the face of disc 2 (the face from which the bearing protrudes). Then insert the protruding bearing into the ⅜in (10mm) hole in the rear face of the front. Again, place a piece of scrap ply over the bearing and disc 2 and tap home with a hammer until disc 2 is firmly against the rear face of the front. Allow the glue to set.

Saw to shape the disc (1) and eight paddles (3) that form the sand wheel (*see* Fig 24.2). Cut out the slots in the disc to the dimensions shown on the plan and glue the eight paddles into these slots. The paddles should be flush with the back of the disc. Fig 24.4 shows the paddles glued into the slots.

Fig 24.4 Eight paddles are glued into slots in the sand wheel disc.

THE SAILS

Cut to shape the spinner (5) and the four sails (4) from the dimensions shown in Fig 24.2. Drill the ¼in (6mm) hole in the centre of the spinner and then glue the sails in position on the 'legs' of the spinner as shown in Figs 24.2 and 24.5. Prime and paint the assembly to your choice of colour scheme.

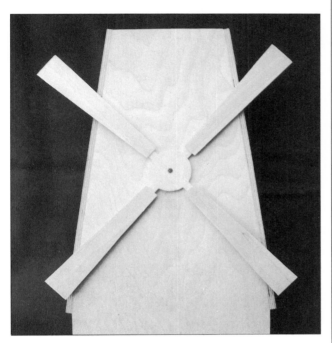

Fig 24.5 A view from the front of the sail/sand wheel assembly.

Fig 24.6 A view from the interior of the windmill housing of the the sail/sand wheel assembly.

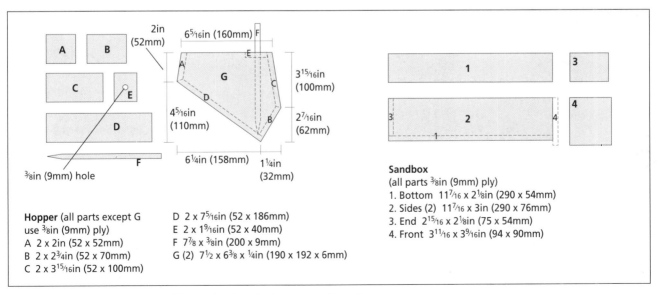

Hopper (all parts except G use ⅜in (9mm) ply)
A 2 x 2in (52 x 52mm)
B 2 x 2¾in (52 x 70mm)
C 2 x 3¹⁵⁄₁₆in (52 x 100mm)

D 2 x 7⁵⁄₁₆in (52 x 186mm)
E 2 x 1⁹⁄₁₆in (52 x 40mm)
F 7⅞ x ⅜in (200 x 9mm)
G (2) 7½ x 6⅜ x ¼in (190 x 192 x 6mm)

Sandbox
(all parts ⅜in (9mm) ply)
1. Bottom 11⁷⁄₁₆ x 2⅛in (290 x 54mm)
2. Sides (2) 11⁷⁄₁₆ x 3in (290 x 76mm)
3. End 2¹⁵⁄₁₆ x 2⅛in (75 x 54mm)
4. Front 3¹¹⁄₁₆ x 3⁹⁄₁₆in (94 x 90mm)

Fig 24.7 Parts lists and assembly guides for the hopper and sandbox.

FITTING THE SAND WHEEL TO THE AXLE

Cut the ¼in (6mm) diameter axle to a length of 1½in (38mm). Refer to the order of assembly detailed in Fig 24.2. Press a ¼in (6mm) starlock washer and cap firmly onto one end of the axle. Pass the axle through the ¼in (6mm) hole in the spinner and place two washers over the axle and against the spinner. Insert the axle through the bronze bearing in the front. Fit two more washers over the axle and against the rear face of the front. Now slide the sand wheel assembly over the axle (the flat side of the sand wheel against the washers), leaving a slight clearance of about ¹⁄₁₆in (2mm) between the sand wheel and the washers. Fix the sand wheel to the axle with epoxy resin. Figs 24.5 and 24.6 show front and rear views of the assembly.

THE HOPPER

Cut out the parts for the hopper (*see* Fig 24.7) and assemble the parts by gluing and pinning together. When the glue is dry, file a flat area on the pointed base of the hopper and drill the ⅜in (9mm) hole as described in detail in Diving Dolphins (*see* page 158). Cut and shape the ⅜in (9mm) pointed dowel (*see* Fig 24.7). Drill the ⅜in (9mm) hole in part E as shown on the plan and glue in position between the hopper sides. When the assembly is dry, glue and cramp to the rear face of the front in the position shown in Fig 24.1.

Fig 24.8 The sandbox fits into the side of the windmill housing.

FINISHING THE WINDMILL HOUSING

Place the back in position between the two sides and screw into position through the previously drilled holes in the sides.

Cut to shape part 3 from Fig 24.1. Part 3 forms the lower side. Glue and pin part 3 in position.

SANDBOX

Saw the sandbox parts to size and glue and pin together as shown in Fig 24.7. The sandbox fits into the gap in the side of the windmill housing at the right as shown in Fig 24.8.

CANOPY

Saw to shape the parts for the canopy (*see* Fig 24.9). The edges of parts 2 and 3 are bevelled to the angles shown in Fig 24.9 to give a neat finish. Assemble by gluing and pinning between the two sides. The canopy simply sits on top of the windmill.

FINISHING

Complete the priming and painting of the toy to your choice of colour scheme.

OPERATING THE WINDMILL

The operation is the same as that of the previous toys in this section. Fill the hopper with silver sand and adjust the pointed dowel by raising from the hole in the bottom of the hopper so that the sand flows smoothly onto the sand wheel, which in turn rotates the sails.

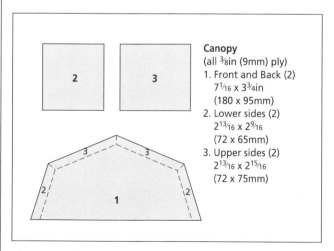

Canopy
(all ⅜in (9mm) ply)
1. Front and Back (2)
   7¹⁄₁₆ x 3¾in
   (180 x 95mm)
2. Lower sides (2)
   2¹³⁄₁₆ x 2⁹⁄₁₆
   (72 x 65mm)
3. Upper sides (2)
   2¹³⁄₁₆ x 2¹⁵⁄₁₆
   (72 x 75mm)

Fig 24.9 The canopy parts, dimensions and assembly guide.

SUPPLIERS

NOTE: A nominal charge for catalogues is made by some of the suppliers listed. Please enclose a self-addressed stamped envelope when writing to suppliers. Other item used in the projects but not listed here will normally be found at your local DIY store.

John Boddy Fine Wood & Tool Store Ltd

Riverside Sawmills, Boroughbridge,
North Yorkshire, YO5 9LJ
Tel 0423 322370

▌ Mail order
▌ Catalogue
▌ Wood, tools, wooden balls, etc.

W. Hobby Ltd

Knights Hill Square, London, SE27 0HH
Tel 081 761-4244

▌ Mail order
▌ Annual Catalogue
▌ Wheels, wooden balls, etc.

Ace Screw Supply Co.

Royle Street, Congleton, Cheshire, CW12 1HR
Tel 0260 278236

▌ Mail order
▌ Leaflets
▌ Many types and sizes of screws at good prices

Classic Wooden Toys

27 Carnarvon Street, Hollinwood, Oldham, OL8 3PW

▌ Mail order
▌ Catalogue
▌ Steel axles
▌ Starlock washers and caps
▌ Plywood kits
▌ Bronze bearings, etc.

House of Harbru

Elton Road, Bury, Lancs.

▌ Brochures
▌ Mail order
▌ Coloured spirit stains for wood, and finishing products

METRIC CONVERSION TABLE

INCHES TO MILLIMETRES AND CENTIMETRES						
mm = millimetres cm = centimetres						
inches	mm	cm	inches	cm	inches	cm
⅛	3	0.3	9	22.9	30	76.2
¼	6	0.6	10	25.4	31	78.7
⅜	10	1.0	11	27.9	32	81.3
½	13	1.3	12	30.5	33	83.8
⅝	16	1.6	13	33.0	34	86.4
¾	19	1.9	14	35.6	35	88.9
⅞	22	2.2	15	38.1	36	91.4
1	25	2.5	16	40.6	37	94.0
1¼	32	3.2	17	43.2	38	96.5
1½	38	3.8	18	45.7	39	99.1
1¾	44	4.4	19	48.3	40	101.6
2	51	5.1	20	50.8	41	104.1
2½	64	6.4	21	53.3	42	106.7
3	76	7.6	22	55.9	43	109.2
3½	89	8.9	23	58.4	44	111.8
4	102	10.2	24	61.0	45	114.3
4½	114	11.4	25	63.5	46	116.8
5	127	12.7	26	66.0	47	119.4
6	152	15.2	27	68.6	48	121.9
7	178	17.8	28	71.1	49	124.5
8	203	20.3	29	73.7	50	127.0

ABOUT THE AUTHOR

Terry Kelly has been working in wood since he was
eight. In 1980, while teaching woodcarving and toy
making part time, he set up a small business in antique
restoration that expanded into furniture making, toy
making, woodcarving and rocking-horse making.
More recently, he has concentrated on designing and
making wooden toys in his home workshop and
writing the occasional article.

OTHER TITLES AVAILABLE FROM
GMC PUBLICATIONS LTD

BOOKS

Woodworking Plans and Projects *GMC Publications*

40 More Woodworking Plans and Projects
    GMC Publications

Woodworking Crafts Annual *GMC Publications*

Woodworkers' Career & Educational Source Book
    GMC Publications

Woodworkers' Courses & Source Book
    GMC Publications

Green Woodwork *Mike Abbott*

Making Little Boxes from Wood *John Bennett*

The Incredible Router *Jeremy Broun*

Electric Woodwork *Jeremy Broun*

Woodcarving: A Complete Course *Ron Butterfield*

Making Fine Furniture: Projects *Tom Darby*

Restoring Rocking Horses *Clive Green & Anthony Dew*

Heraldic Miniature Knights *Peter Greenhill*

Practical Crafts: Seat Weaving *Ricky Holdstock*

Multi-centre Woodturning *Ray Hopper*

Complete Woodfinishing *Ian Hosker*

Woodturning: A Source Book of Shapes *John Hunnex*

Making Shaker Furniture *Barry Jackson*

Upholstery: A Complete Course *David James*

Upholstery Techniques and Projects *David James*

Designing and Making Wooden Toys *Terry Kelly*

Making Dolls' House Furniture *Patricia King*

Making and Modifying Woodworking Tools *Jim Kingshott*

The Workshop *Jim Kingshott*

Sharpening: The Complete Guide *Jim Kingshott*

Turning Wooden Toys *Terry Lawrence*

Making Board, Peg and Dice Games *Jeff & Jennie Loader*

The Complete Dolls' House Book *Jean Nisbett*

Guide to Marketing *Jack Pigden*

Woodcarving Tools, Materials and Equipment *Chris Pye*

Making Tudor Dolls' Houses *Derek Rowbottom*

Making Georgian Dolls' Houses *Derek Rowbottom*

Making Period Dolls' House Furniture
    Derek & Sheila Rowbottom

Woodturning: A Foundation Course *Keith Rowley*

Turning Miniatures in Wood *John Sainsbury*

Pleasure and Profit from Woodturning *Reg Sherwin*

Making Unusual Miniatures *Graham Spalding*

Woodturning Wizardry *David Springett*

Furniture Projects *Rod Wales*

Decorative Woodcarving *Jeremy Williams*

*GMC Publications regulary produces new books on a wide range of woodworking and craft subjects; and
an increasing number of specialist magazines, all available on subscription*

MAGAZINES

Woodturning   Businessmatters   Woodcarving

All these books and magazines are available through bookshops and newsagents, or may be
ordered by post from the publishers at 166 High Street, Lewes, East Sussex BN7 1XU,
telephone (0273) 477374, fax (0273) 478606

Credit card orders are accepted. Please write or phone for the latest information